A WALK OF FAITH

A WALK FOR TIM TO THE WORLD CUP

To Simona

with love and very best wishes

John Reeve

A Walk of Faith : A Walk for Tim to the World Cup
Copyright © John Reeve 2007

All rights reserved.

No part of this book may be reproduced in any form by
Photocopying or any electronic or mechanical means,
including information storage or retrieval systems,
without permission in writing from both the copyright.
owner and the publisher of the book.

ISBN 978-184426-434-6

First Published 2007 by.
UPFRONT PUBLISHING LTD
Peterborough, England.

Printed by Printondemand-Worldwide Ltd.

A Walk of Faith

For Tim

He died young but lived strong and will always be our inspiration

£5 from every sale of this book is being donated to
The Leukaemia Research Fund
For its work with teenagers and young adults

http://www.lrf.org.uk/

John Reeve

Contents

Chapter 1	Tim's Story	11
Chapter 2	100 Days to Go	30
Chapter 3	Ready, Steady……	47
Chapter 4	A Walk of Two Starts	65
Chapter 5	A 21st Century Pilgrimage	83
Chapter 6	Across Flanders Fields	102
Chapter 7	Hard Times and Good Friends in Belgium	122
Chapter 8	A Chateau, two Casinos and the Millennium Stadium	144
Chapter 9	Walking in the Hills	160
Chapter 10	The Rhine and the Main	187
Chapter 11	Frankfurt – a City En Fête	217
Chapter 12	A Journey without End	238

John Reeve

Foreword

This book was inspired by love and fashioned out of despair; both will endure. Just as the walk itself was an amazing emotional journey, so writing the book has given me a huge amount of pleasure as I read through my diary, looked at the photographs and remembered. I wrote for myself, selfishly in the knowledge that it was another step forward for me. Many times, I remembered vividly the feeling and emotions of the walk and they will stay with me for ever.

The decision to make the walk was confirmed over beer and nibbles with Norris and Joan Silk, Ted Herring, Peter Shields, Malcolm Tilsed and Simon Philips and my thanks to them all for their friendship and unerring support. The walk was put together in 100 days and has helped to raise over £100,000. Neither would have happened without the support of many kind and generous people, too many to mention but certain individuals at key moments made a real difference in moving us forward when it all seemed too much and helped us keep on track. Lloyd Scott, Geoff Marshall-Clarke, James Gilby, Rachel Baird of the Daily Express, Angela Lodge of BBC Essex, Phil Smith from the FA, Andrew Doherty and Matt Davey from Tesco, Julian Caruso, Marie Cole and Tristan Barrett are some of the people who stood out. Gemma Herring became my web-wizard and marketing marvel and was always there when I needed an idea, something printing or a media contact.

Ninety three people walked with me for some of the way from St. Bartholomew's Church in Essex to the Waldstadion in Frankfurt and my thanks go to all of them for their solidarity, companionship and support. Sixteen people caught boats and trains and planes to join me during the European leg but one person has to be picked out, Phil, who flew from Spain, not once but twice, to join his sister and honour the memory of his nephew.

Schools played an important part in the walk; Sandra came back to England from Liege with Great Totham School; Chipping Hill Infant School supported Sandra throughout; the Anglo-European School with the backing of the Co-Head Jill Martin arranged accommodation for us at Wegimont and in Frankfurt and; teacher, Ursula Schoelzke, Rosella and Oleg and the other students of the Goethe-Gymnasium were brilliant hosts during our visit to their city.

We were met by kindness and sometimes by gestures 'above and beyond' during the walk, sometimes by people whose names we never found out. The hotel owner in Bourbourg who drove Phil and Anne Hurst to find our hidden chateau; the car driver in Koblenz who drove 10 miles out of his way to find the motor home are but two examples. Sylvia Pratt at Talbot House and Mehmet Fistik in Stadtkyll are two hosts amongst many who looked after us wonderfully well and added enormously to the journey.

The Leukaemia Research Fund does a fantastic job of supporting research into blood cancers. Their independent panel of specialists make sure that research bids are carefully scrutinised and only the most worthwhile are supported. The Head Office team are totally committed to their cause, very professional in their approach and together with branch members believe in creating a family atmosphere where everyone feels 'at home' and gets the support they need. Cathy Gilman, Annette How, Kate White and all the team made Sandra and I very welcome when we first came to talk to them and have been there to help us ever since. Our grateful thanks go to them for all their kindness and support. Joyce Young from Redbridge, Kym McMillan from Medway, Linda Pagdin from Ashford and Val Ackroyd from Huddersfield are just some of the LRF branch members who gave up their time to help us during 2006.

So many people helped and supported, it was a humbling and a wonderful thing to receive their help, kindness, love and money. But five people stand out, without them I might not have made it to Frankfurt. Ted Herring has been the 'diamond geezer' who I can always rely on, a true friend. My brother, Chris, has been and continues to be totally committed and he and his family have done so much to help us and Tim's Trust. Dan has talked to me almost every day since his brother died, some days his words have kept me going. I believe in you too, Dan.

Sandra is my rock and my anchor, she keeps my feet on the ground and picks me up when I'm down. Thank you for going there with me, I know it was far harder for you to make the journey than it was for me.

And that leaves the 93rd person who joined me on the walk. Whose face is in none of the pictures but who was with me, every step of the way. My inspiration!

I was asked recently to go along to a meeting at Deloitte to say a few words to a group of important people. They are the 30 champions who voluntarily lead the organisation's efforts to raise money for the Leukaemia Research Fund and their other charity partners. Thinking about what I wanted to say, I came up with the theme of dreams and dream makers.

We all need dreams, without the freedom to dream and the courage to think the unthinkable, little of real note would happen in our world. What matters just as much of course, is what we do with our dreams, how we turn them into action and persevere to reach our goals; but without the dream...? No one needs dreams more than young people setting out on their adult lives, challenging the prejudices and boundaries of their parents and dreaming of a better world.

There are fewer things worse than seeing someone's dreams, one by one, get smashed and squashed in front of their eyes whilst they are doing everything in their power to keep them alive. Every one until there is only the final gasp of air. I walked to Frankfurt to keep one of those dreams alive, to see it come true and I got there. You and every other person who buys this book, supports Tim's Trust and the LRF is a dream maker. Your support will mean that more and more of the 'forgotten tribe' will survive the scourge of leukaemia and live to see their dreams come true.

THANK YOU

John Reeve

Tim's Story
He lived strong with courage and bravery

I will always remember those few days back in the autumn of 2002 culminating in the words that every parent dreads to hear, *'Your child has got cancer'*. Tim had not been well for a month, the after-effects of a minor operation to remove an abscess, or so we thought. He had just started at Portsmouth University, was settling in well, when chatting to him one November evening on the phone, he broke down, *'I need to come home dad, I feel awful'*

I was working in the Isle of Man but took the first flight out the following morning and was in Portsmouth by 10.30am. He had been home only 10 days before but seeing him as he came out of the student hall was a terrible shock, he had lost weight, was deathly pale and shuffled to the car like an old man. We called at the local hospital on the way home but the doctor clearly thought that he hadn't been looking after himself and sent us on our way – perhaps he thought that Tim was a 'typical student' into drugs or alcohol. Some pampering by his mum appeared to do the trick for a day or two but he didn't recover. A visit to A&E at Chelmsford and a chance blood test brought a more urgent response and the following day, he was in an isolation room at Broomfield hospital – we knew then it was serious! The next days were a blur but I remember sitting with Tim listening to Coldplay's 'The Scientist', both of crying our eyes out and wondering *'Why me?'* and *'What's going on?'* The doctors were reluctant to tell us anything at Broomfield and for four days we were in limbo, knowing nothing, fearing the worst and all the time Tim's condition was deteriorating. The doctors were nervous about prescribing any treatment until they had a diagnosis. finally, a Consultant Haematologist told us that Tim had a serious blood disorder and he was offered a bed at St. Bartholomew's in London. After an all-day wait for an ambulance, off we went, arriving at 10.45pm.

At Barts, our middle-of-the-night reception was great. Tim was given his own room and made comfortable. He was looked after immediately and the family was made welcome. We were told what was going to happen and why and immediately felt confident in the people caring for Tim. He was asked lots of questions and described to the doctors, what we found out later, were many of the classic symptoms of emerging leukaemia – tiredness, night sweats, aching bones, bruising and weight loss. The following day he had his first of many bone marrow tests and then the confirmation, *'You've got leukaemia'*. He was just 20 years of age, beginning to find his way in the world, growing in self-confidence, a talented athlete looking forward to a world full of opportunities and possibilities. Little did we know what the future had in store for us.

Leukaemia has a high profile in the UK. It is the most common form of cancer amongst children and our natural sympathy for childhood sufferers has been built on successfully by people like Gary Lineker and Geoff Thomas and the work of the Leukaemia Research Fund. But most people are ignorant of what it is and what it involves – why shouldn't they be? There are six major kinds of leukaemia, each with different variants. In addition, there are other lymphomas and cancers of the blood and lymph system. The type of leukaemia that Tim had is one of the most aggressive – acute lymphoblastic leukaemia - known as ALL. Research into the childhood version has produced huge improvements in treatment and a cure rate of 80-90%. But the same is not the case for the adult variant. Tragically, only around 30-40% of teenagers and young adults survive long-term. Blood cancers are the most common cause of non-accidental death amongst 16-34 year olds in the UK and very few teenagers and young adults take part in clinical trials of new drugs and protocols compared to children. To quote a recent paper in a scientific journal, *'Teenagers and young adults with acute lymphoblastic leukaemia languish in the shadows of the success of therapy in childhood leukaemia ... they are the 'Forgotten Tribe'.*

There is much conjecture about the causes of leukaemia. Essentially, nobody knows for sure; if they did, it would make finding a cure that much easier. There are theories that in some cases there is a genetic predisposition with the disease being triggered off by a virus or some external trauma. Others argue a link to exposure to certain types of toxins or radiation and certainly the increase in the incidence of leukaemia during the last 50 years supports this view. As a parent, not knowing only compounds the inevitable self-doubt – *'what did we do wrong'?*

Leukaemia is cancer of the blood, it's not a tumour in one of more parts of the body that can be pinpointed and attacked, it gets everywhere, its effects are dreadful and its treatment is tough. I quote from a recent article *'Doctors in the future will look back on early 21 century chemotherapy with the same contempt that doctors today have for leeches. It is a blunderbuss. Yes, it kills the cancer cells (sometimes) but it also kills many other things especially fast-growing cells like hair'* It also compromises the immune system, devastating the white blood count of people who are already ill and making them vulnerable to bugs and infections that you and I would throw off without knowing.

The protocol for Tim involved 12 months of chemotherapy and radiotherapy. They knocked him down, as hard as he could take it, let him recover just enough and then hit him again – for 12 months. And he didn't complain once.

Tim was frightened and scared – who wouldn't be. The treatment started on December 1, 2002. Initially, he was in a single room in the attic of the East Wing. He was very poorly, the leukaemia had reached an advanced stage and he needed help just to get up and go to the toilet. He was put on steroids to build his appetite and strength before the cocktail of poisons began. Soon he was able to move around more easily and was out of immediate danger. He spent most of December in Bodley Scott 2 Ward, in a small four-bed room with patients many of whom were over 60 and with few facilities for young people. We had a cake for Sandra's 50 birthday by his bed and then he developed cellulitis in his arm. Incredibly painful, but his arm responded to antibiotics, and he came home on Christmas Eve. He loved Christmas and we had a wonderful time at home where he felt safe and secure. And then it was back for more. He had visits from some of his friends to help keep him sane but the family, his mum Sandra, brother Dan and me made an unspoken pact and one or more of us visited Tim every day he was in hospital throughout his illness.

It was a hard time but it was also a positive time. At least now, he knew what he was fighting against and could get on with it. He was soon into remission, quickly began to think ahead and make plans and he focused. They say that when we are under pressure, our core personality comes to the fore. In Tim's case, this meant a pragmatism, a focus, a determination and a positive attitude that will always amaze me as I think about him. I've been lucky enough to know and work with some incredibly talented and able people but I have never come across anybody with Tim's spirit, quiet determination and sheer willpower.

He quickly got into a routine. Found out about all his drugs – the chemo pills and the antibiotics and knew what each of them was for and their potential side-effects. He was absolutely disciplined about taking them. As soon as he could, he started walking to get some exercise and transformed his diet to eat only healthy food and he cut out alcohol.

And so 2003 passed on a rollercoaster ride of uncertainty, fear and hope. Every time he came home we celebrated and every time he went back for treatment, we hoped and prayed. Initially, Tim continued to lose weight - over 30 kilos at one point - and looked pale and gaunt; his hair fell out and he lost much of his self-confidence but not his self-belief. His body was struggling but his spirit was strong. We held fundraising events during that summer to raise money for leukaemia research; Tim was always the first to put his hand in his pocket to contribute. As well as his regular visits to the day unit for chemotherapy and transfusions of blood and platelets, he was an in-patient on several occasions when his white blood count was flat and his immune system compromised. Being Tim, he got on with it, hardly ever complained and concentrated on getting well.

One time when he did complain was a night during early April. Sandra was visiting friends in Walton-on-the-Naze and Tim had gone to bed as normal but woke up in great pain sometime in the early morning. Both his knees were excruciatingly painful, the slightest touch or movement wracked him with waves of pain. He couldn't move and yet he couldn't get comfortable. We had some pain killers but they did no good. What was going on? As always, we rang Bodley Scott Ward at Barts, 50 miles away, and they advised us to go to the nearest A&E unit and ask them to get in touch with Barts. It took us 20 agonizing minutes to get down 13 stairs and into the car. At Broomfield Hospital, the night doctors didn't know what to do apart from increase the dose of painkillers and gradually the pain became more bearable. In the morning, he was given a bed, his knees were easing but his temperature spiked. Later that day, he was transferred to Barts and was soon stabilised. It transpired that he had suffered an acute attack of gout, a symptom caused by the recent withdrawal of the steroids he had been taking.

When he was able, he liked to walk and soon established a regular route around the village, past St. Bartholomew's church, round by the apple orchards and back home. Two miles in total but as the weather improved, Tim, Sandra and I came to love that walk and the opportunity to talk and think in the fresh air and the beautiful Essex countryside. It made us realise, even more, how lucky we were to live in such a nice place.

Gradually, Tim started to enjoy life again, saw more of his friends and had the occasional night out. At the end of the year, protocol completed, we went to Tenerife and for the first time in 18 months, Tim got some sun on his back. Even that trip was eventful, the night before we flew from Gatwick, his temperature went up to over 38C and we held our breath to see if it would come back down – it did. In Puerto de la Cruz, Tim was tired out and struggled to walk anywhere. Christmas dinner was corned beef, tinned potatoes and carrots in our apartment.

In February 2004, Tim started at Anglia Uni. He'd taken Maths A level, always enjoyed working with figures and decided to switch from Sports Science to Finance and Accounting, quite a change of direction. He was going for fortnightly blood tests and taking chemo tablets as part of his maintenance treatment but the message was – *get on with your life, do what ever you feel you are able to.* He wanted to begin re-building his life but stay close to where he felt safe. The first term was boring – the work was easy. He went to the gym, began to regain his fitness and was well. In the summer, the lads went off to Newquay camping. Tim was not impressed with camping but had a great time and there are many stories about his exploits.

Tim was strong and powerful and had a physical presence that was added to, when he wanted, by the steely determination in his eyes. If he wasn't sure or didn't see the point, he kept his mouth shut. At other times he could be loud, brash and 'in your face'. He was hard to get to know, he could blank you and be absolutely ruthless, but once you broke through into the circle of trust, he was great company, considerate and a loyal friend. He was stubborn and impossible to shift if he didn't agree with something, but give him time and he often came round. He had a sharp intelligence and quick and very dry sense of humour – he loved Peter Kaye, the Simpsons, Little Britain and The Catherine Tate Show. His answer phone message was pure Homer. He was an excellent mimic, Lou and Andy and Vicky Pollard from Little Britain were his favourites as well as *'How very dare you!'* and the foul-mouthed granny from Catherine Tate.

In September, he moved into uni accommodation but came home most weekends to play football for Bicknacre (and get his washing done). Uni was good; he did well in his exams and with a different perspective on life, wanted to make the most of his opportunity. He enjoyed cooking for himself and adopted a healthy diet using organic food whenever he could. Some of his friends were back from university and he met up with them and kept in touch with others who were away from home.

In April 2005, we had a family long weekend in Barcelona. Dan had bought us tickets for a Barcelona match as Christmas presents. Tim loved that holiday, going to the Nou Camp with 90,000 other people to watch the 3-3 draw against Real Betis, strolling up Las Ramblas, soaking up the atmosphere of a great city. But he was starting to feel tired and after a standard blood test, it was agreed that he should have a bone marrow test.

It was 11.15am on Tuesday, April 26, when he rang us to say that IT was back. We were all devastated but soon became positive again and determined that we could beat it for a second time. Tim wanted to delay the treatment for three weeks because he had exams coming up but the Professor advised not to lose any time and the treatment re-started at the beginning of May. The plan was to get into remission again and then have a bone marrow transplant. There are only 350,000 people on the bone marrow register in the UK. We raised funds for the Anthony Nolan Trust, organised a donor recruitment session. A donor was found. There was a chance. After chemo, the lymphoblast count fell to under 5%. It was working, then disaster!

Barts is a wonderful hospital because of the people, their expertise, world-leading in some cases, and their love, care and concern. But in many areas it is essentially a Victorian hospital trying to operate in a 21 century context. Ambitious plans are in place to change all that but at the moment hygiene is difficult even if the systems are right.

Tim's pick line in his arm was sore and he came into the Day Unit to have it taken out. Because his white blood count was low, the doctors decided he should stay in as a precautionary measure in case of an infection in his arm. Two days later, after having walked from Liverpool Street Station to Barts, he picked up an e-coli bug on the ward whilst his immune system was still compromised. He nearly died in late June. His temperature was over 39°C for a week and peaked at 40.6°C. He had several attacks of uncontrollable shaking – 'the rigours' - but he was stubborn and he battled back.

He loved music and needed things to look forward to. I had texted 150 times for tickets to Live 8 and got two. We were going to go. A friend of Sandra's, Sue - bless her - got us VIP passes the night before the event. Brilliant! But Tim wasn't well enough to go and watched it on TV instead. He insisted I go so I went along with Dan. We stood 10 rows from the front of 150,000 people and listened to Coldplay playing 'Fix You' tears of hope for Tim streaming down our faces. And then I went back to be with my other son in hospital.

The e-coli wasn't the problem, Tim *devoured* that BUT it delayed his treatment for a month and during this time the leukaemia took hold. Even worse as we now know, it developed a resistance to all the poison that was being pumped inside him. But still he soldiered on, staying positive and being Tim. He was on steroids and put on weight. He went to V 2005 for a day and saw Oasis and the other bands. That was the last time he saw his friends.

At the end of August, Tim had the terrible news that the conventional treatment hadn't worked. Because the cancer cells had developed immunity to the drugs, there was no point in repeating the protocol. Added to that the cumulative effect of all the poison meant that Tim had almost reached the limit of chemotherapy drugs that his body could take. It was time to make some tough decisions. By carefully controlling his drug intake, it might be possible to slow down the leukaemia and with good palliative care, he could hope for a reasonable quality of life for a period of time **or** he could risk all and try one of the new, experimental treatments currently under test. At age 23, with what should have been a lifetime ahead of him, the decision was quick and easy, *'If there is a chance of getting into remission and being cured, then I want to go for it!'*

A few days after the dreadful news, we had a message from one of the nurses who was involved in a charity, the Willow Foundation, helping children and young people with fatal illnesses to *'have their wish come true'*. They do wonderful work enabling children to visit Disneyland or meet their favourite celebrity. She asked if Tim had a wish. He was quiet at first but then replied with total certainty. *'Let some other person who can't afford to, have their wish come true. All I want is to live!'*

The team at Barts used their contacts around the world and quickly established that chlorfarabine, a new drug, currently under test and not yet licensed in either the UK or the USA had the best chance of success. Nearly all the testing had involved children with good results and the drug was just starting to be tested on adults. Permission was granted to use the drug on a compassionate basis and arrangements were made for a course of treatment. The plan was to have one dose of chlorfarabine per day for five days, allow his blood counts to recover and then repeat the dosage. Tim went into hospital on September 18 and we waited and prayed. The effects of the new drug were savage. After three days, much earlier than normal, his blood counts plummeted and his temperature spiked to over 40°C but the treatment continued – he was strong. After another 10 days in hospital, his blood counts started to pick up. He came home and a few days later, had a bone marrow test – *the moment of truth*. Sadly, the gamble hadn't worked. The cancer had not gone away. Only worse, it had grown further in strength **and** the poison had destroyed almost all of Tim's remaining healthy bone marrow.

In October, at a fateful meeting with Professor Lister, Tim was told that there was no point in completing the second half of the course of treatment; - it would probably have killed him! *'Take a couple of weeks off and decide what you want to do. We can try to control the leukaemia for a time but a cure is not expected.'* He didn't want his friends to know. We pleaded with him but he didn't want them to see him ill, wanted them to remember the old Reevo. He didn't know what to say.

One of the consequences of a long period of medical treatment is the risk of becoming institutionalised. Even if you are at home for much of the time, it is so easy to become totally reliant and dependant on the doctors. Especially when the treatment has worked in the past, the tendency is to go along with what they say and in some way to almost give up personal responsibility for making decisions about treatment, what to do and what not to do. There is comfort and certainty, after a fashion, in following an established routine. Belatedly, we had already started to look for a second opinion - was there nothing that could be done? - and arranged to see another UK expert. We had also researched alternative therapies, spending hours on the internet.

It was surfing the net that Sandra came across Nicola Bradbury and the superb work she is doing from her new base on the Isle of Skye. Nicola's own story is an amazing tale of courage and determination to overcome a serious accident and illness. She now offers a range of complementary treatment to patients with serious illnesses. She has an impressive record of helping to make a real difference to the health of her patients and their quality of life. Tim was sceptical but talked to Nicola one day on the phone and 20 minutes later was ready to give it a try. Nicola sent us a range of natural supplements and treatments to boost Tim's red blood count and immune system and advised him on which foods to eat and which to avoid. She also talked to Tim, on the phone, helping to maintain his positive attitude.

The attitude of the majority of the medical profession in the UK towards alternative therapies appears to vary from condescension and polite sufferance to outright opposition – *'meddling in things they don't understand'*. Despite the tremendous advances in medical science, there are still many things that we don't know or understand about the human body and the treatment of illnesses. A small but growing number of hospitals are beginning not only to offer but to promote other therapies alongside conventional treatment. We believe there is a huge amount that complementary medicine has to offer and only wish that we had been made aware of what was available alongside the conventional treatment that Tim went through when he was first diagnosed. We are convinced that the treatment helped Tim and that had he started much earlier, it would have made a real difference.

With his complementary treatment underway, Tim was given a large dose of steroids to kick start his remaining healthy bone marrow back into producing blood cells and told to go away and do what he wanted for two weeks.

Mum and son on holiday in Spain just six weeks before Tim died

He wanted to go to Spain to see his uncle, aunt and cousins. So off we went to Nerja, strolled on the Balcon del Europa and had four great days – *'I'll always remember watching him trotting after 4-year old Jo on the beach.* He seemed so well and so strong, it was hard to believe he was dying! Back home, we went to see Leeds play at Reading. We watched Athlete at the Hammersmith Odeon with Dan. At the start of November we went to Paris. He had been once before to Euro Disney but wanted to see more of the city. We went First Class on Eurostar, stayed close by the Sorbonne, had lunch on the Seine and went to Montmartre, seeing all the sights.

We came home from France on November 6 and that night, we descended into Bedlam. He had picked up a bug, somewhere, and developed legionnaire's disease. He was on oxygen, in great pain and the doctors told us to expect the worst. I stayed by his bed-side throughout that night and helped him to find his 'happy place' - a special holiday that he had really enjoyed - to leave the pain and torment behind and go to that 'happy place. He said later that it had really helped him get through the night.

The following day, Tim was moved into a room by himself, a room to die in! The Prof. told him *'to lie back and think of England.'*

'What was that all about?' Tim said afterwards. He wanted to live every day, every hour and every minute of his life. That evening I rang my brother in Huddersfield and told him the dreadful news. Chris, as always, listened and said what he could but I could tell he was stunned. The next morning, after another night at Tim's bedside, my mobile phone rang about 7am and it was Chris. He had driven down overnight, arrived in London about 4am and sat in the car and visited the early morning cafés next to Smithfields until he felt he could ring. I let him in about 7.30 and he tiptoed to the room to see Tim whilst most of the patients were still in their beds and the night staff getting ready to finish their shift. It was an emotional moment, each knowing that they would probably not see each other again. And then Chris left and drove back to Huddersfield – sometimes you just have to do these things!

Yet again, Tim fought back. Mornings were the hardest for him, it was as if he was summoning up the will to face another day but he gradually improved during the morning and as each day passed by. We had some special times, watching his favourite DVDs in the evenings, pain-free, breathing more easily with the oxygen turned down, imagining a different world from the one that was his. Two weeks later, he walked out of the hospital to the smiles and surprise of many of the nurses but again the infection had allowed the leukaemia to get even stronger.

To enable him to come home we had arranged for oxygen to be available both from canisters and via a condenser and he was on oxygen for long parts of the day. Getting up and down stairs was difficult but he was determined to sleep in his own bed. The help from local community services was good with equipment for the bath and a chair that could be raised and lowered. For another 10 days he battled on, using his determination, sense of humour and spirit to get through the days and long nights. The leukaemia was everywhere, he ached everywhere. Soon his testicles became hugely swollen, and then his eyesight started to fade and he couldn't watch the TV and DVDs which had become one of his few remaining pleasures. At times, the pain from his inflamed lungs reduced him to tears but still he didn't complain. He knew he was dying then and asked his mum, what she thought it was like to die – now there's a question for a mother! For Tim, there was only one thing to do, as always – *to get on with it*. On November 29, he wrote some words to his family that we found after his death – they are etched forever in my heart.

On the night of December 5, Tim couldn't settle, the pain was bad and breathing more and more difficult. At one point he threw his mask off and said he had had enough but we worked out a plan. We managed to get him downstairs and with the oxygen on full, he was more comfortable and we decided to wait until 6am and then drive into Barts. This time I talked to him about my special place, a holiday when he and Dan had been young boys and helped Tim to bring back the distant memories.

He knew as he struggled out to the car that he was leaving home for the last time. The oxygen had almost run out by the time we reached the hospital, and when he got onto a bed in the day unit, he was exhausted.

Tim's Story

Struggling for oxygen to stay alive, he was having a cannula put in by Sam, the nurse who has cared for him more than any other over the three years of his illness and had become a good friend. She was pregnant, expecting her first child and had told Tim confidentially, before she told anyone else at the hospital. Tim was gasping for air, Sandra, who was sat out of sight to Tim, was sobbing quietly and on seeing this, Sam started to cry silently, tears rolling down her cheeks. Tim saw this and when she'd finished he gasped *'piece of paper'* and shakily wrote *'Sam's getting upset, not good for baby, think I should have another nurse.'*

After transfusions of haemoglobin and platelets, Tim's breathing became a little easier for the next 48 hours but it was a temporary improvement. His morphine dose increased and he dozed for long periods. But every time his drugs were administered, he knew exactly which pills he was due to take and questioned and corrected the nurses, if they didn't get it exactly right. Getting up required an enormous amount of concentration and willpower but he continued to get up to go to the toilet and eat the small amounts of food he was eating, in a comfortable chair. Even on the evening before he died, he was thinking ahead and making plans with the doctor for more treatment the following week.

The end came relatively quickly and despite everything, took me by surprise. Tim seemed to be relatively stable, he had chatted to Dan in the afternoon and Dan said he'd be back the following morning. Then at 8pm, after four days of normal temperatures, his temperature started to go up but not excessively, we'd seen much worse before. He found it hard to settle down to sleep, but that had happened before and we all got ready for another uncomfortable night. It seemed as if his body had reached its limit and his incredible willpower couldn't hold things together any longer. His final few hours were desperate as he fought right until the end. He died at 5am on the morning of Sandra's birthday – the one day he desperately didn't want to die on. He had a card and a present for her. He died as he lived, with courage and bravery.

So that's Tim's story.

Some of us were lucky enough to know some part of the boy and the man that was Timothy Paul or Tim Reeve or Reevo but none of us knew his full extent, the strengths and quirks that made him unique and what he might have become.

He was passionate about sport – especially football. Leeds United and England were his first loves. A few days before he died, he said to his brother that he would give anything to be able to kick a ball around again.

He loved music and films. He downloaded 4,049 songs onto his laptop (ready for the transplant that never came) and had a DVD collection into the hundreds. He knew film scripts - the Shawshank Redemption, Pulp Fiction, Star Wars and the Lion King to name but a few, word perfect, and he loved to sit with his mates watching a film, each with a part they were playing.

He was catapulted from teenage angst and stroppiness to maturity and then to a wisdom that was scary. Towards the end, he could make me feel like the kid with his perception and perspective, his ability to sit me down and put me straight when I was loosing it. Mum, dad, uncles, teachers, doctors, professors all had their feet returned firmly to the ground on occasions by an unerring ability to cut through the crap in a few words.

What did Tim believe in? He believed in people; his good friends but above all else, in his family and in himself. It was a deep-rooted belief that formed the basis of his determination. During that long and painful autumn, he came across a saying that he liked a lot. It was in a football magazine, 'Four Four Two'. The words are Vince Lombardi's and they have become a motto for me.

'The darkest moments of our lives are not to be buried and forgotten, rather they are memories to be called upon for inspiration; reminding us of the unrelenting human spirit and our capacity to overcome the intolerable'

Tim is and will always be our inspiration

During those last few crazy weeks before Tim died, I asked some friends, *'What do you hold on to when all hope is gone?'* Steph answered, *'Cling onto love, it's the only thing you have left'.* And so that's what we did on that fateful December morning. We left the hospital feeling cold and totally drained and drove to find Dan. It was 6am on a dark, cold and wet Saturday morning and we drove through London to the Health Club in Kensington where he works, unsure if he had started an early shift, but he hadn't. Thirty minutes later we were banging on the door of the house where he lived in Earlsfield and knocked up a startled Chris who let us in. No words were necessary, our faces said it all. Dan was fast asleep in bed and he and his mum clung together desperately as we told him the terrible news.

He drove us home and I began the job of phoning people. I was exhausted and angry but frightened to lie down and relive the nightmare in my mind. I was probably rather brutal as I shocked family, close friends and Tim's closest pals telling them the tragic news in a direct, matter-of-fact sort of way – perhaps, it was the only way I could do it. I even began looking for Funeral Directors and made appointments to see two on Sunday. Finally, late in the afternoon, I went to sleep for a few hours. We didn't see anyone on that Saturday although everyone we spoke to sent their love and condolences.

The next fortnight was a blur with one shining exception – Tim's Thanksgiving Service. There were so many things to do and people to see and right away I slipped almost automatically into survival mode, keeping busy. The Service was arranged for Monday, December 19 and we spent hours discussing the Order of Service. Tim didn't believe in God and we felt it was important to have prayers that weren't religious in the traditional sense, as well as some of the music that Tim loved so much, rather than hymns or carols. So we had many family discussions and a fair few passionate arguments before we finalised the arrangements and signed off the Order of Service for the printer. At the same time, I threw myself into writing Tim's story which I managed to read out at the Service without too many tears and which forms the greater part of this Chapter. Faye, Dan's girlfriend, came up on Sunday to be with him, helped us to choose the music for the

Service and was a great support to us all. On Tuesday, Dan and Faye went back to London and Sandra and I got on with the arrangements.

Family and friends were on the phone and calling round to see us every day and were so loving and supportive that it did us good to talk about Tim and share our grief with them. All the time Christmas was getting closer and closer but we didn't even begin to think about what we would do.

The day of the Service was bright and mild for December. The house was full by 10am. Two hundred people attended the Thanksgiving service, to remember Tim and celebrate his short life – many of them his friends from school and uni. It was a bitter sweet occasion with a lot of tears but also many smiles and happy memories. We sang one of his favourite happy songs, 'Amarillo' and nearly raised the roof in the church. Many of his friends came along and shared their memories of Tim with the family. We began to realise the full extent of the impact he had on many people's lives.

We had three readings at the service and I'll remember them all for different reasons. This one was read by our good friend Ted.

After Glow (by unknown)

'I'd like the memory of me to be a happy one,
I'd like to leave an after glow of smiles when life is done.
I'd like to leave an echo whispering softly down the ways,
Of happy times and laughing times and bright and sunny days.
I'd like the tears of those who grieve, to dry before the sun
Of happy memories that I leave when life is done.'

Even before Tim's funeral, in the midst of the sadness, despair, anger and confusion, I knew I had to focus on something positive, something that would be a challenge and might just result in some good coming out of the tragedy. Sandra, Dan and I had talked about not having flowers at the Service but asking for donations for leukaemia research and establishing the Tim Reeve

Charitable Trust. Already in my mind, I had an idea for the launch event for Tim's Trust.

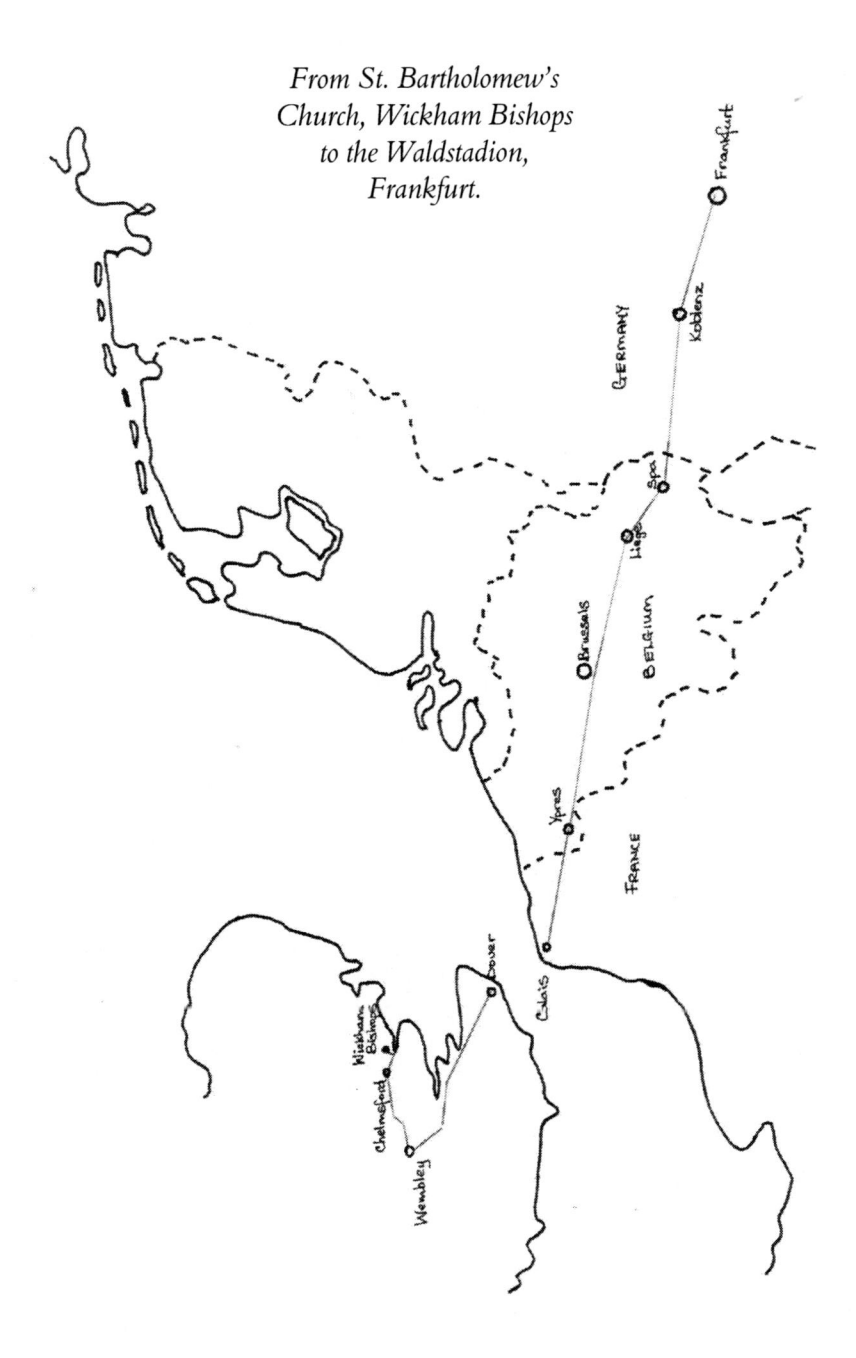

*From St. Bartholomew's
Church, Wickham Bishops
to the Waldstadion,
Frankfurt.*

John Reeve

100 Days to Go
'Getting on with it'

During Tim's illness, one of the things that helped him through the bad times and kept him positive was having things to look forward to. One of his most vivid dreams was to have a transplant, get well and travel to Germany to support England in the Football World Cup finals. He applied for tickets in the on-line lotteries and we talked many times about making the trip. So for me, the idea of Walking to the World Cup was a 'no brainer', it ticked all the boxes. As a '50-something', I was battered by 30 years of playing rugby, triple jumping and road running but still fairly fit and was confident I could walk 500 miles, although the thought of walking every day for a month made it seem enough of a challenge to motivate me. It was a way to honour Tim's dream – a walk for Tim, a journey that he would have loved to have made to a destination and a tournament he would have loved to have visited. It provided an opportunity, in what would be a huge media spotlight around the tournament, to raise awareness of the plight of 'the 'Forgotten Tribe' and raise funds to improve treatment and care, to make a small difference and try to make some good come out of Tim's death. I knew also that for me, I had to keep busy, have a focus and as Tim would say, 'Get on with it, Dad'. Otherwise… I didn't want to go there.

That was my logic and those were my needs. But grieving isn't about logic and it wasn't all about me. Christmas was a haze, a time to slow down and allow the grief and anguish to replace the gnawing fear that had been our lives for the past eight months and beyond that, for the last three years. Dan joined us for Christmas Day, friends were kind and caring. We went up to Yorkshire, as we always did, and saw Sandra's dad and our families and then came home for New Year – and getting on with the rest of our lives!

In those first few days of the New Year as we started to think 'what now', I wanted to charge into this new project at 200 miles an hour but Sandra was different. Sandra and I have been married for 31 years, teenage sweethearts; she has always been the girl for me. We know each other well and know our differences. Sandra wanted time and space to grieve, she had given up her job to care for Tim, he had become her whole life for the last eight months. The last thing she needed was to set out on a new venture that would require a huge amount of planning, preparation and organisation. She wanted time for herself, 'time to be' as Pat later said. And so, I was cautious about telling her about my idea, tried to pick my moment and think through the issues involved. Like Tim, Sandra speaks her mind; she is a Yorkshire woman, naturally spots drawbacks, disadvantages and risks in any idea and tells it straight. Like Tim, she is also a perfectionist and needs to get things right, so once she commits there are no half measures.

Could I have picked 'the right moment'? I doubt it. But I chose a time after the first week of January was over and launched my scheme. Her immediate reaction was that it was a good idea but totally impractical and that we couldn't do it properly in the time available – simple as that. It was a view shared by other people. What's more she didn't want to and couldn't get involved in something like this, so soon after Tim's death. For two weeks we wrestled with the idea between us. She knew I wanted to do it and wasn't easily diverted, could see that it was a good idea but felt overwhelmed by the scale of the challenge. I talked to Dan, my brother Chris and to friends about it. Everyone was supportive, some thought we should go for it, others cautioned not to go ahead – the jury was split. The more Sandra and I talked, the more she helped us to think through the issues and the more determined I became. But I knew I couldn't do it without her commitment and support – *I* would be walking but it was for *our* son and brother and friend and lots of people would need to be very actively involved, her especially; I wanted her to be. And all the while, time was passing by. Each day meant less time to plan, to organise, to train and to make it happen.

We agreed to hold a 'summit meeting' and ask our trusted friends for their considered views. Following that, we would make a final decision. Ted, Peter, Norris and Joan, Simon and Malcolm came round on Wednesday 25 of January for a beer and nibbles and we talked it through. I had outlined an agenda including our initial plans. There were three key areas: planning the logistics of the walk, raising awareness and funds, and getting fit so as to arrive at Frankfurt without any lasting damage. Everyone was asked for their honest views and after a long conversation, they gave them and still the jury was split – one half said, 'Go for it' and the others, 'Great idea but you haven't got the time to do it the way you would want to'.

Sandra says that I had already made up my mind and she is probably right. The meeting helped to flush out yet more considerations and things to be done, enlisted some of the people to provide help – although I know they would have done so anyway – and convinced Sandra and I that we should do it. We reasoned that we would work hard for two months to build some momentum behind the walk and take stock at the end of March. If needs be, we could decide then not to go ahead without losing too much. And so the battle plan was drawn up – we had almost exactly 100 days to get everything into place.

I started walking everywhere. Sandra and I went out for our first walk the Saturday after the meeting and covered 16 miles over five hours with a pub lunch at Woodham Walter in the middle. It was a bright January day and Sandra was remarkable as someone who had taken virtually no exercise at all for months. She only started slowing down in the last few miles but was very stiff the following day. I began keeping a diary recording the main events of each day, the successes and disappointments as we moved forwards, noting down where and how far I had walked and reflecting about Tim – using his inspiration to fuel my determination.

I hit it hard. Meetings took place over the next two weeks with: the Leukaemia Research Fund - initially with Annette How who visited us at home, Cathy Gilman - Head of Fundraising in London to talk about their involvement and support, Malcolm Tilsed - manager of the Meadows Shopping Centre in Chelmsford to discuss a local media campaign, Lloyd Scott to pick his brains about how to prepare for this crazy venture, one of Norris's friends who had walked from John O'Groats to Land's End and the entire length of New Zealand when in his fifties.

A Walk of Faith

Within a week, I had sent off over 50 letters and 250 e-mails asking for help and support from a whole range of people. Geoff Clarke, an old Uni friend and now a Marketing Consultant, helped us to design a sponsorship form and arranged a free charity mail drop from Vernons Pools. Gemma Herring, who helped massively in all sorts of ways and works for Malcolm, commissioned the design of a website for Tim's Trust. We were up and running, well walking.

The original idea was to walk from Elland Road, home of Leeds United, to Frankfurt, where England played their first game of the World Cup on June 10. I had worked out via the internet, that it was a distance of about 700 miles and that assuming I walked an average of 20-25 miles a day, it would take me around 30 days to complete the walk. I looked to see when Leeds last home game of the season was. Could I tie in the start of the walk with the game? The uncertainty was that they looked destined for the Play-offs – the timing might work but it might not. Then meeting Lloyd Scott at the Brentwood Hilton gave us another idea. Why walk from Leeds? Wembley is the home of English football even though it was still a building site, so why not start the walk from there and why not start on cup final day? At that time in early February, the game was still scheduled for Wembley and although it appeared unlikely, we reasoned that a Wembley start might still be a newsworthy item and provide some much-needed positive publicity for the stadium. So Wembley it was and cup final day, May 16, fitted perfectly with the outline schedule that was emerging. That meant 500 miles instead of 700 although I decided I should walk from home to Wembley first – as a sort of warm-up for the main event – so add another 50 miles for good luck.

Lloyd Scott was a great encouragement. He was so positive and yet told us about some of the pitfalls and hard lessons that he had learned from his many charity events. One excellent piece of advice was to get three different sets of footwear from different manufacturers. *'When you are on your feet for so long, no matter how well the trainers or boots fit, you will develop pressure points. Get three different makes that all fit well, break them in so that they are all really comfortable and then keep changing them as you complete the walk'.*

Advice so good that, subsequently, I had only one blister in 550 miles of walking. He also advised me to break the walk down into three sessions a day with a break for food between each session. The pattern for the walk was set.

One thing that made the walk easier to organise was the fact that I work for myself as an HR Consultant and so had no boss to talk into giving me yet more time off. What I did have were a number of long-standing clients who had been very supportive when Tim was ill and when I told them about the Walk, were very understanding. I was selective in the work I undertook during the January-April period and from May 9 to June 12 I would be 'otherwise engaged'. So for much of the first four months of the year, I was working a seven-day week. Three days each week earning money and four days planning, talking, organising and training for the walk. Sandra had started doing some supply work as a primary school teacher and her involvement started more slowly, but soon she was getting more and more involved.

In terms of training, my aim was to walk at least four times a week and cover a minimum of 30 miles. This would build up gradually and the week before Easter I covered 102 miles in a week, walking six days with four of the walks covering distances of 20 miles of more. I found the walking good. I soon got into the habit of taking a note pad and pen with me and wrote down all sorts of ideas and things to do whilst I was out walking. It was great thinking time, a chance to clear the head, a chance to think about Tim, to think about the dark times but also begin to remember the 'bright and sunny days'. Each week I would complete at least one long walk of over 15 miles and this was often at the weekends and with Sandra. There are lots of beautiful places to walk either from our home or a short drive away and we came to know our part of Essex much better after living here for 20 years. You see so much more at walking pace than flying by in a car.

I have always been fairly competitive especially at sports and anything physical and always timed my walks and checked my pace. I could comfortably walk 20 miles at 3.75 miles per hour pace and covered 10 miles at 4.2 miles per hour on a number of

A Walk of Faith

occasions. I had several regular walks, into Chelmsford and back (10 miles each way) being one of them and each time I kept a close check on my pace and timing. This was made even easier with help from Colin Gibb, an experienced long-distance runner and friend. I met up with Colin for lunch and he loaned me a wristwatch-style GPS system that measured distance covered to within 20 yards and pace to the nearest tenth of a mile per hour. So my ability to measure became even greater but at the same time, I tried hard just to walk, not to count down distances. To check times and speed but not think about how far I had come or had to go. Just Walk. I knew I would need this attitude when I set out on May 6. Colin persuaded me to invest in some walking sticks, invaluable he said, for the steep climbs and descents and for spreading the effort across arms as well as legs.

Colin also loaned me two skin-tight tops that draw out the sweat and help to keep you dry, cool when it's hot and warm when it's cold. Magic really, but they proved really effective. I wore them out training and every day on the walk – one became the infamous Yellow Jersey but more about that later. By this time, Leukaemia Research had given us 50 T-shirts with 'Walking To The World Cup' printed in red on the front. Walking around Essex, with a T-shirt over one of the tops, I started to get toots of support from passing motorists who had seen me out before or had heard about our plans for the walk.

I bought each of my three pairs of footwear at separate times I started off walking in an existing pair of Asics running shoes. First I went to Runners World and bought a new pair of Asics. In early March, I discovered a great chain of shops called Runners Need; there is one at Holborn, near the LRF Head Office, and I called in one day after a visit. They have three treadmills set up with video cameras at foot level. They ask you to run (or in my case walk) as naturally as possible for 30 seconds and by the time the treadmill has stopped, the tape is rewound and you can see your walking action in slow motion. I knew I pronated – my feet move outwards as each step moves from heel to toe contact with the ground – but not how much. And I also hadn't realised that the tendency to do so, is less when walking than running – obvious I guess – so the trainers that are just right for running, will offer

35

John Reeve

too much support for walking. Make sense? Well it did for me and the result was I bought a second, cheaper pair of Asics which have become my favourite walking footwear.

I should explain that having checked out a route and rough mileage via the RAC website right at the start of our planning; I intended to buy large scale maps and drive the whole of the route, spotting footpaths and trails that we could include in the route, where possible. But from the outset, our assumption was that in the pursuit of the shortest and most direct route, much of the walking would be on tarmac and on roads. For me walking boots were never a realistic option, good trainers would be much lighter and more comfortable. However, I did need a third pair of footwear and I wanted something waterproof so that if it did rain all day, I wouldn't end up with three pairs of soaked trainers that I couldn't get dry for the following day. So I decided to look for some lightweight, waterproof walking shoes and on April 13 (just enough time to get them worn in) I found a pair I liked at the Cotswold Outdoor shop near Liverpool Street. This time no video on the treadmill but with my 1,000 mile socks on, I tried several pairs and settled on a pair of Meindl Gore-Tex shoes – they turned out to be another good choice.

For three months, I walked pretty much everywhere, down to the station instead of taking the car. If I was working in London, say Victoria, instead of the tube, I would walk. If I was going to the gym to do some training or to a meeting in Chelmsford I walked there (and back). It all took more time but not as much additional time as you might think. It was certainly healthier and it was building up the miles in my legs. The gym sessions were important. I have been going to gyms for 25 years, increasingly so as I began to stop playing sport and running on the road. My weakness, I knew from the outset, would be my knees; I had keyhole surgery on both of them about five years ago and the surgeon likened them to car brakes running without any pads left – metal on metal or bone on bone. They became swollen and were sore whenever I did anything slightly excessive. Walking on tarmac four times a week was painful, what would walking 20 miles plus a day for 28 days be like? So the gym sessions had three purposes as Dan, my personal trainer son told me. Firstly to build up stamina without impact using bikes and cross-trainers, secondly to exercise and strengthen the muscles around my knees to provide more support and thirdly to stretch and try to maintain and improve my flexibility. I tried to have a workout with him in London at least once a week and go through the pain barrier of a serious stretching session. But gradually the gym sessions became less frequent as walking and other things took over.

Early on as my knees began to suffer, Sandra came across some Glucosamine Gel Patches. As well as Glucosamine they have chestnut as a soothing balm and menthol to cool. They can be used on any joint and can be left on for 2-3 hours to allow the ingredients to soak in. Their effect on me was immediate. Whereas, before, I would wake up feeling sore and uncomfortable in the middle of the night with my knees aching, often struggle to get back to sleep and feel stiff and sore the following day, with the patches the aching was far less noticeable and it was much easier to get going again the next day. The downside was that the patches were not cheap - £10 for five – and as I needed one for each knee, it would be expensive. To the rescue, however, came David Wilkie, ex- Olympic swimmer and MD of the firm who make the patches. I wrote asking for his support and he generously sent back 10 packs free of charge – one of so many kind and generous gestures that gave us hope and strength to see the walk through, especially in those early days when there seemed so much to do.

Walking near my home in Essex is great. There are lots of 'big skies' to enjoy, waterside as well as open countryside. There are quiet roads and plenty of footpaths for a change but there aren't any proper hills. Now that may sound like a benefit but I knew that our route was likely to take us up into the Belgium Ardennes, through the hilly Eifel region of Germany, climbing up to over 2,000 feet at times and that I needed to get some hills into those legs as well.

So when Sandra went up to Barnsley to see her Dad, I tried to go with her and walked up into the foothills of the Pennines, out towards Hoylandswaine and Penistone. Not as high as the terrain we would encounter in Europe but some steep climbs and drops – and for me the downs were at least as difficult as the ups. I had two glorious Sunday mornings, one in February, the other a month later, when I was out and walking before 9am. On both occasions, the ground was damp and it was chilly with a cold breeze, but the sun was shining and I was well wrapped-up. I had a glorious time, enjoying the views into the valleys and across to the higher ground. Exploring narrow country lanes and finding a secret stone cottage in an idyllic setting as the morning started to unfold. Often, when the sun was on my back, I sensed that Tim was with me and amongst all the sadness and dark thoughts, there were moments of joy and peace as I felt him close by. I'd walk hard up every hill, the steeper the hill, the harder I'd walk, getting hotter and hotter and as the miles unfolded feeling tired but good. I covered 15 miles the first time and over 18 miles on the second walk and then it was back to Hoyland and Sunday dinner with roast beef and Yorkshire puds.

The other place I got my hill walking in, was on the Isle of Man. I visit regularly for work and have done for six years. I almost always enjoy the visit, the people, the pace of life and the country and seaside. During March and April, I made at least four visits and was working for five days at the Old Church Farm at Lonan, about five miles from the hotel where I was staying in Douglas. My routine became: breakfast at 6.30am, walk at 7am, arrive at the farm for 8.15am, change and then prepare for the training session that day. At the end of the day, I'd walk back. Another 10 miles covered with a long drag up out of Douglas along the coast road to the north but some wonderful views, seeing the sun rising and sometimes the lights of Douglas twinkling as I walked back down onto the Prom.

Towards the end of March, Sandra went over to Spain with her father and sister, Anne, to see her brother, Phil, and his family at Moclinejo. Whilst she was away, I was working in Shropshire and drove up to Derbyshire on the Friday evening to stay with my brother-in-law Anthony. On Saturday, we drove out and walked the 18 miles of the Tissington Trail, another change of scenery and another great walk. Anthony would be coming out to walk for five days with me and was in training himself.

Walking became my pastime and sometimes, my pleasure. It became my routine, something to do and be done, an opportunity to let my thoughts free-wheel, think about Tim. Many times I felt he was there walking with me. But the same didn't apply for Sandra. She wasn't doing the walk, she was trying to get back into the routine of work after almost a year and felt even more overwhelmed by the scale of the project. Many evenings included tears and difficult conversations. Many times, I asked myself, was it fair to place this pressure on her, to go ahead with this crazy idea.

Walking also became my opportunity to talk to people. My office became the great outdoors and with a mobile phone and a signal, I spent literally hours on the phone, talking to people, asking for help, making arrangements, conducting radio interviews. All on the move, all with the hopefully faint sound of traffic and my heavy breathing in the background.

As a sometimes management coach, one of the principles that I use most days in my professional work is *'be clear about your goals'*. If you don't know where you want to get to or the outcomes you are looking for when you go into any situation, then how can you expect to achieve the best result? Looking back now, I realise that we did work out some specific, measurable, realistic and time bound goals for the walk but certainly, not from the start and not on my own.

I wanted to walk from home to Wembley and from Wembley to Frankfurt to arrive by June 9. Walking 20-25 miles a day, I would need to set off on May 6 – that's pretty specific and very time bound. But was that all? Why was I doing it? I talked at the 'summit meeting' about raising awareness and funds. Someone, I'm not sure but I think it was Norris, asked how much did I want to raise? Without too much thought, I replied £50,000 Many people said that was an awful lot of money and did I realise how hard it was to raise money for charity without a public profile and with so many competing causes, but the figure stuck and so that became another factor in the goal.

Cathy Gilman at LRF asked the same question, 'How much do you hope to raise?' and this time followed it up with *'and how are you going to raise £50,000?'* My instant reply was to rattle off a list of ideas and fundraising opportunities that I think made her realise that we were reasonably serious, but it was another great question that was forcing me to think through what we wanted to achieve and what we needed to do to achieve it. A friend asked whether this was a one-off event or the start of a longer-term effort to help young people with leukaemia. In my mind it was definitely the latter, but another question that helped to shape the purpose and objectives of the walk and position it as the launch of our campaign, a journey to launch a much longer journey and a different context for the Charitable Trust that we were establishing in Tim's name.

Summing it up and I think we reached this by the end of February, my aims were to walk to the World Cup to honour Tim's dream, arriving safely in Frankfurt in time for the England-Paraguay match, to raise a minimum of £50,000 to support research and other efforts to improve the treatment and care of teenagers and young adults with blood cancers and to launch Tim's Trust in order to raise funds and awareness of the plight of the 'Forgotten Tribe'.

So how were we going to raise £50,000? My response to Cathy had been a gulp and then a plunge into a list of ideas – a wish list. A sponsorship form to enable people to sponsor me by the mile, the day or for a total amount; an offer of a free mail drop to 250,000 homes; interviews and appeals on local radio and newspapers; targeted approaches to local businesses where family and friends had contacts; targeted approaches to large corporations where we had specific contacts; enlisting the support of Tim's friends and a reasonably wide network of contacts to organise other fundraising events; coverage by the national media – radio, press and TV - as the World Cup came closer; a website to include information about Tim's Trust and the walk and with an on-line donation capability; contacting the FA, Leeds United and the football community in general to get their support and backing for the walk. So much to do. Where to start? At times it seemed overwhelming and many entries in my diary talk about my head spinning with the scale and the speed of it all – but then I do love juggling. I also love planning but mainly at a high level, getting the overall strategy in place, generating ideas, looking at possibilities, something of a 'dreamer' who needs to keep his feet on the ground.

A Walk of Faith

Tim, on the other hand, was a pragmatist, organised and structured and very good at dealing with detail. He shared his mum's perfectionism, perhaps too much for his own good as he set himself very high standards and expectations and worried too much about whether he could achieve them. Despite an 'easy-going, take it as it comes' appearance that he presented to other people, he liked to be prepared, to plan ahead and as far as possible to avoid the unexpected. He used to help me a lot with preparation work for my business when he was at home and was totally reliable; I knew he would always get it 100% right. His course work for the Home Accounting Course that he had started just four months before he died was immaculate; he would have become such a good accountant. It was also one of the reasons why it often took him time to come round to a new idea; he needed to think through for himself exactly what would be involved and be convinced that he could do it to the standard he required. We would have made a great 'double act' organising the walk. Me with the sense of direction, the ideas and the energy; Tim keeping me on track, sorting out the detail and making sure we had covered all the angles

Logically, some of the opportunities could wait, others were immediate priorities. We needed to design and print a professional and compelling leaflet and sponsorship form that was available for mid-March; we needed to list the local and national companies to contact and a standard letter that would be tailored to send to them; we needed a press release that we could use to give to local media for the start of the local media campaign which we reckoned ought to begin in March; we needed work to begin on the website so that we had something in place for April; we needed to set up the Charitable Trust and open a bank account.

Still an awful lot to do but straight away it seemed a bit more do-able and there were friends, contacts and supporters to help us. Geoff Marshall-Clarke, my friend from Nottingham University days, produced at least three improved versions of the leaflet that we had drafted out. Malcolm Tilsed from the Meadows Shopping centre produced a list of local media contacts and promised to help us with a local media campaign. LRF put together an initial press release and printed T-shirts to advertise and promote the walk. Gemma Herring, Malcolm's assistant, persuaded their website designers, SOLTEC, to design a website for Tim's Trust – free of charge. Tom Holmes, Gemma's boyfriend, who works in publishing, researched specialist football and other media contacts. We met up with Smithy and Alex, Tim's two closest friends and they offered their support and also put us in touch with Tristan, who would later become a key member of the WTTWC team. I set up the Charitable Trust with the help of CAF and Sandra opened a bank account for the Trust with HSBC. We also set up a PO Box (very easily) for the increasing volumes of mail that was starting to arrive. A web page, Walking to the World Cup, on the Justgiving Web Site soon followed. Sandra and I brainstormed people we knew and organisations to get in touch with and I put together letters and e-mails and sent them off, not quite to anybody but a lot of them.

The first positive response came early – February 17 – and an e-mail from the FA, saying that they couldn't sponsor us but would donate a signed England shirt and give us a page on the FA website – thank you Phil Smith. The following week, Tim's godfather sent through a cheque for £500 and the week after that, a friend sent through a cheque for the amazing amount of £2,000 – both letters made us cry. It was a busy, busy time. Often I'd be working in London, get home by 6.30am, have a meal and then work until 11am, reading e-mails, sending more and writing letters. The pattern emerged early – letters and gestures of support that took us by surprise, made us sad but at the same time even more determined to make the walk a success. And then letters of rejection or being ignored. The rollercoaster ride that had been our lives for the previous nine months continued. And all the time, the sadness and the despair, the nights of tears and feeling that it was all too much and did it matter?

But the good news and the offers of support continued to arrive. The local Tesco store, where Tim had worked for 2 years as a part-time shelf-stacker, after an initial misunderstanding offered to help us by collecting money in store and providing fantastic support with a long shopping list of energy drinks, food, medical and other supplies that we would need for the journey.

A Walk of Faith

The Daily Express responded saying they would like to run a feature story based around a copy of Tim's story (Chapter 1) that I had sent them. James Gilby, of England 06, someone whom I had send an e-mail about the World Cup merchandise he was selling on-line, replied saying that he would be delighted to give us some England flags and caps and would let us have 1,000 England '06 wrist bands that he was selling for £1.99 each, for 20p. On March 3, the Essex Chronicle ran a half-page story with a front-page lead and picture about the walk for Tim and stories followed in the Maldon and Burnham Herald, the Colchester Evening News and the East Anglia Times. I had my first radio interview with Angela Lodge of BBC Radio Essex on March 9. She was well-prepared, very kind and supportive and we had several follow-up phone calls from listeners. Other interviews followed quickly with Essex FM and Dream FM.

On March 27, Dan rang to say that, through a good friend of his Rob, Peter Crouch would be donating one of his Liverpool shirts signed by the team and that another friend of his hoped to get a Michael Essien shirt from Chelsea. A donation of £1,000 came from the charity committee at Baker's Oven and many smaller donations, often of £5 or £10 were starting to arrive. Arsenal, via Geoff Marshall-Clarke, sent through a signed shirt and Alastair Cook, who as a boy lived in the village and went to school with Tim, gave us a signed shirt that he wore on his Test debut in India. By the end of March, we had raised over £8,000, the sponsorship leaflets had arrived and were excellent, the website was up-and-running and would become a major awareness and fundraising tool and we had received many offers of support. I wrote in my diary that *'The force is with us'* and there was no need to review our progress to decide whether the walk would go ahead or not, we had built the momentum and were pretty much on track.

By the end of March, we had also made huge progress with the third strand in our preparation, organising the logistics for the walk. On Sunday, February 19, Sandra and I had driven the proposed route from Wembley to Dover. It had been quite an experience. Setting off from the landmark arch at 10am, we were back there 20 minutes later, having had our first blazing row of the day. Sandra couldn't navigate and take notes at the same time, so we started again. This time with her driving and me taking notes. We found where we would get on the Grand Union canal as intended and then picked up the route again at Paddington. The route would take us through the Royal Parks, across Westminster Bridge, out of London along the A2 and then Shooters Hill towards Bexley Heath and Dartford. I took copious notes of road signs and landmarks, potential stopping points and measured distances for each stop and the end of each day's walk.

Photos for the local papers, a necessary evil

We got seriously lost around the 'black hole' that is Dartford and only passed Bluewater Shopping Centre and drove into the Kent countryside around 2pm. But the 50 miles from there to Dover were much quicker (to drive), the route following the old A2 through Chatham and Faversham and then onto Canterbury was straightforward. After a slight delay to find the footpath where we would pick up the North Downs Way near Bridge, we were on our way again and arrived at Dover by 5pm. The following week Sandra typed up my notes. It was 84 miles – four days walking and we had a detailed itinerary for each day.

A Walk of Faith

By the end of March we were ready for stage two of route planning, a much more ambitious foray across the Channel. Four days to check out the route from Calais to Frankfurt. We left home on March 29 and drove down to Dover, via Wingham, to see Linda and Gordon Pagdin, LRF members who had a guest house in a converted Oast house and had offered to put us up during the walk. Having found our way there, we finished the drive to Dover, stayed at the Premier Travel Inn and talked to the manager about sponsoring us during the walk.

The following day we were on the 6.30am ferry and followed our proposed route through NE France and into Belgium. We had our first road closure after five miles but did OK until we got to Ypres and then it all went wrong. Sandra was driving, her first time ever outside the UK, I was taking notes and navigating, again taking copious details. My proposed route, using a Belgian cycling map, was to pick up a long-distance cycle path and to follow it most of the way south of Brussels and towards Liege. What I hadn't counted on, however, was the total maze of cycle paths, criss-crossing and inter-connecting without any obvious (to us) signage. After 90 minutes of driving around in circles, we came to the conclusion that cycle paths were out and it would be back to roads. Some quick re-planning was called for and fortunately, many of the Belgian roads are straight and have good cycle paths alongside, so we picked up our journey heading east. That night we stayed in Brussels and it was past midnight by the time I had finished typing up my notes from the day's journey – it was now or never whilst I could remember the detail of what I had written – and planned out our revised route for the next day. Day two took us towards Liege, through the city (we didn't try to map out the detailed route here) and followed the rivers Oudre and Vesdre up into the Ardennes towards Spa where we treated ourselves with a stay at the Raddison hotel. A work-out in the gym to clear the effects of 10 hours in the car, a nice meal in a near-by restaurant and then more typing up notes and hoping tomorrow's route into Germany would be more straightforward.

April 1 started with a skirmish at the hotel reception. Whilst, I was loading the car, Sandra had gone to pay the bill, to be told that the credit card machine was broken as she would have to go to a cash point to get cash to pay the bill. Was it a Belgium April Fool? When I returned she was ready for battle but we managed to get sense to prevail and left the card number for them to process later. On our way, we drove into the fabulous Ardennes countryside, very hilly and tough walking (I measured 18 miles of almost constant uphill over one stretch) but with incredible views and lots and lots of trees. The route followed roads all the way across the German border and we came to the first point where I intended to follow a long-distance footpath. This time the signs were much better. We drove round the roads to pick up the route later and continued this criss-crossing of the route for 2-3 hours through the German Eifel region. At some points the ride in the car up and down steep hair-pin roads was hair-raising. What would it be like walking?

That afternoon I texted friends that the WTTWC Expeditionary Force under the leadership of General Sandra Reeve crossed the Rhine at 1600 hours. We stopped in a small hotel in a German village that evening. We ate in a busy but very friendly restaurant, where no one spoke English. Neither of us was quite sure what we had ordered but the meal was fine and we walked back to more typing and route checking before our last push towards Frankfurt.

Day four left us with the last 60 miles to drive and we accomplished this by 12 noon. We reached as far as Hattersheim on the outskirts of Frankfurt, reasoning that we could be met by our hosts here and complete the final stage of the walk, to the Waldstadion, about 10 miles, with directions from the locals. We had a coffee and sandwich in a café, asked a waiter and customer to point out the stadium on our map and then hit the autobahn and the route back to Calais. After 3½ days of tortuous driving to get there, we got back to Calais in five hours and caught a ferry one hour earlier than scheduled. We arrived back home by about 8pm exhausted but feeling that we had done a good job and another important piece of our preparations was now in place.

Ready, Steady.....
Final preparations – training, logistics, awareness and fundraising

The weekend after our European reconnaissance, we travelled up to York for the Leukaemia Research Fund Annual Conference. Apart from the obvious connection, one of our reasons for working with and supporting LRF was the fact that their 2006 campaign was to help teenagers and young adults with blood cancers, our very cause – it was the right and the natural thing to do. Cathy Gilman had invited us to attend during our first conversation with her, the date had been in the diary for two months and my brother, Chris, was coming over from Huddersfield for the day on Saturday.

Typically, my diary was full for the Friday before. I walked into Chelmsford and had a meeting at noon with Martyn Stokes and his team at Duke's nightclub. Tim had been a member and a regular before his illness and Dave Valentine, the regular Saturday night DJ had an idea for a 24-hour 'mixathon'. He had lost his cousin to leukaemia a few years earlier, had been wanting to do something to help the cause and this seemed like just the opportunity. We had a very positive meeting, agreed a date of June 16 for the mixathon, after we returned from Germany and right in the middle of the World Cup. They had some great ideas to use the Decadence Bar for the mixathon, charge an entry fee and set up chairs and tables with 'live music' on the patio area at the front of the club. The idea was to create a carnival atmosphere and all proceeds from the entrance charge and collection, would go to Tim's Trust. I agreed to send through more information about Tim's Trust and the team at Dukes would produce their own poster and media PR for the event. Another example of some brilliant support and great ideas

Eventually, we set off for York around 1pm, beating the Friday afternoon exodus but the road works on the A1 were not so kind and it was 6.30 pm before we arrived at the hotel. Dinner was at 7.30 with a drinks reception beforehand. So it was a quick shower, change and down to dinner. We were looked after very well by our hosts and joined a table for dinner along with Richard Delderfield, a trustee of the LRF, his wife, one of the original Calendar Girls and her partner and Dr. Ron Chakrabarty, a consultant from the Royal Free Hospital, who was talking at the Conference the following day. The evening was relaxed with a real family atmosphere. I sat next to Ron and was very interested in his research and clinical experience and he, in turn, was very kind in his support for our walk and promised to mention it at the start of his session.

One of the highlights of the Conference was a presentation by Professor Tim Eden of Manchester University who talked about the *'Forgotten Tribe'* and put into context the stark difference between the survival rates for children sufferers from ALL and young adults and the difference in outcomes for young people treated on the paediatric protocol rather than the adult version. It seemed so obvious to Sandra and me that we couldn't help but wonder why Tim had been treated on the Adult protocol, which had been first introduced 20 years earlier. I became even more convinced that I had to try and do something to help young people with leukaemia. The survival rate for children with leukaemia has improved from 20% to over 80% during the last 15 years. Each death of a teenager or young adult is a tragedy and the same improvement in treatment, care and survival rates must happen for young people, only much faster.

In the afternoon, Geoff Thomas, who was in remission from Chronic Myeloid Leukaemia, talked about his amazing cycling journey around the Tour De France route. Sofie, partner of Floyd London, bass player from *The Almighty*, talked very simply and incredibly movingly about coming to terms as a carer, with the person you love being diagnosed with a life-threatening disease. Many people in the audience, Sandra, Chris and I included, cried during her presentation and it was a fitting finale to a good event.

We drove back to Sandra's dad's house on the Saturday evening and stayed with him. On Sunday morning, I went out for a long walk; we had lunch and drove home. Arriving back on

A Walk of Faith

Sunday evening, exhausted but feeling good, we realised that we had 25 days to go before the start of the walk. The pace that had been stiff until now was going to move up at least another two gears as we raced to get everything in place.

The week that followed leading up to Easter was to include the furthest distance covered in seven days during my three months of preparation. After 21 miles on the Sunday, on Monday I spent the morning with phone calls, sending e-mails and then walked down to the gym in Maldon and from there into Chelmsford (16 miles) and quiz night at the Meadows. As usual, Ted's team had three times more people than any other team and we managed to come second. Malcolm and Gemma were sweet and presented me with a birthday cake in front of 100+ people – a kind gesture on a most un-birthday-like day.

Tuesday was my day off from walking. Sandra and I went down to Heybridge to look at a campervan owned by Dennis and Anne which they had generously offered to lend us for the walk. It was ancient but in immaculate condition and gave us a good fallback position. We had also been offered a Volvo Estate by Ray Cawston, a long-standing friend and Volvo dealer from Bury St. Edmunds but our first choice was a sponsored motor home from Marquis Motorhomes. I had contacted them back in February because of their connection with the Daily Express who were going to run Tim's story. They had expressed an interest and were considering our request but hadn't given us a final answer.

On Wednesday, it was 21 miles into Chelmsford with Sandra, lunch with Malcolm and Gemma and then when Sandra caught the train back to Witham, I retraced our route on foot, talking to Essex FM and Ladbrokes, who had offered some sponsorship support, along the way.

Thursday was another quiet day. Up at 7am and walking by 7.30 over to Tiptree, had my hair cut – Dave offered to pay me to give me a skinhead haircut next time! – and then back home. Two hours at home, more post, more letters and e-mails to write and then the train into London, bought my walking shoes, then walked to Covent Garden and Stanford's, the best map shop in the world. From early school days, I have always enjoyed studying maps and spent a happy 90 minutes picking out more maps of

49

Belgium and Germany. The ones we had taken on our route-planning journey weren't up to it and we needed some larger-scale maps. In the end, I bought a total of 14 maps for the walk. Some of them stayed at home but others were invaluable. Then from Covent Garden, I walked over to Victoria, a meal with Sandra, Dan and Faye and an evening show (15 miles).

On Good Friday, it was back to correspondence in the morning whilst Sandra went shopping to prepare for my brother, Chris, and his family who were visiting for the Easter weekend. In the afternoon, I walked over to Tiptree, to Jan and George's and had a cup of tea and dropped off some leaflets. When I arrived back at home (eight miles), Chris, Anne, Tom and Kathryn had arrived. Dan soon followed and the seven of us had a very nice roast dinner – only problem was, one person was missing but I'm sure he enjoyed watching us enjoy the meal.

Saturday was a shopping expedition to Bluewaters for the females whilst the four men went for a walk. The only part of the route down to Dover which remained uncertain, was around the 'black hole' of Dartford, so I had agreed that we would walk from Bluewater towards London as far as Shooters Hill, then walk back out as we would do on May 7. With two very fit young people we set a good pace (4.2 miles at hour) and cracked on past Dartford and Crayford and into Bexley Heath. We had our WTTWC T-shirts on and had many looks and comments from shoppers, 'You're walking the wrong way!' being definitely the favourite. I wished I had brought some collecting tins with me, I'm sure we could have had raised a lot of money as the town centres were packed with shoppers.

As Shooters Hill loomed large, the boys picked up the pace and disappeared as they raced towards the top. Chris and I kept up a decent pace but took more time to see the Easter lambing event that was taking place with hordes of young children and their parents visiting the lambs and other young animals at Shooters Hill. We were some distance behind when we reached the Bull pub, right on the top of the hill, our destination for lunch. We had walked 10.2 miles in 2½ hours – good going for me, especially on the back of 80 miles+ already that week.

A Walk of Faith

After a quick bite and watch of the football – it was FA Cup semi-final day - it was back down the hill, stretching the legs out and then along the flat, back to Bexley Heath and towards Dartford. The weather closed in about halfway and it started raining. As we climbed up the steep hill out of Dartford, we were coming near to the spot where we lost our way on the route-planning journey back in February. Chris and I were lagging behind again and as we passed a woman carrying two bags of shopping, I asked her for directions to the hospital. If we made it to there, I knew we would have found our route. She pointed us in the right direction involving the next two roundabouts ahead and then as we set off again, called us back saying. 'I'm almost home, if you give me a moment, I'll run you up there in the car'.

Thanking her kindly, we declined the offer but walking on, realised we must have looked quite a sight - hot, wet and bedraggled and she probably thought we were in need of the hospital ourselves.

By the time we reached Bluewater and the ladies arrived at the 'pick up' spot, the rain had stopped and I stretched down slowly. The last few miles had been hard and I was sore and tired – 20 miles for a total of 101 miles in seven days. I would start reducing the distance over the last three weeks before the start. I was confident I had enough miles in my legs. That evening, the seven of us went out for a Chinese meal, tired but feeling good.

Chris and family went home on Sunday and Sandra and I had a quieter day, just a seven mile afternoon stroll. On Monday, I decided to walk along the Chelmer canal and check out the route into Chelmsford – it would be embarrassing to get lost here. After some work in the morning, Sandra drove me down to Tesco in Maldon and I walked along the towpath. It was a glorious spring day with sunshine and a fresh breeze, good for walking and it reminded me of a walk with Tim on Tollesbury marshes, almost a year before.

I spotted where we could stop for lunch at Paper Mill Lock and then Sandra rang to say that Dan had locked his keys in the car boot whilst they had been out shopping. We worked out a plan whereby he would bring my car, pick me up at Chelmer village and the two of us would drive into London to pick up his

51

John Reeve

spare key and then drive back home. So the rest of the day gave me some unexpected time with my son.

On Tuesday I completed the walk into Chelmsford, had interviews with two radio stations and photographs with Peter Crouch's shirt for the local paper. On Wednesday, I flew over to the Isle of Man to work for three days. But there was no escape. The Daily Express, last minute as all newspapers are, wanted a photograph to go with the picture of Tim for the article due to run the following week so I had my picture taken on Douglas Prom just as the light began to fade. I was having problems with my laptop and sending e-mails, for some reason I could receive them but not send. I had two long conversations on the phone with Sandra, talking her through where to find and how to send the letters and other documents that needed e-mailing urgently.

Back home, Sandra was progressing two other important aspects of the logistics for the walk. Supporters and accommodation. We had decided early on that, ideally, we would have a minimum of three people as the core team for the walk. Me, as main walker, someone to drive the support vehicle and a third person to share the driving, do some walking and also be available to sort out other things along the way. More than that, up to a point, would be fine but as Sandra was going to be with me for all but one week of the walk, I didn't want her left driving the vehicle all the time on her own. Family and friends had offered to help and given us an idea of availability. Once we had the route finalised after our expedition to Frankfurt, we were able to send round a schedule and start to make firm bookings.

Dan was going to walk with me for seven days, in England for four and catching the Eurostar to Lille along with Jono and Jay to walk for three days in Belgium; Phil was going to fly up from Spain to meet us at Dover, stay with us for five days and then re-join us later in Germany with his son, Sam, who was desperate to be part of the walk; Chris and Tom (despite A level exams) were flying out to Brussels to walk for seven days through Belgium and into Germany; Anthony was coming out with them and would fly back from Cologne, a couple of days before Chris and Tom returned; Ted and Dave Cobb, the Tumble Tot Twins, were travelling out to Brussels to walk through central Belgium; Peter and Elaine Shields would join us for the walk through Liege and into the Ardennes; Tris and Will were going to fly into Frankfurt and join us for the last few days; Anne and Geoff Hurst kindly offered to walk with us for our first day in France; Mick Waite would walk from Canterbury to Dover to join Barry Cotgrave who lives locally and David Rawnsley, from Manchester, who was going to walk for two days; the first weekends from home and from Wembley would see many people starting the walk including Al Hepworth, our best man from 30 years ago, who would drive down from Derbyshire to join us. In total 18 people walked some of the route in Europe and another 75 joined me for some of the journey through Southern England. In the event, I walked on my own for only two days on the entire walk (the only two days I got lost!)

Fantastic support from many people who I hope all believed it was worthwhile. But it all needed organising, co-ordinating, putting into place and that was one of Sandra's tasks. It also meant arranging accommodation and that proved to be an even greater challenge. Without any certainty, even at this stage about the support vehicle, we would need accommodation for three or four or seven (that was the most) of us each night. The one thing I knew I would crave at the end of each day was a soak in a hot bath, so that became a priority as we started to make arrangements. Certain parts of the walk fell into place easily. In England, we would stay at home during the walk to Wembley and the night of the 13th (a short hop back across the QE2 Bridge), stay with the Pagdins for two nights and at the Premier Travel Inn in Dover.

From early route planning, we realised that we would be passing very close to Wegimont Chateau near Liege. This magnificent building was home to visiting school children (and walkers, cyclists etc) from all over Europe. Both Tim and Dan had been on visits from their Primary and Secondary schools. With the help of Marie Cole and Jill Martin from the Anglo-European School in Ingatestone, we arranged to stay at Wegimont for three nights; at nine euros a night it made sense. The Anglo was very supportive and helpful and also offered to help us find accommodation in Frankfurt. The school has a long-standing relationship with the Goethe-Gymnasium in the heart of the city. They put us in touch with Ursula Shoelzke and it was agreed that we would stay with a German family for our four nights in Frankfurt.

That left accommodation for 18 days to arrange. The problem was that we were keeping off the main routes and out of the big cities and towns wherever possible. Whilst it would be fine to make a short drive to our accommodation, we didn't want to be driving miles and miles. Sandra speaks little French and no German or Flemish, it was difficult. During our recce, we tried to pick out possible small hotels or B&Bs but we didn't have time to stop and enquire, just pick up the brochures we could find and press on. Chris, kindly offered to try and book accommodation for the time he was with us and that was a great help. Eventually, with the help of the internet, from Dave Cobb and other friends, and after much biting of finger nails and translation of e-mails, we started the walk with accommodation arranged for 12 of our 24 days in Europe. The remainder we would find on the day, it would be something else to do!

I arrived back home from the Isle of Man on Friday morning, only two weeks to go. It was good to be home and Sandra and I both cried as we hugged each other and talked about Tim. And then it was off again with more preparation to be completed. Donations were starting to come through in some quantities – often 10 or more cheques per day. Keeping a record of them sending 'Thank You' letters – we have tried and I think, pretty much succeeded in sending a letter of thanks to every person who has made a donation, no matter how large or small, if we had their address – was becoming a major occupation in itself.

On Saturday, after some prep work in the morning, Sandra and I walked from Heybridge Basin along the Blackwater to Goldhanger and lunch in the pub. A walk we had made several times with Tim. A walk of many memories, we needed to let the happy ones in and begin to restore the balance of the nightmare of Tim's decline and painful death, memories that were always close to the surface. We walked back to Heybridge and then continued along the canal, and up onto the Blackwater Rail Trail and back home, 15 miles in all. That evening we went to an engagement party for Nick and Laura – a happy occasion for two smashing young people – but again there were the inevitable bitter sweet thoughts.

Sunday was a miserable day, cold and grey. I walked down to the gym, did 60 minutes hard cycling and walked home. Sandra was deeply sad. There was a sense of knowing that we would have to concentrate all our efforts and energy into the walk and this was the calm, the time to reflect, before the storm. Although there are many similarities, often superficial, between people, we are all essentially unique. The particular combination of personality, attitudes, values, and experience that makes up an individual is almost always complex and often paradoxical. It's what makes people interesting and thank God for the differences. We all find our own ways of coping with crisis, with tragedy and grief. Loosing a child goes against the scheme of things, it's not supposed to happen. Although, intellectually, I can understand that there are worse things that can and do happen, for me and I think Sandra, Tim's death was truly the worst thing that could possibly happen in our lives.

Sandra was brought up at chapel, sang in the choir, was a Sunday school teacher when I first met her, but was not especially religious. She had wanted both boys to be baptised at church but didn't attend regularly and didn't want to force religion on to them both.

Tim was a rationalist and a pragmatist. To him, things were clear cut, were 'black and white'. He liked the certainty of 'A' level Maths. Like his dad, he was an introvert, thought too much at times – he often accused me of the same thing – but had no time for things he couldn't understand or couldn't be explained to him. Keep it simple, keep it practical and get on with it – those were some of the things he stood for. He didn't believe in God. He told us once, when he was very ill, that he preferred to believe that there wasn't a God who could allow him to go through such pain and torment. His note to us, which we found after his death, talked about heart but not soul and yet who knows…?

As for me, I was brought up as a Catholic by my mother. My dad was an atheist but my mum lived and died a devout Catholic, part of a strongly Catholic family. As a boy, I embraced the faith, took my first Communion, was confirmed, went to Catholic primary schools and was taught by strict Irish nuns and priests. I became an altar boy, took Lent and the Stations of the Cross very seriously. And then, as the sixties rolled on and I entered my teens, I began to doubt. Not God but the disciplines and ritual, the compulsion and the 'all or nothing' nature of my religion, or certainly the role models I saw each week at Mass. Would I really go to hell for missing Sunday Mass? Were all the strict rules and obligations really necessary? Could I not find God, wherever and whenever I needed to? And so like many, I guess, I revolted, not suddenly and until I left home at 17, I maintained a pretext of adherence. It hurt mum badly, I know, when she realised that her eldest child would not stay true to her religion. We were both stubborn and strong-willed but it was an argument she could not win at the time.

But I don't think I ever lost my faith. My belief that there are many things that we don't understand, that we can't explain by reason and logic, that science for all its advances and its certainty, is still primitive when faced with the incredible wonder of the world and the universe that we live in. That faith itself was about believing in something that you couldn't explain. That I could talk to God, in the countryside as I was walking, at home at the end of the day or in a cool church with its calmness and quiet grandeur.

The death of a child is likely to challenge the faith of many people, certainly it did mine. I was, and to some extent still am, so angry about everything, anger directed at most everybody. As Colin Gibb recognised perceptively, one of the challenges of the walk for me was to channel that anger positively and not allow it to take over or make me push too hard. I was angry with the nurses who had failed to look after Tim properly at the end when he needed them most, with the doctors who had failed to make him better, with God for doing nothing to save his life and deserting him in his hour of need and most of all with myself, for failing in the most important job of my life – to protect my child. For three years, every single night since Tim was first diagnosed, I had prayed for our family and friends, for other people we knew who were ill or worse, but most of all for Tim to get well. My greatest dream and most fervent wish, was that one day, he would say to me 'Dad, I'm clear'.

After his death I was distraught, exhausted, in despair, trying to care for Sandra and Dan, grateful for the wonderful love and support of family and friends but smouldering beneath all of that was my anger. And yet, I knew somehow, instinctively, even on the night after Tim's death that I had to keep on saying my prayers, I had to hold onto my faith. I had to believe although I couldn't possibly understand. I didn't want to do it, I recited my prayers as a ritual, spat the words out silently but I did it, I tried to hold on to my belief. I said to Tim, at some point during the bedlam, that I believed in him. I'm not sure he knew what I meant. That I believed in his spirit, in the force of nature that was the man, that I believe his spirit does and will always survive. I told him that he and I will meet again, he looked at me with that 'dreaming again Dad' look but I meant it and always will.

So that's about faith and me. It's about how I cope, it's about times when I'm out walking, an unexpected moment at home, going into Tim's bedroom each night to talk to him. It's about how I survive. It's about what helped me to feed off that belief in him and those memories, bad and good, to make the most of those last few days before the walk began.

Tuesday, April 25, was a big day in moving towards our aims. It was also a strange and almost surreal day at times. I caught the train into London for a meeting with a client at the Tate. Picked up a Daily Express at the station and scoured it for our article. It was supposed to be in the Health Section, just after the middle. I found the section, looked through it, plenty of articles but not ours and then working back towards the middle I saw it. A double-page spread right across the middle of the paper. Rachel Baird, the Health Editor, having said she would have to drastically cut down the piece I had submitted, had printed over 2,000 words and produced an article that stayed absolutely true to Tim's story. I cried to myself as I read it. Proud, elated and incredibly sad, all at the same time. The article included contact details for Tim's Trust and we received many letters and donations as a result of the article.

John Reeve

Then, part-way through the meeting at Tate Britain and with the agreement of my client and good friend, Colin Coombs, I was whisked away by car, to the BBC studios just down the road at Millbank, for an interview on Radio 5 Live. After the rush to the studio, I was kept waiting and left alone to listen to the programme through my headphones and then had my two minutes on the Victoria Derbyshire show. By now, I knew the message I wanted to put across, could usually do it without blubbering and it went fine. Back in the car, on the three minute drive back to the meeting, my phone was hot from friends and family who had heard the interview. Tim would have hated the spotlight but for the first time, the walk and Tim's Trust was reaching a truly national audience; we were beginning to create a profile.

A Walk of Faith

The third piece of good publicity that day was much lower profile but still important to me. A small article in 'Shoot', a specialist football magazine, entitled 'Walk of Faith' along with a picture of Tim and me sitting in the square by the fountain at Bart's Hospital.

After the meeting, I had lunch with Dan, chased around unsuccessfully to find Lloyd Scott on his marathon walk as St. George in full armour and towing dragon and then headed to City airport and the Isle of Man again. Another three-day visit with the same combination of working hard during the day, walking in the evening and sending e-mails and letters late into the night. I spent a very pleasant couple of hours with Nick and Jane at the Liverpool Arms and talking to Dan and Sandra, both seemed well and positive. Back home on the Friday evening, I dived straight back into the arrangements and pulling things together.

On the following morning, I was up early and walking down to Tesco at Maldon with Sandra by 7.30am. We had a breakfast meeting with Andrew Doherty, the manager and Matt, his very able assistant, to check through the supplies they had put together for us and run through the arrangements for the event at the store on the following Saturday. They had had huge banners made to publicise the walk, had T-shirts printed for the staff to wear and Matt had pulled out of his hat 200 large England flags to decorate the store. (He later gave us 100 flags to take with us to Germany).

Tesco were doing great and then we walked over to McDonald's who had agreed to provide prizes and drinks for the children's penalty competition that would be taking place near their restaurant as part of the launch event. Next it was back home, Stephanie Cook called round and then off to Leyton Orient for a collection at their last home game of the season.

Ted Herring, a lifelong Os supporter had organised the collection, we had a small article in the match programme and after waiting for accreditation, we met up with the two representatives from LRF who were collecting with us. Collecting before the game was slow, there was a big crowd and a 'must win' game as promotion was on the cards. At half-time, we collected some more money and then Annette How from LRF decided that

59

they would go. We stayed on, met Ted at the final whistle to celebrate the victory and then, as the fans started to leave in high spirits, Ted went into action, as only a true East-End man can. Shaking his bucket, smiling and looking people straight in the eye, he talked non-stop at the crowd as they moved past us for the best part of 10 minutes. The majority of people put their hand in their pocket; those that missed Ted were tripped up by Sandra. In 10 minutes, they collected nearly £300. But that was to be outdone shortly afterwards.

Taking us up into the hospitality area, where Ted had been for the day with his brother and friends, we were able to collect from the tables of guests. One kind man, offered to take me into the Boardroom. In 20 minutes, we collected another £400. Enjoying a cup of tea afterwards with Ted, Barry Hearns came over and presented us with a signed Leyton Orient shirt – a great day and some very kind and generous people.

The next day, Sandra was up and drove up to Yorkshire to visit her Dad, the last time she would see him for six weeks. I walked from Margaretting to Ongar following the St. Peter's Way and the route we would take from Chelmsford. Again taking notes, checking the route and spotting places to stop, pubs to visit. It was a bright, sunny morning, everywhere seemed sleepy and I felt close to Tim. On the way, I had a call from Pat Jones, of the Yellow Advertiser, a Sunday morning interview from a very nice lady who promised to publicise our cause and pressed on. I had lunch with Keziah, Tim's former girlfriend, at Ongar and decided that the pub we ate in, the Two Brewers would make a good lunch stop on Day Two of the walk. They were happy for me to make a collection when we called. Then it was another eight miles back along the route to Margaretting and the car. I counted the styles on the way back; there were 19 in the last three miles and heavy going with tired legs. That would make for a challenging start the following week.

May Day started wet but the sun soon came out and started to dry things. I was going to finish the walk from Ongar through to Epping, a walk of about 10 miles. Sandra drove me over and dropped me off at Ongar and I followed the road through to Toot Hill, then picked up the Essex Way heading towards Epping

Forest. I crossed some huge fields of clay soil still wet and clingy from the rain and struggled through the ups and downs of the terrain, carrying half the field with me on my walking shoes. Then on the edge of the forest, I met a group of walkers with the BBC team led by Angela Lodge who were completing the Essex Way – west to east. I literally bumped into Angela on a footbridge over the M11 and we chatted briefly about her walk on Friday when I would be joining her for a second BBC Radio Essex interview.

Ploughing on through the forest, I was appalled by the state of the path- the county's premier footpath and it was little more than a bog in parts. There are lots of demands for local services but if walking is to be encouraged and footpaths promoted, then keeping a very popular stretch of footpath in a reasonable condition seems fairly basic to me.

Finding my way to the car park at Epping Tube Station, right by the start of the Essex Way, Sandra was there to pick me up and it was back home by 3pm and our last appointment of another busy day, a barbecue at Ted's. When we arrived, all our friends were there to welcome us and wish us well for the walk. They had all given us cards, good luck wishes and sponsorship donations. To cap it all, they had all gone in front of camera to produce a Good Luck video for us. It was an emotional afternoon and a wonderfully warm and loving send off by some very good friends who have stood by us in our time of need.

Tuesday began early, of course, with another walk. This time into Chelmsford for a live interview with Dream FM. Both Dream and Essex FM wanted to keep a regular diary update during the walk and we talked about how they would ring me from Dream, around 10.45, European Time for a live interview whilst I walked. On the way into town, I rang Marquis Motorhomes for one last check about the motor home. Emma Franklin had been on holiday after Easter and had promised to get back on the case, she needed the agreement of the MD, I didn't hold out too much hope. Yet to my surprise and delight, she confirmed that they would sponsor us and provide a campervan and not just any old campervan but a brand new, six-berth, 22-foot motor home. Fantastic! It would provide the option to sleep in it, if we needed to, had its own toilet and shower, a fixed double bed, where I could rest when tired and a huge external store that would take all the provisions Tesco were providing. It was perfect! The only trouble was they needed copies of the driving licences of all the people who would be driving the van, each driver had to have a short driving lesson (to validate their insurance cover) and we needed to go down to Newbury to pick it up. The latter was no problem, the former a challenge, as the six prospective drivers including Sandra and myself, lived in Derbyshire, Yorkshire and Spain! And yet with the wonders of technology and some inventive planning, it was all done within 10 days.

That evening, I drove to City Airport again and my last trip and piece of paid work for six weeks. This time, a two-day visit, two busy days with some good people and some tremendous kindness and support from Joan and Glynne, Andy, Anne x 2, Mark, Sam and Laura. When I returned home, Sandra was stressed out. She had worked so hard and had boxes and boxes of things ready for the motor home, all with written instructions and lists of contents. Some more very touching letters and e-mails, including one from Julian, a football referee who included in his message, the line 'every step is a step forward for someone else's future'. Words I remembered many times during the walk. Thank you, Julian.

And so many things were in place. Not least, the website was set up with the walk itinerary and I would send back a daily diary entry and photographs. Tris had designed a second website – www.walkingtotheworldcup.com – which was easy to remember and give out to people and with a direct link through to the Trust website and the 'Justgiving' page. Over £2,000 had already been donated on-line. He had also bought a thousand red wrist bands with the strap lines *'Walkstrong'* and *'Helping Young People with Leukaemia'* which we would give to people along the way, in return for a small donation.

The last day before the start was a beautiful morning. I was walking with the BBC Essex team and would be meeting them at the start of the day's walk at Great Waltham. They were completing the walk across Essex over four weeks, with interviews and live broadcasts each day. On Day Five of the walk, a group of around 30 people joined the reporters and crew. I had met Diane, one of Sandra's teacher friends and now Head of Great Waltham Primary School, at Terling where I would end my walk, and travelled with her to Great Waltham. I had a cup of tea at school before the walk began, met the caretaker and cleaner and some of the other teachers, had my photograph taken with Diane and the cleaner gave me a £10 donation– so kind.

It was a lovely day for a walk, fresh and clear but with the prospect of getting warm later. We walked by bluebell woods at their gorgeous best, over streams and rivers and across beautiful countryside. I did my interview with Angela at Chatham Green, in the pub car park and felt so small and so sad. Then on again, talking to Pete Moore, an amazing man who was walking the Essex Way as part of his own journey – managing pain. He worked in the NHS, helping to train people to help patients cope with and manage chronic pain. Every step of the way was difficult for him but he kept going, chatting away, a wonderful example of the strength of the human spirit and how we can learn to cope and deal with incredibly difficulties.

As planned, I bailed out of the walk at Terling, too many things to do. Picked up the car, headed home and went to the Meadows and then to Tesco, delivering wrist bands, posters and collecting tins for the following day and picking up England flags and T-shirts.

Back home it was a busy evening, finalising lots of things for the following day, making sure we had everything in hand for next week. We added up the money we had received already in donations. Before I took a single step towards Frankfurt, we had raised £20,000 – we were on our way! The evening culminated in Dan and Faye arriving at midnight (he had worked until 10pm) with a car full of clothes and other things from his house in London – he was moving home when he got back from his trip to Germany and needed somewhere to store things.

The way we had planned the walk meant there would be two starts. Firstly, a local start, from St. Bartholomew's in the village before three days walking into London. It was a kind of warm-up for the main event which started the following Saturday, cup final

John Reeve

day, from Wembley. In between, we had four days left to finalise the arrangements, pick up the motor home from Newbury, collect all the provisions from Tesco, load the van and lock the house up. I would be away for almost a month. Oh and there would be one or two more calls from the media to deal with as well.

A Walk of Two Starts
From apple blossoms to Shooters Hill.

Sandra and I clung to each other for a few precious moments before we got up, just after 7.00, on Saturday, May 6. Neither of us quite knew what to expect. I had my usual breakfast of cereal and two extra pieces of toast, not feeling nervous or anxious, just wanting to get on with it. It was a dull morning after the good weather of the last few days and the forecast talked of rain. Did I look as if I cared?

By 8.30, I was dressed with top, T-shirt, 1,000-mile socks (Vaseline between my toes), walking shoes (it could be wet on the towpath), light backpack with drink, energy bar and fruit and my walking sticks. Dan emerged from the shower, having just surfaced and Sandra and I drove up to the church car park where we had arranged to meet and where the walk would start. The car park was already beginning to fill and more people arrived; lots of greetings and people catching up with each other.

By 8.50, there were 30 people and I had to slip off into the church. I had a feeling, deep in my stomach, of being ever so slightly overwhelmed. All these people had come today to support Sandra, Dan and me and to be part of honouring Tim's dream. I needed a few moments on my own, talking to my son, remembering him in 'his fire and in his flood'. And then it was back outside and ready for the off.

By 9.05, there were over 40 people present who had come to join us for the start of our adventure. I called them together, talked through our route down to Maldon and from there into Chelmsford. Of the first 12 miles, only 400 yards would be on tarmac roads, so it would be safe for us to walk as a fairly large group and on a route designed so that people could drop out at various points along the way. I thanked everyone for coming, for their support and love and for all the help and encouragement we had been given, in making the walk happen. I finished by telling people that the first 400 yards of my journey of 550 miles followed the path of Tim's favourite walk. A walk he had made many times, a happy walk. I was sure he would be with us as we set off and with us for every step of the journey.

I led the way out of the car park at 9.10, ideal to get us to Tesco on schedule, and we were soon walking down through the apple orchards, the trees laden with white blossom. The rain was holding off and it was a warm and muggy morning. After ten minutes, I decided to get into a rhythm and set a decent pace and as we crossed the Maldon road and followed the Blackwater Rail Trail, the group were strung out over quite a distance. Many local people had never walked the Trail and there were comments about it being an interesting walk.

After 1¼ miles we crossed the road again and followed a footpath across open fields. At this point the rain came, not heavy but enough to get the waterproofs out. The grass on the path was long and many people were wet by the time we reached the end of the path. At the front, I slowed the pace so we could all arrive at Tesco at about the same time. The rain had stopped. The store was decked out with flags and banners, staff were collecting donations, Carol was selling wrist bands, John Whittingdale, our local MP had arrived and Albert and Roger from Maldon Saints (Tim played as a boy for the club teams for five years) had set up the penalty competition. Some friends said their goodbyes, others went for the free breakfast that Tesco had very kindly offered us and I went to meet John Whittingdale, score two of my three penalties and had a radio interview with Essex FM, their Black Thunder van had come to Maldon to meet us.

A great reception and send off but it all took time, more than I had anticipated and we were 20 minutes behind plan as we picked up the canal towpath that ran alongside the store and headed towards Chelmsford. About 20 people started this second stage of the day and I set a faster pace to try and make up some time with Dan, Faye and I pulling about 400 metres ahead of the main group. So many shades of grey in the sky but it was getting warmer and even more humid, very still and calm. As the rain came gently down, we walked through countryside looking fresh and green and passed a beautiful, tiny old church right at the side of the canal. As we came nearer to Paper Mill Lock, the rain came on more heavily. After warding off two wildly-barking terriers with my walking stick, I broke one attacking nettles that blocked our path and we arrived hungry and thirsty at the Lock café for lunch.

It was the only day of the entire walk when I was trying to stick to a definite schedule to arrive in Chelmsford in time for a planned reception. We were still running late but fortunately, Carol and Sandra had lunch ready for us and after a quick stretch, the ham salad sandwiches tasted real good. After 20 minutes we were ready to go again and just as some of the stragglers arrived for their lunch, seven of us set off for the next six miles into Chelmsford, having been joined by Graham and Paul Jeater.

The rain held off during this part of the walk, all seven of us were prepared to up the pace and we made good time. Leaving the canal as it turned on a big loop away from Chelmsford, we took the tunnel under the A12 into Chelmer village and cracked on along the roads, past Barnes Farm, where we met Tristan (he had torn ligaments in his leg and couldn't walk) and then picked up the canal again for the last mile into the town centre.

As we neared the centre, Sandra rang and said something about slowing down. It sounded like 'so the belly dancers can come and meet you' but I decided I must have misheard her. The seven of us had kept together well and with the *'Walking To The World Cup'* Banner held high, we came towards Backnang Square to, indeed, be met by a dozen or so belly dancers who ran towards us. I was feeling tired and thirsty from the fast pace but suddenly thought, *'Is this real? Am I hallucinating?'* But it was real, the belly dancers came in all ages, shapes and sizes and were all doing their thing.

After a brief pause for photographs for the local paper, we crossed the bridge to be met by yet more dancers, this time the Centre Stage Dance Troupe from Gt. Dunmow. These I had been expecting, the belly dancers were a nice surprise from Gemma! To the tune of *'Amarillo'* we entered the square full with about 100 shoppers, supporters and onlookers and a stage set up for outdoor entertainment – an amazing welcome. After a very short and quite emotional interview and thanks, especially to Gemma and Malcolm, I was given a chair as guest of honour and

John Reeve

both sets of dancers performed routines to the audience to loud applause. Soon I needed to stand up and stretch and almost got dragged into the dance routine.

The start of the walk at St. Bartholomew's Church, Wickham Bishops.

With John Whittingdale MP and friends at Maldon Tesco

A Walk of Faith

Strutting my stuff, stick in hand

With Sandra at the Meadows Shopping Centre

We had a longer-than-anticipated break at the Meadows. I talked to lots of people all wishing us well and including Gordon Williams from Chelmsford City (Tim's second club side) who was running another penalty competition for children to raise funds for Tim's Trust. After an hour, more of the walkers had joined us whilst others had got lost and headed home. Six of us including Sandra, who would re-join us for the last walk of the day, were going to follow the London Road, out of Chelmsford and as far as Margaretting. The Red Lion was our stopping point for the day after 20.4 miles. Carol was bringing her car to take us home.

We set a very gentle pace out of town, feeling stiff and then picked it up to something more respectable along the old A12. Chatting away, we came up with the idea of a Yellow Jersey award for the best walker of the day. The joke part was that the winner would have to wear my Yellow Jersey the following day and it would pass from wearer to wearer unwashed, all the way to Frankfurt. It was very uneven and difficult to walk on the wide grass verge and it slowed us down until we came to the A12 roundabout and the last three quarters of a mile, back on pavements, to the pub. There were cries of 'How much further?' every 50 metres but at 4.45 we arrived. I bought a round of drinks to celebrate our first day and found out that the Os had won promotion with a last-minute goal. A great start, 20 miles gone, 530 to go. Winner of the first Yellow Jersey award went undoubtedly to Faye. She had walked the full distance and kept up with the boys when we stepped up the pace into Chelmsford.

Back home, Al, our best man, was waiting on the drive. It was good to see him after a long, long time. A big meal of lasagne and salad, soak in the bath, stretch by Dan and Glucosamine patch on my right knee, e-mails and a chat to Al with a glass of red wine. Bed by eleven, tired but satisfied.

After heavy overnight rain, Day Two started dry with the promise of sunshine later. We were up at 7am and after cereal and a bacon buttie, three cars set off to Epping and the Tube Station Car Park. We left two cars there, headed back to Ongar and picked up Sandra and Faye, who left their car at the Two Brewers – it was like some sort of puzzle. We were back at Margaretting by

8.40 to be met by Ted and Theresa who were joining us for the walk and Richard Quy and Mark Kidd, two of Tim's school friends, who had come to check about sponsorship money and the walk from Wembley.

Seven of us set off at 8.45. It was wet underfoot but not soft. Nineteen stiles in three miles meant that our pace was steady, just right for a Sunday morning, we were in no rush. We carried on straight past the Cricketers, past the big houses at Beggars Green, following the St. Peter's Way – an old footpath stretching right out to the chapel of the same name at Bradwell. Our first stop of the day was planned for Blackmore and as we walked across the open fields, we could see the pretty village nestling in the bottom. The village green at Blackmore is a haven of peace and beauty, a chance to sit on the bench and watch the ducks and fish in the pond. But not this Sunday, as we came off the footpath, we could hear engines revving and saw the green filling up with vintage motor bike and grey haired bikers kitted out in leather. I sat on one of the benches, had a drink and biscuit and watched more bikes arriving, lovingly-preserved chrome shining in the sun that was starting to break through. Ted and Al grabbed collecting tins and some of our leaflets and were soon amongst the bikers who gave generously. One or two had been in Chelmsford the day before, others had heard about the walk on local radio.

Off again after 30 minutes, we walked through the village and back onto the footpath which took us through a large field of rape. The yellow flowers were taller than me and wet through after the rain. Leading the way, by the time I reached the far side, I was totally drenched from head to toe. Luckily, it was warming up and my clothes would soon dry. Across more open ground towards High Ongar. The fields were clay and it hung heavily on our shoes.

As we came off the path onto the road in High Ongar, we stopped to scrape the mud off our shoes. Suddenly, there was a shout from the nearby house, someone was hanging out of an upstairs window, shouting abuse and telling us not to leave mud on his driveway. I looked around, we were scraping our boots on the pavement edge and I could see that others had done so before us. I looked up, said sorry and we started to move off. A few moments later, two women, wearing dressing gowns come out of the house, one older carrying a broom, one younger and started sweeping the drive and yelling abuse at us. Foolishly, I turned around, asked them if they wanted me to sweep it up, told them to stop being so abusive and walked off.

Seconds later, as the seven of us were nearing the bottom of the road, a voice shouted, 'What did you say to my sister?' and we heard someone charging towards us. I turned around; he was the same height as me, 6'3" but heavier, looked fit and in his late twenties, interesting! I learned many years ago not to turn my back on dogs when I was out running and it seemed like a good idea now. I stood still, facing him, and he ran right up to me and put his face close to mine, still shouting and swearing. I stared back at him and then he took half a step back. At that point, Ted, all 5'4" of him, but strong and not to be messed with, stepped between us and 'laddo' gave Ted a shove in the chest and pushed him away. At this point, the situation could have got out of hand, he was big and strong but heavily outnumbered, Dan had moved to one side ready for a punch to the head, but sense in the form of Al prevailed. In true Head Teacher fashion, he stepped between us, calmed the situation and we all started to move away. It was all over in 60 seconds, something and nothing but quite a welcome to High Ongar. After so much kindness and support, it seemed to make this incident even odder. I reflected afterwards that my anger was never too far from the surface and I was partially to blame. Humming the theme tune to *'Deliverance'*, we walked up the hill into Ongar. Strange, this little bit of Essex.

We soon arrived at the Two Brewers and our second stop for lunch. Keziah joined us with her family and during the meal I took the collection tin around the pub. It wasn't very busy but most people donated and I stood at the bar for a few minutes. One man was particularly interested in any TV coverage that we had organised for the start from Wembley and a few minutes later, he came over and gave me his business card and suggested I gave him a ring. After I'd finished my lunch I went over and chatted to him again. Turned out, he was a retired outside broadcast engineer and had managed operations for the major TV networks at two previous World Cups. He promised, if I rang him that evening with details, to contact people at Sky and ITV to add his support to them running our story. We were to keep on having lucky coincidences in meeting people throughout the walk.

Al had done brilliantly to cover the 13 miles to Ongar. He was unfit and not in the best of health so he, Sandra and Faye (who was still tired from her efforts the previous day) drove back to Epping. Al was going to then take his car and drive home to Derbyshire. It had been great to have his support and company for the morning walk. Four of us, Theresa, Ted, Dan and me set out on the road towards Toot Hill. It was warm, the sun was out and soon the trouser bottoms were zipped off, I exposed my knees for the first time on the walk. We picked up the Essex Way after 1½ miles and climbed uphill through woods and open fields to Toot Hill, stopping briefly for a drink from our packs outside the Green Man, resisting the temptation to go inside.

Fortunately, the fields were drying fast and the stretch leading into Epping Forest, where I had been badly clogged up the previous week, was fine and we made decent progress. Theresa was walking easily but Ted was beginning to tire and we waited a few times for him to catch up. As we left the forest, we skirted a cricket pitch with an early season match in progress. Soon we passed the Theydon Oak with Ted tiring rapidly. The last section of footpath was overgrown and still very wet and muddy; we were pleased to come out onto the road, just short of the end of the Essex Way and the car park.

Sandra was waiting for us there. Ted and Dan headed across the last field to the car park but I decided to follow the road, skirt round the edge of Epping, head towards the larger section of the forest and the route into London. I reckoned that an extra couple of miles would make the next walk, to Wembley, just that little bit easier. It was a steep climb up two hills to the Loughton road and for the first time, Theresa began to slow. She was without doubt the Walker of the Day and the winner of the Yellow Jersey award. Later she was to suffer with severe bruising and two black toenails but she stayed with me all the way. As we came to a bus stop, half-way between Epping and the roundabout in the middle of the forest, Sandra picked us up. Another good day with good company and some interesting and unexpected incidents.

Monday was a day off from walking, I had to go down to Basingstoke for a meeting, there were final calls and e-mails to the media about Wembley, messages about accommodation and lots of people to talk to.

Over 40 people started Day One, seven Day Two but on Tuesday morning, it was just Sandra and me who set out from home for Epping. We had agreed that she would drive me back to the bus stop, take the car on to Loughton station and then walk along to the Ridgeway to meet me as I came out of the south side of the forest. I enjoyed the chance to walk on my own and let my thoughts run free. After the Old Orleans restaurant, the side road through the forest was much quieter and relatively free of the morning rush-hour traffic. I thought about Tim and how he would have enjoyed the walk and marvelled at so many shades of green. After the Information Centre, there were more houses and one sign he would have loved, *'The very latest in luxury chalet accommodation for cats'*.

Shortly afterwards the road veered to the north, just as the map said it would and I continued south, following a footpath, also shown on my map. Almost immediately, however, I came across several other paths that crossed over each other. I walked alongside the edge of a golf course and was looking for a second course, the Royal Epping, when a jogger came by. He kindly stopped and gave me directions for a short cut. After missing the turning, I walked on too far but turned back, picked up the right track and came out onto the golf course to be met by a wonderful view looking down on a bright spring morning onto Loughton and the north-eastern suburbs of London. The views were uplifting and I exchanged greetings with a few friendly golfers and then saw the same jogger running round a long loop and heading back towards me. He stopped again and we chatted. He was amazed at my answer to his question, where was I headed for and seemed genuinely moved when I explained the reason for my journey. As we parted, he wished me 'God's speed'.

I arrived by a slightly different route than planned at the Ridgeway and sat on a bench for a quick breather until Sandra returned; she had gone looking for me. We set off together and after an abortive attempt to cut through the Lea Valley, we reached the North Circular and our first break at Tesco with a drink and mid-morning bacon and egg sandwich. I used the break to check the route and ended up re-drawing large sections of our way to Wembley – last minute as usual.

It was getting warm and slightly hazy as we set out again and we were glad to turn away from the noise and pollution of the North Circular. We crossed the A10 at Edmonton and headed on towards Muswell Hill Golf Club. We walked through some of the many diverse communities that make London such a wonderful city, Greeks, Jews, Indians, Italians, all with their distinctive shops and culture. Climbing up towards Muswell Hill, we turned off towards Bounds Green and found a pretty, very clean pub, the Windsor Castle at East Finchley, where we had a late lunch – club sandwich and chips. Over lunch I took a phone call from a film producer who had been commissioned to make a documentary about the World Cup and wanted to meet in Frankfurt to interview us. As we were leaving, the Evening Standard phoned chasing a photograph, it looked like they were going to run a story. I phoned Gemma, gave her the contact details at the Standard, asked her to phone and then e-mail through a photograph. It was great having someone 'back in the office' to handle all sorts of things whilst I was out doing what I was doing.

We'd already covered 15 miles by now. Sandra was doing really well but we both found it hard to get going on this third stretch of the day. Our route took us back towards the North Circular, we found Brookside and walked alongside the stream, amongst greenery, with the traffic noise all around us and the busy dual-carriageway just yards away. From the green of Brookside, it wasn't long before we crossed Hendon Park and the A41, by Brent Cross. For a moment I thought I had got our route wrong, the road ahead looked impassable but looking right, there was a crossing just 200 yards away and we were off again. We had caught glimpses earlier of the new Wembley arch in the distance but as we crossed the M1, it loomed large straight ahead.

Sandra was walking well with bursts of energy and a steadfast determination but she was starting to tire as we came to Welsh Harp and an opportunity to walk alongside some more water as we neared the stadium. A little boy played in a tiny stream of water, jumping up and down in his wellies whilst his mother watched. There were a few dinghies out on the water, the breeze was picking up and the haze had cleared.

We seemed almost on top of Wembley but had to walk right round the northern side to the new tube station and Empire Way as it is now called. We took lots of photos of each other to send to the Standard, walked up close to the impressive new stadium and then wearily caught the Tube back to Loughton. It had been another good day, especially to walk with Sandra on our own. Another female winner of the Yellow Jersey award. I was tired but feeling fine. It has turned out to be a good warm-up for the real thing starting on Saturday.

Walking towards Wembley had set me thinking about Tim and the old twin-towered stadium, Tim and his love of football. As soon as he was old enough to run, Tim would chase after Dan, wearing a tiny red Liverpool shirt down to the field near our home in Groby, Leicestershire. He was well co-ordinated, big, strong and fast for his age and when Dan started training, by now on the Prom in Maldon, Tim would often come along and could hold his own with boys two years older than him. He was seven when he went to Wembley for the first time, to see England play and beat Poland in a World Cup qualifier in 1989. He played in his primary school team for three years, captained the side in Year Six, played for the District Schools team and was a regular for Maldon Saints, playing with boys a year ahead of him at school.

He generally played centre-half but often surprised opponents by having a good touch and the ability to beat a man by skill and pass the ball well. It was in 1991, when Leeds United won the Division One title, the last season before the Premier League was introduced, that Tim became a Leeds United supporter. I remember taking him, Dan, Tim Wardrop and Matthew Collins to Chelsea to watch them play Leeds for Tim's birthday. Standing up on his seat to look around at halftime, Tim was proudly wearing his Leeds shirt and I quietly suggested that he get down as soon as I saw some of the Chelsea thugs pointing down at Tim, muttering away, threatening looks on their faces.

The day we walked to Wembley

He loved everything about football, supporting a club and his country, going to Arsenal which we did many times in the late '80s and early '90s, before the Hillsborough Disaster, when you could squeeze down to lift him over the front to sit on the barrier alongside the First Aiders. He loved watching football on TV, watched tapes of Leeds's glory years endlessly, could quote statistics and who scored which goal with an incredible memory and even came to Barnsley with me the day we won promotion into the big time in 1997. We travelled up to Oakwell for home games (we only missed three) during our season 'in the sun'. He was also with me and Dan and 20,000 other Barnsley fans back at Wembley again, when we lost the 2001 play-off final to Ipswich. It was the last competitive game at the old stadium and Tim was there. It seemed more and more appropriate that Tim's walk would be starting from Wembley in four days time.

Most of all, Tim loved playing football and just messing around with a ball, up on the playing field or in the garden. One of the last things he said to Dan before he died, was a wish just to be able to go outside and kick a ball about.

The first edition of the London Evening Standard is available mid-morning and the following day, I had a phone call from a friend, in the midst of more e-mails and packing, asking if I had seen the day's edition. They had run the story over half a page with photo and map of our journey to Frankfurt. Elizabeth Hopkirk who had interviewed me over the phone to research the piece had done a great job and provided a wonderful publicity boost, just at the right time. Sky News and Sports were soon on the phone asking for interviews and confirming they would be at Wembley. London Tonight picked up on the story and there were numerous phone calls from other local newspapers wanting to run a piece. My mobile phone was getting even busier.

On Thursday morning, we were off early, driven by Ted, around the M25 and west on the M4 to Newbury, to pick up the motor home at the Marquis Motorhomes dealership. When we arrived and were shown the brand new motor home, we were all gob-smacked – it was superbly equipped with loads of space but just so big. Sandra and I had road tests, we were given a 30 minute induction tour of the facilities and Sandra drove all the way home. On the way back, we called at Tesco and loaded up the pallet of provisions they had organised for us.

Friday morning started badly, we couldn't unlock the external store on the motor home. The lock had seemed dodgy the previous day. Dennis and Anne, experienced camper-vanners, arrived to help with setting up the vehicle but after another 20 minutes Dennis couldn't open the lock. Calls to Newbury and the technician who had shown us around the previous day didn't help and it looked like I was going to have to drive the vehicle round to Harpenden to get the lock sorted out. Then just as I was arranging for someone to be available when I got to Harpenden, Dennis managed to get the door to open. More importantly, we had fathomed out how the lock worked, there was only one way and it had to be followed precisely to lock and unlock the door.

The rest of the day for me was taken up with phone calls from the media and well-wishers, the last after 9pm. I carried the heavy gear but basically Sandra loaded the motor home, our base for the next four weeks. Anne and Anthony (Sandra's sister and her husband) arrived around 10pm, we had a glass of wine and went to bed after midnight.

I was the last up, at 6.20am the following morning. Breakfast of cereal, bacon butties and hard boiled eggs whilst the thunder and lightning crashed around us outside. The three of them were sat in the car by 7.30 when Ted arrived and we were off. I was feeling quiet and subdued, with thoughts of Tim and the scale of what we were about to do. The drive to Wembley was easy and quick and the sun was shining as we arrived at Olympic Way.

The Sky News crew was already in place and Dan, Nick and Jono arrived at the same time. By 9.15, there were 20 of us and the others held the banner and waved as background to 'live' interviews with Sky News and Sky Sports at 9.30. One horrible moment when mid-interview, the voices of the studio presenters was replaced by a high-pitch noise in my ear-piece and I gazed stupidly into the camera, not knowing what to do or say.

Cup final day and ready for the off

Photos for local photographers followed but still no sign of London Tonight and at 10.40 (forty minutes later than planned) most of the group set off and I waited with Dan and the boys for the ITV London crew. When they arrived, they wanted shots of the group, so we agreed to catch up with the others and the crew would follow in their vehicle and find a suitable spot, hopefully with a backdrop of the stadium.

So, stiff from too much standing around and almost an hour behind schedule, we set off walking fast. Almost immediately, a big stretch limo pulled alongside, the window came down and the driver shouted 'Good Luck! Just saw the interview on Sky!' Next a Reuters cameraman ran ahead of us taking shots and arranged to meet us again as we crossed Westminster Bridge. Shortly after we crossed the North Circular we saw the main group with the London Tonight crew in a small park at the side of the road. Another 15 minute delay for interview and filming of the group walking and then we were off again.

We were soon at the Grand Union Canal but only to find that the towpath had been blocked off by the Met Police, a few weeks before, because of a body found floating in the canal. We had 20 people who didn't know where to go and were over an hour behind schedule – what a start!

There was no immediate way of picking up the canal as it ran alongside railway sidings but Faye took the map and worked out another route to join the canal a mile away and for the first time that day, we were able to settle into a rhythm. Past a beautiful canal-side garden and what looked like a Buddhist shrine and on to Little Venice where we waited for the group to catch up. David and Mark Kidd and Keziah and her friend decided to leave us here and the remainder of the group headed off to Paddington, then towards Hyde Park. The day was cloudy but by now, it was warm and the park was busy with tourists and strollers enjoying the Spring colours.

Sandra had already phoned several times, she couldn't find our stopping point at the New Cross Tesco. I stopped to talk to her again whilst the others continued and then cut around in front of Buckingham Palace, through St. James's Park and across Horse Guards Parade to rejoin the group in Parliament Square. We met up with the Reuters cameraman and had a hilarious few minutes walking slowly across Westminster Bridge as he walked backwards ahead of us taking photographs of us with Big Ben in the background, knocking tourists all over the place with his large camera bag strapped on his back.

Twelve of us crossed the river and headed for the Elephant and Castle. Sandra rang, she had found the Tesco store, at Southwark, not New Cross. It was all my fault but she had arrived, the store manager was willing to look after us with food and drink in the staff restaurant and even better, it was only one mile ahead.

By the time we arrived, we had walked 12 miles and were all tired and hungry. The FA Cup final was on the TV in the staff restaurant and after a stretch, a drink of Ribena and a plate of chips, sausage roll and beans, I felt much better.

Anne and Ted decided to stay with Sandra and nine of us set off for Bexley Heath as West Ham took a 2-1 lead. We attacked the second half of the day's walk and Dan and I pulled ahead of the others as we walked along New Cross Road and into

Lewisham. It was good to walk and talk with my son. Then Anthony caught us up and the three of us continued to set a pace with the others some way behind. Dan was getting regular updates on the cup final as the score see-sawed backwards and forwards. We walked up and over Blackheath, the first hill of the walk, past the A2 turn-off and onto the long climb up Shooters Hill. Dan pulled away as we climbed the hill, I tried to keep with him but couldn't and Anthony fell behind. It was good to reach the top and the pub where we had lunch a few weeks earlier but we continued down the other side. It was painful going down the steep slope and Dan and Anthony decided to stop at the pub at the bottom of the hill and sat outside drinking shandies before going inside to see the re-runs of the big match. I carried on and covered another two miles through Welling and towards Bexley Heath.

Yellow Jersey award shared by Faye and Nina.
Distance covered - 22.4 miles.
Total distance covered - 85.2 miles.

Sandra picked me up almost as soon as I stopped and took me back to the John Barras pub where the others had stopped. A stretch, sit down and welcome pint of orange. Ted and Anthony collected money in the pub, full after the cup final and I had an emotional chat with a kind and friendly fireman, who pledged his support for our cause.

Then it was back home for the last time for four weeks. I was cold and sore but a hot bath, Glucosamine patches and a take-away Chinese helped to restore me. I finished the diary just before midnight and knelt down to talk to Tim, at the side of his bed.

A 21st Century Pilgrimage
From the City through the 'Garden of England' to the Sea

I had mixed feelings as I woke up and faced Day Five of the walk. I was looking forward to getting on with the real walking, out of London, with no media distractions, seeing if we could make all the planning turn into reality. But it was hard leaving home. I was used to going away on business or holiday but never for four weeks and it seemed like such a long time with so much to do before I'd be back. It was our family home, a house that all four of us had come to love, a home of happy memories. Tim, perhaps more than the rest of us, had always felt a special affinity with the house. He was only four when we moved in and all his memories were of this home. He had gone away to university twice but had always liked to come home, back to his own bedroom and his own things. *'I've almost got it perfect,'* he said, not long before he died. It was somewhere where he felt safe and secure, a house full of love.

Once I was up though, there was much to do, final checking of all the packing that Sandra had done and getting my things ready for the day. Anthony and I were going to drive back to Bexley Heath and the pub where I had stopped the night before and Sandra and Anne would drive the motor home and meet us en route, the real adventure was beginning.

The roads were empty and we arrived at the pub in good time. Anthony checked with the landlord that it was OK to leave his car in the car park and I rang Dan. He was not far away and by 9.45 a.m. – a lie-in concession for a Sunday - five of us set out including Dan's housemates, Nick and 'Big Guns'.

Through Bexley Heath, people were waiting for the shops to open at 10am and the lads detoured to McD's for breakfast but caught us up as we walked down the hill towards Crayford. It was a bright morning, cloudy but with the prospect of sun later, a

John Reeve

slight breeze, good walking weather. Not long afterwards, Sandra and Anne passed us on their way to our first stopping point by Bluewater Shopping Centre. There was more traffic on the roads now but the centre of Dartford was empty and we climbed the hill out of the town, past the point where we had got lost doing the recce and towards the General Hospital. Sandra rang and asked for directions to our meeting point. She had taken a wrong turning further back (one of very few on the entire journey) but we were able to easily get her back on course and saw the motor home cross a junction ahead as we walked along Watling Street; now there was a road made for walking.

For the first time, we saw open fields and began to leave London and its sprawling suburbs behind. Just over the crest of the hill, on a slip road to the Shopping Centre and almost blocking the coach lane, was the motor home. We'd covered six-and-a-half miles in about an hour and a half, a little early for a stop but still very welcome, nevertheless. Sandra had hot drinks, bacon butties and energy bars ready but I made sure I followed my routine of stretching exercises before sitting down – they were to become essential as the walk progressed.

After 30 minutes we were ready to go again. The next part of the walk was to take us as far as the outskirts of Rochester and the Medway towns and involved one of the most problematic stretches of the entire journey, a six mile walk along the busy A2 dual carriageway. We would leave as it blossomed into the M2 but there was no alternative without a very significant detour. From our preparation, I was fairly certain there was a path we could follow, we had caught glimpses of it amongst the trees and bushes of the verge when we drove the route to Dover, but there was no telling whether it ran the full route or what sort of condition it would be in. I didn't fancy walking on the hard shoulder for 90 minutes but we would soon find out.

As we joined the A2 we had to navigate across two busy slip roads and along the hard shoulder for 800 yards and then picked up the path at the first junction. It ran high along the top of the grass verge, surrounded by trees, bushes and thick undergrowth and for long stretches was completely covered over. It was a strange part of the walk; we had to walk in single file knocking

A Walk of Faith

brambles and branches out of the way at regular intervals, up and down following the contours of the road, having to almost shout to be heard by the person in front or behind because of the din from the traffic. At each junction, the path headed up the slip road and deposited us at the inevitable roundabout at the top and we would cross over, find the path again and continue on our Kentish jungle walk. There were the occasional signs of life, various sorts of litter sprawled across the path but generally the impression was that very few people used the path and those that did weren't doing so for the walking.

It was the only day that Nick and Big Guns would join me on the walk and not a very inspiring landscape for them to enjoy. The undergrowth shielded us from the sun but also from any breeze and we were soon hot as we stepped out to get this stretch of the walk over with. I'd seen an e-mail the evening before from Paul Jeater who'd walked with me on the first day from Chelmsford, saying that a doctor friend of his, Andrew Harris, another Wimbledon AFC fan, had heard about the walk, was very involved in offering help and advice to leukaemia sufferers and arranging donor recruitment sessions for the Anthony Nolan Trust locally, and would be trying to meet us on the route. As we walked along one short stretch of roadway running parallel to the A2 a car drew up and it was him. The others continued slowly and I stood and chatted for five minutes, thanked him for coming out of his way to meet us and set off to catch the others with his best wishes for a successful walk. By now the others were 400 yards ahead and I enjoyed walking by myself for 20 minutes, catching occasional glimpses of them in the distance and gradually hauling them in before we reached the start of the M2.

By this time, we had covered about 13 miles, it was 1.30 pm and we were getting ready for lunch. Sandra and Anne had been in regular telephone contact but had been having difficulty finding somewhere for us to stop but just as we were leaving the A2 they rang with good news. They had found somewhere, literally 100 yards off our route and about one mile ahead. Getting onto the old A2 was no easy matter, as the path was talking us up the first exit and the A286 towards Hoo St. Werburgh. We had to drop down and cross the dual carriageway,

85

climb up and over a steep verge covered in very dense undergrowth and then onto the hard shoulder of the slip road up to the roundabout and the road to Rochester.

By the time we had reached the roundabout, we were all ready for a break and after another five-minute walk, right on cue, Sandra and Anne appeared at the next roundabout and directed us to our second stop of the day, the Three Crutches pub at Strood. We didn't find a more aptly named resting place along the whole of the walk and after a compulsory team photo to capture the moment for posterity, the others piled in for a drink and some food, I did my five-minute stretch-down and went in to join them.

The pub was busy with lots of families out for Sunday lunch. It was one of those pubs where you found a table, checked the table number and then ordered your food at the bar. It was good to sit down, have a drink and get away from the traffic noise. Sandra seemed to be coping well with the motor home and it was good that she was with her sister for her first full day in the driving seat. The landlord had spotted our T-shirts and said he had heard a radio interview earlier that day about the walk. He very kindly gave us our lunches for free and allowed us to make a collection around the pub; we weren't intending to make a major effort to collect money along the route preferring to concentrate on the walking but always carried a collecting tin with us.

We stayed nearly an hour at the Three Crutches, a friendly pub with good food. Nick wisely decided to call it a day at this point; he had exacerbated a slight injury and would take weeks to fully recover. I needed to stretch out and warm up and the four of us set off for Part Three. The road took us downhill, gently at first but ever downwards as we headed for the Medway Bridge and Rochester. We were back on the route of Watling Street, the very first Roman 'motorway', from Dover to London. The road narrowed from a tree-lined avenue to a narrow stretch of busy road past shops and offices and finally we came to the bridge. There were road works and traffic lights over the bridge with pedestrians having to navigate around the repair work. Not watching my feet closely enough, I managed to trip and fall straight onto my arm so stopped for a few minutes to brush myself down and get my breath back. As we stood over the middle of the river, we could see the imposing ruins of Rochester Castle ahead and to our right.

The first castle was raised here at the time of the Norman Conquest and is mentioned in the Domesday Book in 1086. Rochester was an important centre in medieval England, the castle was the scene of many battles and sieges during the reigns of William II and King John, and was attacked by Simon de Montford and his men during the rebellion against Henry III.

Even further back in history, the Medway became the dividing line between the territories of two invaders, the Saxons who retired north and west and became Kentish Men, and the Jutes who settled to the east and were known as the Men of Kent - descriptions that have survived the test of time.

Looking more carefully now at the debris on the floor, we crossed the remainder of the bridge and walked through the town centre. It was 3.45 pm and there were lots of people out for a Sunday afternoon stroll, window shopping. The old town reeked of history and in places it was easy to imagine scenes from 'Pickwick Papers' or 'Great Expectations'.

But we had a walk to complete and moving quickly onwards, many shoppers stopped and looked at us as 5 men in Walk to the World Cup T-shirts passed by. By now, I had already experienced many people asking 'Are you really walking to the World Cup?' I nearly always answered, 'Yes, from Wembley to Frankfurt' as I continued on my way but was getting increasingly irritated by the regular follow up 'How are you getting across the Channel?' Most of my replies are not to be printed here.....!

As we headed towards Chatham and Gillingham, the group of five of us began to split up, with Dan and me leading the way, and the others walking comfortably but taking their time. We needed to ask directions on a couple of occasion and this gave the others the chance to catch up but as we headed up Chatham Hill and towards Gillingham, the gap widened again. It was a good climb up the hill, Dan stopped for a natural break and I waited for him at the top, admiring the beautiful exterior of St. Augustine's church.

We had only one-and-a-half miles to go but would be passing the house on First Avenue where I had lived for a short time as a five-year-old. It was only 30 yards off our route and very vague memories returned; I imagine the road itself had changed relatively little over the intervening 48 years apart from the cars outside the houses! But the main A2 road certainly had changed. As we continued towards the motor home waiting for us, it was a classic early 21 century edge of town scene, fast-food outlets, DIY and furniture stores and the inevitable supermarket. It was the Tesco sign we were looking for. It was 5pm by the time we arrived and the car park was empty except for one vehicle and three people waiting for us.

We'd covered 21.8 miles on the day, stepping out at a good pace for most of the way, a total of 107 miles in all. The Yellow Jersey award went to Anthony for two days' solid walking. He and Anne headed back to Bexley Heath with the three Londoners to pick up their cars. I would see Dan again in five days' time at Ypres and Anthony was flying out to Liege for the walk up into the Ardennes. After fond farewells, it was Sandra and I who drove the van south-eastwards towards Canterbury and our accommodation for the next two nights.

It was a 25 mile run down to Wingham. We had called in on our way to Dover and our drive to Frankfurt back in March, but at the end of a day's walking, the ride from Canterbury seemed to take for ever. We remembered the turning, sharp right in the middle of Wingham and then left, out of the village and after fun and games getting the motor home into the drive way and the car park, we eventually arrived. There we were met by Gordon and Linda's daughter, Helen, and their son. He was recovering from lymphoma, looking well, building up his strength by doing some physical work around the house and was very positive about the future.

Danbridge Oast House was a beautiful resting place on our journey. As well as the main building converted from the old Oast House, there is a second smaller cottage and two blocks of Charolais cottages converted from the old milking parlours. The feel of the place is friendly, well-furnished and decorated but somewhere to feel comfortable and relaxed in. Our room was in

A Walk of Faith

the main building, up on the second floor with a good, big bed and a well-equipped shower room.

After a hot shower and a change of clothes I was feeling more human but by now it was 8pm. It was too far to walk into the village for a pub meal (certainly for me) and we didn't fancy talking the van out again down the country lanes. So we had our first evening meal away from home, in our room eating sandwiches and cakes from the motor home but they tasted really good and after some food and a hot drink, I settled down to check e-mails and write the web diary for the day. My laptop would receive e-mails but not send them which was frustrating and by the time I'd finished this and wrote my personal diary it was time for bed.

On Day Six of the walk, a collection on behalf of the Leukaemia Research Fund was taking place at the Gillingham Tesco store where we had finished walking the evening before. The local Medway branch was organising it. Sandra and I both wanted to spend some time with them collecting and had agreed to meet them at 10am. Driving down to Wingham the evening before, Sandra had the good idea of doing the first stage of the walk in reverse so that I could walk the first four miles or so of the day back to Gillingham and when we left the store, I would already have that under my belt.

Up at 7am and cereal and tea in our pretty room, we were on the road by 7.50am. It was a cool and grey morning but the traffic was light around Canterbury and we made good progress back to the M2 junction when we were held up in the busy commuter traffic. Sandra was looking noticeably more confident driving the motor home and she dropped me off at a lay-by at Newington to start my walk for the day. Stiff legs made it hard going to begin with but there was no need to rush and after 20 minutes I started to move more easily. The traffic was heavy on the relatively narrow road and I slowed down through Rainham and took a picture of St. Margaret's Church with its Cross, right in the middle of the town.

Continuing towards London, I avoided any 'you're walking in the wrong direction' comments despite the T-shirt and the fact that the town was busy with people going to work and early

89

shoppers. I was surprised to see the Tesco symbol appear in the distance sooner than I had expected, as I walked along a foot/cycle path running alongside the now much wider A2.

As I came into the car park and saw the LRF table and collectors by the store entrance, my mobile phone rang and it was Tracey from Dream FM calling for the first of many 'live' radio interviews. The interview went fine; I had talked to so many people about Tim, his bravery and our despair, about the walk and our hopes that I knew what I wanted to say. She was very kind, the interview went on for several minutes and after we had gone off air, she expressed her sadness at Tim's death and empathy as a mother. She promised to ring regularly for an update around the same time; 9.45am (or 10.45 in Europe) was to become my Dream FM interview slot.

Interview over, I said hello to Pat from the Medway Branch of LRF and her colleague. Sandra was collecting with them and she introduced me to Steve Peelin, the store manager and Liz Caswell, the Customer Service Manager. I also saw another member of Tesco staff, Julie, looking upset with red eyes. When I said hello, she explained that her eight-year-old son, Jake, had the same type of leukaemia as Tim and she was overcome with the emotion of the visit. We chatted for a few minutes and I tried to reassure her that the prognosis for Jake as an eight-year-old was very good. She agreed to take some of our England '06 wrist bands to sell and raise money and I promised to bring back a World Cup programme for Jake.

Eventually, I went inside to the restaurant area to have my second breakfast of the day and sat down for 20 minutes. Sausage, bacon, beans on toast and a large mug of tea – yum, yum. I managed to say hello to David Rawnsley, my new walking companion for the next two days. David had driven down from Manchester to join the walk. His family are close to Sandra's parent's family. His niece, Joni, also eight, has aplastic anaemia, another serious blood disorder and was undergoing chemotherapy in preparation for a bone marrow transplant. David was a fellow Barnsley supporter and I was looking forward to the opportunity to talk some football as we walked. He was raising his

A Walk of Faith

own sponsorship for his part of the walk and later sent through a cheque for the amazing amount of £1,500 that he had raised.

The team at Tesco Gillingham were very supportive and offered us more supplies of energy drinks and food but we still had 18 miles to cover and after compulsory team photos David and I were ready to go.

Lunch at the Three Crutches at Strood

With the LRF Medway branch and Tesco teams at Gillingham

Sandra promised to return to help the collectors again but drove us back down the A2 to Newington, it seemed easy to David; four miles and he hadn't felt a thing.

David was good company and happy to walk at my pace. We talked about football and Barnsley a lot including our favourite team across the years, University (where he worked), our families, the state of the nation and walking; he was a keen rambler. The miles passed easily as we walked through Sittingbourne and its pedestrianised area and back out into the countryside of Kent. Always the busy A2 traffic close but also alongside us were fields of apple orchards, trees full of blossom, white and green, fresh and bright. Fields of hops with canes tall and straight, looking like regiments of wooden soldiers standing to attention. As we passed the Wyevale Garden Centre, we decided it would be a good place to stop for lunch and I rang Sandra who was on the way from Gillingham, having sold some more wrist bands and filled up with petrol.

We had lunch in the motor home, used the toilet in the Garden Centre – we were trying to minimize the use of the toilet in the van – and then were off again. We soon passed the Faversham stone chapel beneath Judd Hill, the site of a rare seventh century Saxon Church, Our Lady of Elwarton. Although it fell into decay more than 400 years ago, the stone chapel is one of the most unique church buildings in England, the only one known to incorporate the remains of a pagan shrine or mausoleum. You could see the different bricks, tiles and stone work through the ages, unique in the UK and we took the compulsory photograph.

In Roman times, the area was quite heavily populated. There was probably a Roman camp on Judd Hill, and a cemetery of substantial size has been found a few hundred yards to the east of the church. A number of Roman artefacts have also been found in the field in which the church stands. The "Itinerary" of Antonius places the Roman station Durolevum 16 miles from Rochester and 9-12 miles from Canterbury. It is quite possible, but so far unproved, that the site on Judd Hill is this station.

In AD 601 Pope Gregory directed St. Augustine not to destroy pagan buildings, but to adapt them for Christian use. King

A Walk of Faith

Ethelbert of Kent allowed St. Augustine to build and repair churches in the area. It is tempting to think that this little church was one that St. Augustine converted, but there is no proof that the fabric is of this early a date. As it is, the remains are a unique record of the adaptation of a pagan Roman building for Christian use, and are preserved for that reason[1].

Striding out, we were hit by a mini dust-storm, caused by the dry weather and the lorries thundering by, as we walked through Ospringe and the outskirts of Faversham. From the A2 we caught glimpses of the Shepherd Neame Brewery, a famous name in English beer-making but missed the centre of this pretty Kent town with its history going back 2,000 years. It is thought that Faversham takes its name from the old Latin word Faber, the town of blacksmiths.

Chatting away as we crossed the M2/A2 roundabout, we almost missed Sandra parked in a nearby lay-by. She had stopped to let us catch up but couldn't get the handbrake off and had to shout two or three times before we stopped and came back to help. Vehicle restored, we continued on a B road through Baughton under Bean and up the long hill towards Dunkirk. The sun had come out by now and it was warm at the bottom of the hill. As we climbed the steep hill, we walked into the wood and shade and passed children on their way home after a day at school; at least they could walk downhill at the end of the day, I wonder if they walk up in the morning?

A short stop just before we rejoined the A2 and we covered half a mile along the busy A2 before turning off again, for a short-cut through Upper Harbledown and towards Canterbury. We were both getting warm now and starting to tire as we picked up the dual carriageway and the main London road into Canterbury. I hadn't decided where to stop for the day. It needed to be somewhere with a decent car park, as we had more walkers joining us for the walk to Dover and after navigating the first three roundabouts, we settled for the Habitat store, right by the road where we would leave Canterbury for the A2.

---

[1] *Text courtesy of Clive Foreman, Warden of the Stone Chapel at Elwarton*

Walking the last two miles into Canterbury, with the cathedral looming large and other signs of antiquity around us, had set me thinking about the medieval walkers who had journeyed from all over England and beyond on their pilgrimages to one of Britain's holy places. My walk to Germany was in many ways a pilgrimage, a walk for Tim but also a walk to a football tournament, the modern day religion of many. They walked in groups and told each other stories about their lives to pass the time and I had my companions joining me for different stretches of my pilgrimage. How difficult their route along the Pilgrim's Way must have been, compared to my stroll with a motor home in attendance. But still many similarities and it felt like a sense of connection across the ages as we walked closer to the cathedral that dominated the skyline with St. Mildred's and the old castle just across the busy road from us.

22.9 miles covered in the day for a grand total of 129.9 miles. Yellow Jersey award to David Rawnsley for his good company and chat.

Then it was back to the Oast House, fortunately with a much shorter journey. David was booked in for one night and after a shower and update for the website, we were ready for a good meal. We wanted to eat in a pub with TV and the Sky Sports channels. The Bat and Ball by the country cricket ground was recommended so the three of us took a taxi and 20 minutes later arrived at the pub. Despite the fact that it was now the cricket season and the pub was be-decked with cricketing memorabilia, it was football we had come to watch, specifically the Division One play-off semi-final second leg between Huddersfield and… Barnsley!

The pub was fine, the mixed grill was good and filling and we sat back to enjoy the football. Despite having lost the first leg at Oakwell, 1-0, David and I were both quite confident that Barnsley's counter-attacking style could do the business and after a quiet start Barnsley rose to the challenge. As the first, then second and then third goals went in, the noise we were making in the pub increased and the landlord explained that there had been 30 Barnsley and Huddersfield fans in the pub for the first leg – Yorkshire had been playing Kent across the road. Good food and a great result, only problem was that I would still be walking and miss the big day out in Cardiff.

Back at our lodgings, I managed to get some e-mails sorted out and with Helen's help sent them through. Tired but satisfied after another good day, it was bed at 11.45 – no problem sleeping.

Day Seven began with breakfast in our room again and then downstairs to sort out the lock on the motor home. We had been unable to open it the evening before and it seemed it would become a regular irritant. Sandra was the expert and soon had it opened. As long as you put the key in the correct way, made a quarter turn to the right and pressed on the door at the same time, it was fine. Anything else and the key just revolved until the whole locking mechanism could be taken out. Whilst she was doing this, I said goodbye to Helen and her friend who gave me £20 towards our sponsorship money and went to check that David was ready.

The evening before I had spoken to the other walkers who were joining us for the day and told them about the Habitat car park and we quickly completed the short journey into Canterbury. Mick Waite, a friend over many years was already waiting for us in the sunshine. He had been up at 4.30 and driven from Dorchester to join us; it was great to see him. Reg and Jennie, our next door neighbours soon appeared with Rachel, their younger daughter, at uni in Canterbury, and her friend who was working as a Red Bull rep. A case of Red Bull soon joined our other refreshments in the store and we drank a stimulating toast to Barnsley's victory.

We said goodbye to Sandra who would meet us for a first stop just before we joined the North Downs Way and set off at 8.45 am. Traffic was heavy queuing in the opposite direction and a few drivers with their windows down in the warm Spring sunshine, shouted across to the five of us, 'Are you really Walking to the World Cup?' That question again! We met Barry Cotgrave, another former work colleague of mine at the top of Old London Road, close to his Canterbury home and the six of us continued past the Bat and Ball pub and out of Canterbury. After 75 minutes and my regular radio interview with Tracey and Dream

FM, we reached Bridge and decided to look for a shop to buy lunch.

We were going to walk for three hours on the North Downs Way and for the only time along the entire route, would be meeting the motor home only once during the day, so needed some food for our back packs. We stood outside the village shop talking and looking in through the window, but as I was about to enter, an elderly man across the road shouted, *'You don't want to go in there, go the baker's at the end of the High Street instead'*. Local knowledge usually pays off, we thanked him and were soon following our noses as the wonderful smell of fresh bread wafted towards us. The shop was busy but the wait was worthwhile, the ham sandwiches looked good and the ginger spice cake irresistible.

Up the hill, out of the village and we met Sandra by the lane leading over the A2. She had prepared fresh melon and a plate of apple pies and buttered malt loaf – as well as walking to the World Cup, I was going to eat my way there – and enjoyed a coffee and mid-morning snack. After 20 minutes we left Sandra to drive down to Dover, crossed over the A2 and turned immediately right picking up the North Downs Way which ran parallel to the dual carriageway for a time before turning away and talking a more direct route towards Dover for 8-10 miles.

So far that day, we had walked on pavements alongside often busy roads with hedgerows and Spring greenery restricting the view around us. Now the scene was transformed into the massive fields, the bare chalk surfaces and the huge open skies of the Downs. Magnificent views, a bright morning with lots of sunshine and a light breeze. Space to breath and think. We were walking at a much steadier pace than I had done over the last few days and the six of us chatted easily, changing partners as we progressed over stiles and up and down the rolling countryside.

After three or four miles and crossing three roads, the surroundings became more heavily wooded and just after Womenswold, we missed a stile and footpath sign and headed off into a wood. Barry, as the youngest, jogged off to check the route and came back to report that the path petered out ahead. We turned round and approaching the point where we had turned off, easily saw the offending footpath sign from the opposite direction and realised our mistake. We had walked maybe a mile out of our way and this, together with the easy pace, started to mean that we were getting behind schedule, so I began to gently speed up and the group spread out.

At Shepherdswell, Barry left us to catch a train back to Canterbury. A busy man, it had been good of him to join us and we had enjoyed chatting with him despite the fact that he had got us lost; he had to take the blame as the local man. It was 12.30 now and we were looking for somewhere to stop for lunch. No pubs in sight, we tried the old railway station but it didn't look promising and we decided to rejoin the footpath. As soon as we crossed the first stile and turned a corner, there were two picnic tables perfectly positioned and just waiting for us to use them. With the sun shining and the day becoming warm, the trouser bottoms came off and the knees were exposed again, resplendent with the glucosamine patch that I had left on.

The last few miles of the footpath took us from one pretty East Kent village to another, cutting alongside gardens and beautiful country homes, many with dogs barking behind the hedges. As we crossed yet another road, we turned away from the footpath which veered east and north for a time, and picked up a B road that headed straight towards Dover.

Reg and Jennie were starting to tire and followed behind whilst David, Mick and I forged ahead. We kept each other in sight to avoid them getting lost and after 30 minutes began to hear the traffic of the A2 in the distance. Our road ran parallel to the busy dual carriageway for two or three miles, always a mile away but the traffic noise seemed reassuring, we were getting there. I rang Sandra and told her our expected arrival time. She had checked into the Premier Travel Inn, where the local newspaper reporter and journalist were meeting us at 6.30pm. Before that, we had to visit the Tesco superstore, where more LRF volunteers were collecting money, and walk down to the Ferry Terminal.

We were booked on the 8.45 ferry the following morning and the terminal was two miles from the hotel. I was determined to get down there before finishing for the day to avoid a very early start. The McD's sign appearing amongst the houses meant that we were at the junction with the A2 and just half a mile from the Tesco. Sandra came to pick up Reg and Jennie, and David, Mick and I set off on the A2, walking on the hard shoulder with 42 tonners thundering by. I had told them both to go with Sandra and have a sit down. We had walked 16 miles and they had been good companions but both were determined to finish the day with me – good men!

The alternative route, following a much quieter B road swung round to the west before dropping down into Dover and looked about twice the distance. Although the hard shoulder was not ideal, at this stage of the day, it was the preferred option. The only other possibility was to pick up the North Downs Way again as it made its final approach to the sea. Mick had spotted on the map where the path crossed the dual carriageway and after three quarters of a mile we reached the point, right alongside a slip road. We could see the path on the other side as it came down from the north but on our side, there was nothing but a low fence and yard after yard of brambles, nettles and bushes. Nevertheless, this had to be the path, obviously well-used and the intrepid Dr Livingstone aka David Rawnsley, led the way, machete (or was it walking stick?) in hand demolishing nettles, brambles and all in our path.

After 200 yards and a lot of huffing and puffing, the jungle thinned out and we could see a proper path ahead. It was muddy and wet and almost totally covered over by low trees and bushes creating a tunnel. As we moved forward, the ground began to fall away and steepened quickly. Was this some kind of chute that would send us sliding off the cliff edge? Progress was difficult for me down the very steep slope but after another 10 minutes, the path became firmer under foot and soon merged into a narrow road. We had glimpses of the cliffs around us and the valleys seemingly suspended above the town and continued downhill for another half mile until we came to the first houses and the outskirts of Dover. It was 3.30pm by now and schoolchildren were on their way home. The road flattened out as we reached central Dover and headed east towards the Ferry Terminal and it

A Walk of Faith

Toasting the Reds with a can of Red Bull

Dave and Mick ready for a paddle

John Reeve

was nearly 4pm when we reached the port. I rang Sandra, asked her to pick us up and took photographs whilst we waited.

Back up at the Tesco store we met Linda from the Danbridge Oast House who was part of the LRF collection team. Then up into the staff restaurant where we were made very welcome, a hot mug of tea and a sit down. Rachel had agreed to drive down and pick up her mum and dad, as well as Mick and David, and take them back to Canterbury. Reg was then going to drop David off by his car on their way back to Essex. We thanked them for their company and support and said goodbye – it was already becoming a regular event - and headed for the hotel.

Yellow Jersey award to Mick Waite, a top man.
Distance covered – 18.2 miles.
Total distance covered – 148.1 miles.

I was ready for a hot bath and soak after two nights with a shower and needed to change and recharge my own personal batteries before meeting the local press at 6.30 pm. Our next supporter on the journey was the person travelling the furthest to join us – Sandra's brother Phil, who was coming all the way from southern Spain (he would do it again later in the walk) - to honour his nephew's dream and brave life and support us on our pilgrimage. Phil had flown into Gatwick at lunchtime, picked up a hire car, driven down to Eastbourne to have a briefing and a road test with Marquis Motorhomes and was now driving across to Dover – a quiet day.

Anyway, by the time I had bathed, Phil had not arrived and Sandra and I went over to the restaurant area to meet Carol, the manager and Bob and the reporter and photographer. The restaurant was holding a collection to raise money for Tim's Trust and we chatted and had a drink and then went outside for a photograph with the banner. Phil had still not arrived so we went back to our room and I checked e-mails and did the daily web diary. During this time, Phil rang through to Sandra. To finish off his day, he had arrived at the wrong Premier Travel Inn – there are two in the town and driving in from the M20 route, had arrived at the Inn close to the Ferry Terminal and assumed we were there. After 15 minutes of confusion, they had pointed out there was a second Premier Travel Inn and he was now on his way from the other one. At the same time as I finished he walked through the door. It was good to see him, an experienced motor home driver he would be great support for Sandra as she drove the vehicle for the first time ever in Europe.

Back in the restaurant, the three of us chatted and enjoyed a good meal, kindly donated along with the room charge, by the hotel. Tired but feeling good, we headed back to our room at 10pm. It would be an early start for the ferry and the start of another episode of the journey but it felt like we were getting somewhere and achieving something.

John Reeve

Across Flanders Fields
From a ferry full of Gooners through the war graves of Poperinge and Ypres and a walk with the Three Musketeers

Up at 7am on Day Eight and at the ferry terminal by 7.30 with breakfast planned for the ferry. The cars and coaches queuing for the 8.45 ferry already stretched back some distance and we were met by a sea of red – Arsenal fans on their way to Paris for the Champions League final that evening. P&O were sponsoring our trip across the Channel and had asked us not to collect money on board but Phil and I saw no reason why we shouldn't ask for donations on the quayside and grabbed a bucket. After a few minutes walking up and down the rows of vehicles, we went into the service area packed with supporters queuing for breakfast, all talking about the prospects for Arsenal's big night. We moved from group to group and as soon as I mentioned about Tim and my walk, almost everyone put some money in the bucket and we exchanged their condolences with our best wishes for the big game. After 20 minutes it was time to go back to the motor home but by now the bucket was nearly half full – another generous contribution from the English football community.

As we parked on the car deck, we saw Geoff and Anne Hurst, friends from Wickham Bishops drive on near to us. They were to be our next companions on the walk and we agreed to meet upstairs at Langham's restaurant for breakfast. The ferry was bustling with people everywhere, and by the time we reached the restaurant it was already full and we were told by the head waiter that we would have to wait for 20 minutes for a table. We sat down nearby and I went to get a daily paper. After 20 minutes I went to check in the restaurant and was told that our names had been called and a vacant table had just been given to another group. The waiter could see that I was not pleased and within another few minutes we were seated and starting to enjoy our

A Walk of Faith

breakfast, if rather later than expected. It was worth waiting for, the service was efficient and the breakfast helped prepare me for the walk from Calais.

The morning had been grey and misty in England and right across the channel but as we approached the French coast the sun appeared. It was now 10.45, European time and starting to warm up. With the prospect of a pleasant day's walking ahead, I climbed out of the car as soon as we cleared the customs point and began my walk in Europe.

Phil was joining me for the first stretch and after following the canal for 800 metres, we turned left onto the road for Oye Plage and Gravelines. The signing was not very clear and the nearby adverts had changed since our drive over here. I wondered straight away if Sandra had seen the signs. She was going to meet Anne and Geoff at a nearby car park where they would leave their car for the day and then re-join us on our route, north-east along the French coast.

The sun was warm but with a fresh breeze it was a good day for walking and for an early sun tan. Phil and I soon left Calais and its mixture of chalet houses and warehouses behind and walked out into the flat countryside with the dunes of the coast away to our left. Sandra had indeed missed the turning; it was 40 minutes before she caught up with us and Anne and Geoff joined the walk.

Making a steady 3.7 miles per hour we chatted as we strolled along the road with light traffic, no paths alongside the road but plenty of long, straight stretches and plenty of opportunity for vehicles to see the four of us from some distance. Geoff and Anne were good company. We have known them for many years, they have three sons, the younger two similar ages to Dan and Tim and all went to the Anglo. We used to see more of them several years ago than we had recently and it was nice to chat and catch up on family and the latest things in their lives. We passed Sandra waiting for us at Wagen, after 5½ miles and agreed to have a first stop at Oye Plage another 3½ miles ahead. By the time we reached the outskirts we were all ready for a sit down but the town stretched out alongside the road for over a mile and it took us another 10 minutes before we saw Sandra and the van ahead of us.

After a break, Phil took over the driving, giving Sandra the opportunity to walk for the first time since the two of us had walked to Wembley together, a fortnight before. It also gave her chance to talk to Anne and typically the group split up into men and women and the four of us continued happily along our way. It was afternoon now and the day had developed into an early season scorcher with the breeze strengthening as the sun reached its zenith. The road continued straight and flat, mainly open farmland with the occasional copse of trees. We were intrigued by the roofs of some of the chalet homes along our route. They had a shiny glazed finish to the tiles that we hadn't seen before in England and speculated whether it was done for visual effect or for maintenance purposes, perhaps against the salt in the air from the sea, still only half a mile away. As we passed Phil, Geoff climbed up into the motor home and they drove back to Calais to pick up his car and bring it up along our route. We knew from our earlier expedition that there was a supermarket on the outskirts of Gravelines, which would be a good place to park it and leave a relatively short drive back to their car at the end of the day. By the time, they returned, Sandra, Anne and I had almost reached the outskirts of Gravelines and could see the Super U sign up ahead. The two vehicles continued past us and Geoff rejoined the walkers as we passed the car park.

We skirted round the outskirts of the town and passed the marina, full with millions of pounds worth of pleasure craft. At the tower, we turned inland and left the sea behind us. We were following the road to Bourbourg and covered 2-3 miles on the hard shoulder of a road now much busier with commercial traffic. It was no fun despite the diversion caused by passing a plot of land filled with dolls, often hideous, hanging off gates and fences and looking out of tiny wooden huts – a bizarre sight in the middle of the French countryside.

We had our second stop near here and a longer break. We had broken the back of the day's walk and were all ready for a rest. The sky had clouded over but it was still warm and becoming humid. Phil continued to drive and Anne joined him. She was

A Walk of Faith

ready for a rest but as a fluent French-speaker, she was to be invaluable in helping to find us accommodation – there was the small matter of having nowhere to stay that night. On our recce we had spotted Bourbourg as a likely overnight stopping point but had been unable to book any accommodation in advance. It was now mid-afternoon and time to start looking in earnest.

Consequently, after a 40 minute stop, Geoff, Sandra and I stepped out to walk again and Phil and Anne went ahead to check out the local hotels and B&Bs. Gradually Bourbourg came closer and as we entered the outskirts of the small town, we were able to walk on pavements and give the traffic a wider berth.

Bourbourg is a pretty town, with several churches, a typically French town square with statues, a river and a canal. In the centre, we stopped to check our route and took a few minutes to make sure we were heading in the right direction.

As we left the town, we passed the first military cemetery of the walk, as always immaculately maintained, and were reminded that we were entering the territory which had faced the onslaught of two World Wars as well as being a hotspot for many of the great European conflicts for over a thousand years. It was polder country, flat land with only a few slightly elevated areas interrupting the view to the horizon, dotted with occasional clumps of trees providing shelter for the isolated farmhouses, criss-crossed by canals and a spider's web of ditches and drains; good farming country with open fields and open skies. We were heading for Looberghe, our planned stopping point of the day and the directions told us that when we crossed the larger Canal de la Cer we were almost there.

I had rung Phil earlier to let him know our estimated finish time and he had reported that Anne and he were struggling to find accommodation. Now, as the motor home passed by and then pulled in to mark the end of the day's walk, we wondered whether they had been successful. There was no need to worry. Both Phil and Anne were animated and telling us enthusiastically about the kind hotelier, who having told them that his hotel was full and finding out about our Walk to the World Cup, had offered to lead Phil and Anne, driving his own car, through the town to another place where we could stay for the night – our

105

John Reeve

Sandra and Geoff in the square at Bourbourg

very own moated French chateau!

Le Withof, Auberge du Chateau, lies in a beautiful setting with views over open fields, on the outskirts of Bourbourg. Without help, finding it as a visitor is almost impossible. The route is along the side-streets of the town and then cuts through a housing estate and along a narrow lane, with the chateau hidden from sight until it suddenly appears. Grateful for the kindness of our guide, Geoff, Sandra and I were wide-eyed when the chateau came into view; it was almost too good to be true. Geoff and Anne needed to set off back for their return ferry with Phil driving them back to their car at Gravelines, so we said more goodbyes, thanked them for their company and support and went to find our room.

Yellow Jersey award to Anne and Geoff Hurst, great to see them.
Distance covered – 21.2 miles.
Total distance covered – 169.9 miles.

The house was full of wood panelling and creaking wooden floors. We were shown up to our huge bedroom and sat down for a minute. People were being so kind but we had already experienced several fortunate coincidences, some things are meant to be. I subscribe to the view that you make your own luck, but it made me think?

We went into our daily routine now, bath or shower, sort out feet, knees or whatever was aching the most and then diary. We had arranged to see Phil at 8.30 and drive into town for an evening meal. It was a 10 minute drive, back into town and as Phil drove, I remarked that restaurants often close quite early in small, provincial French towns. So it shouldn't have come as a surprise but we passed the fritterie and the pizza takeaway, both open and serving customers, thinking that we would prefer a sit-down restaurant meal. We had seen one or two on our way through the town. The Chinese restaurant was closed and so was the local French eaterie. The hotel looked as if it was still closed for winter, there were no signs of life and so we decided that maybe it was going to be pizza after all.

The conspiracy theory started when we arrived back at the pizza shop to find that it had just closed and weren't even remotely surprised when we arrived at our last resort – the fritterie - to find that, it too, had shut up shop for the night – were the locals watching and waiting until just before we arrived before closing up? Getting a meal in 'down town Bourbourg' after 9pm was clearly impossible and so, for the second time already on the walk, we went back to the motor home and feasted on bread, pâté and a good supply of Jaffa cakes and yoghurts washed down with red wine. Then it was back up the creaky stairs to our room. Total darkness, absolute silence, shut out the world and rest.

It was getting harder to 'switch on' each morning, the temptation to turn over and sleep until noon grew more each day but on Day Nine, as on every morning, my thoughts as I surfaced soon turned to Tim. He had the same problem, how to face up to another day but for him it was a day without hope or respite but he always did it – so what the hell!

Creaky floorboards, grey sky, toilet in a cupboard. Was I in a bad mood? But then a wonderful breakfast room fit for a chateau, all to ourselves and a simple French breakfast. Fresh baguette with lashings of butter and jam. Yum, yum. Then back to the motor home and the drive back to the canal and the outskirts of Looberghe. Twenty-two miles to walk – 'Just do it, Dad'.

After 20 minutes of aches and twinges my legs calmed down and I settled into a pace. I was walking with Sandra, Phil in charge of the van, and she was kind and understanding in letting me set the pace. Past open fields full with lettuces and other salad vegetables growing in the rich black earth. Into Drincham and out again. Turning left, we aimed to cut off the corner from the route we had driven in March but realised that the road zig-zagged left and right. It was comfortable walking with Sandra, chatting occasionally but both of us content to walk and think as well. Right at the T junction and up towards the water tower, then away from it, then back towards it, as the road continued to swing wildly. The motor home staggered into sight, Phil had found us after our detour and looking everywhere but reported that we had, indeed, saved some time and distance.

Shortly after re-joining our original route, Le Xenon café came into view on the outskirts of Zegerscappel. A small village with a

A Walk of Faith

huge church dominating the surroundings. Everything neat and tidy, most un-French like. For the first time that day, we wondered whether we had crossed the border into Belgium. Later we realised that it was unimportant whether we were in France or Belgium, the important thing was that we were in Flanders with a language and traditions all of its own. Indeed for most of the last thousand years, the people of this part of NE France have not considered themselves to be French at all.

Sandra took over the driving here and Phil joined me for a stroll so we decided to continue into Esquelbecq. He was convinced it was a mirage, - 'not on the map', but it was and real too, much larger than I had remembered it. We stopped here for the first break of the day – 10½ miles and a little too far, I was already starting to get sore again and the pleasure of walking was starting to disappear.

After bread and biscuits, we set off again at 11.30, almost the same time that we had started yesterday's walk from the ferry. It was a busier road now with a cycle path for the first mile but then the need to dodge on and off the grass verge, avoiding the traffic but making sure not to over-balance into the inevitable ditch. We were averaging 3.8 miles per hour, reasonable going and I was happy to work at keeping up with Phil's pace. Next was Wormhout with the sun shining and a strong smell of chlorine from the swimming pool. It was a pleasant enough walk but I was glad to see the motor home in the distance with Sandra parked up for our second stop. Except what was she doing over there? Then as we came closer, the realisation that there were other motor homes on the road, it wasn't her and another mile to go before we saw the Marquis Motorhomes signs and knew this was our stop.

The 16.7 miles were turning into a bit of a slog. Six more to go but if we could reach Poperinge, then we would have started to pull ahead of the schedule and tomorrow was a short walk anyway. Not much to eat this time, just wanted to get on and finish the walk. Sandra joined me again for part three and we chatted happily for the first two miles with cycle paths to follow alongside the road. The next two miles were OK and the final two miles a real grind as my knees started to ache badly.

John Reeve

Poperinge is an attractive Flanders town with a mix of old and modern buildings and a large square, full of bustle and atmosphere in the centre of the town. We arrived by 4pm and Phil had difficulty finding somewhere to park. We had accommodation booked for the night at Talbot House and after we unloaded our bags, Phil went to park the van and Sandra and I went to find Talbot House, and Sylvia. We asked at the Talbot House Museum and were directed in very good English to the big door back on the main street we had just left. Lugging our bags we found the door, rang the bell and were shown into a large, imposing entrance hall, one that had seen better days but looked full of interesting furniture and other artefacts. A lady in her sixties greeted us and showed us into a conservatory-style meal room. 'Would we like a cup of tea?' she asked with a north-of-England accent.

Sandra and I sat down and soon the tea arrived, piping hot in a huge tea pot with three big mugs. The lady introduced herself as Sylvia, the Warden and began to tell us about the wonderful place that is Talbot House. She told us about Tubby Clayton, an Army Chaplain who, together with Padre Neville Talbot opened the doors of Talbot House for the first time on December 11, 1915. The house was named after Neville's brother, Lieutenant Gilbert Talbot who was killed at Ypres on July 30, 1915. Poperinge, she explained had been only a few miles from the Ypres Salient but because the front moved very little over the whole of the War, with thousands of men dying over the capture of a few extra yards of territory, Poperinge remained largely untouched physically by the fighting apart from a very occasional bomb blast. It became the headquarters of the British Army at Ypres and a place where men could take some respite from the battle just a few miles away. Talbot House had been one of these respite homes, not a place for officers to unwind but a place of refuge and relief for the privates and the corporals, the backbone of the British Army. A sign hung over the door read, *'All rank abandon, ye who enter here'*.

During the Great War, Talbot House become famous to the ordinary fighting man beleaguered in the trenches of Flanders. It was a place of calm, a place of peace, a place of kindness and comradeship. A place where men could try to forget the madness only a few miles away for a short time; remember how life could and should be and find new strength to continue. Entertainment took place nightly in the concert hall and the House became one of the most important institutions of the British Army in Belgium.

Sylvia explained that the House was now owned and managed by TOC H, a Christian charity committed to building a fairer society by working with communities to promote friendship and service, confront prejudice and practise reconciliation. Each year, 12 wardens come over from England for one month each to manage the running of the House and May was Sylvia's month. She was a former employee of the organisation and had been visiting warden for several years. She made us feel at home, listened to our stories about the walk and then showed us up to our rooms.

The House has been lovingly preserved as a tribute to the men who visited and the people who cared for them. It is clean if spartan by modern-day standards. Our room, the Blanckaert Room, was on the second floor and after a cold bath and then long, hot soak in the nearby bath, I took a few minutes to explore the rest of the House. Tubby's office remains as it might have been with copies of letters, pens, an Army uniform and other items from the Great War. The garden was beautiful, full of spring greenery and a place of calmness and tranquillity in the midst of the bustling town but best of all for me, was the chapel. Up in the eaves, approached via a steep wooden ladder, it has also been preserved as it would have been 90 years ago. As my head came up through the gap in the floor I found it easy to imagine soldiers ascending the rickety, bare wooden slats to pray for themselves, their comrades and their families so far away. A shaft of early evening sun broke through, shining onto two kneelers by the window and with tears in my eyes, I knelt and said a prayer and had a quiet moment to think about all the people who had fought bravely and died, and my son who fought his own personal battle with such courage and dignity.

By this time, we were all ready to eat and a short stroll around the town centre seemed like a good idea to loosen up my stiff legs. It was a pleasant evening, warm enough with a T-shirt and

111

jumper in case it cooled down later. We settled for a restaurant on the corner of the main square and it proved to be a good choice. Busy with local diners, a steak, a pudding and a couple of Belgium beers seemed like a good idea. The steak was good, the beer was cold and the pudding, a Mazarintaart with cinnamon, honey met ijs, delicious. My 'Eat to the World Cup' was moving up a gear.

Back at Talbot House, we chatted with Sylvia who was watching English TV, filled our glasses with water and climbed the stairs to bed, feeling tired but good.

On Day 10, Friday May 19, I was up at 7am. It had been an eventful night. Dan, who was coming out on Friday evening by Eurostar to Lille with two friends, had texted at 12.30am to say he couldn't find his passport. I rang and then texted him back, disturbing Sandra in the process and with my knees aching, it took a long time to get back off to sleep. I was up at 4am to go to the loo and my left knee nearly gave way under me. I came round slowly; it was as if my body knew it was a rest day with only 10 miles to walk. On my way down to breakfast, I came across the following poem, written on behalf of the men of the Royal West Kent Regiment. It seemed to sum up Talbot House well.

Talbot House

Behold a gleam of light, amid a world of gloom,
For those who bravely fight, defying threats of doom.
Here is a place of warmth, when all around is chill,
Here is a place of health, despite pursuing ill.
This is a place where love, in its most useful form,
Awaits the warrior worn, cold, weary and forlorn.
In this House we forget, for moments all our foes,
A welcome smile, a cup of tea, bids farewell to our woes.
More, in the Upper Room, the hurt souls feel release,
The wounded heart, the shattered nerve, can share in God's own peace.
For this is Talbot House
And Tubby Clayton's here,
The Salient's far away
With thanks, we raise a cheer.

A Walk of Faith

Touched by the words and with a fresh perspective, I enjoyed the croissants and jam for breakfast and looked forward to the day, to reaching Ypres and seeing Dan again.

Sylvia, a lovely Sheffielder, gave us 10 Euros towards our cause and let me use the internet access to check e-mails and send my diary update. She wanted us to come back for a second night. We had nowhere planned to stay, but it would have been 10 miles back in the wrong direction so we said our goodbyes and set off.

Phil was driving and Sandra and I soon found our road out of Poperinge and gradually settled into a rhythm, a leisurely 3.4 mph pace. The wind was gale force and gusty with thick, dark clouds scurrying by and light rain coming occasionally, almost horizontal. The wind, which we later found had been part of major storms in the UK was from the west and blowing us forwards on our journey east. The road was flat and straight, cycle path alongside the main drag and not too much traffic with very few big wagons. There was a motorway running parallel to our route a few miles away and we were being passed mainly by local traffic on the N308.

We shouted over the noise of the wind but mainly walked silently together. More and more military cemeteries were appearing. Walking steadily, we could see far more that the passing vehicles and soaked up the atmosphere created by the sight of so many graves and the sound of the storm around us. It felt very appropriate and fortunately, the wind was so strong, the rain held off most of the time. After a mere five miles, we saw Phil, who had cooked some bacon and enjoyed hot bacon butties with brown sauce just outside the town of Vlamertinge.

Sandra and I continued our walk and the cemeteries, all lovingly cared for, became even more numerous, their names taken simply from the nearest building or place name. Names like Red Hill and Hop Store, some tiny areas with two dozen white headstones, other far larger with many hundreds of graves. On the outskirts of Ypres, or Leper as it is now known, we stopped for a coffee and chatted to the locals who had seen our T-shirts. We didn't mention Tim and talked mainly about whether Rooney would be fit and the Belgium Under-19 side – the team of the future.

John Reeve

As we walked into Ypres, we were aiming for St. George's Church. Sylvia had recommended that we visit it, as the British Church established in the 1920's as a memorial to the Troops who had fought and died during the Great War. Without diverting from our route, we bumped into St. George's and took another short stop, this time in the quiet and peace. It was a typically British church, simple, strong, full of plaques to the heroes of the Western Front – one plaque pays tribute to 5,600 men who died. I learned that Churchill and Montgomery, names associated with other times and other battles had fought at Ypres. Sandra took my photo by the plaque of the famous *'In Flanders Fields'* by John McCrae.

Field Marshal Sir John French, Earl of Ypres, a former Army Commander, appealed for a British memorial church to be built in Ypres. Land was allocated, planning permission was given by the town and on Saturday, July 30, 1927, Field Marshal Lord Plumer laid the foundation stone of the church. The church was dedicated for worship by the Bishop of Fulham on March 24, 1929. As well as the plaques, the history and bravery of the regiments and individuals who fought at the Salient are reflected in the church windows, dominated by the Window to the Guards Division.

With Sylvia in the garden at Talbot House

Coming out of the church we lost our bearings and wandered around the old town for a few minutes before heading out towards the north instead of continuing east. The map got us back on track and we walked for another 40 minutes out of town, past the huge Menen Road Cemetery and the ring road and onto the N8 where we found the motor home and Phil waiting for us.

We decided to have some lunch in a nearby café and then look for somewhere to stay for the night. Back in the van, I retired to the double bed to lie down and Phil and Sandra drove around for 45 minutes looking for somewhere to stay. Dan rang to say he had his passport. It had been at our house and Carol had found it and sent it to him by courier – 'just in time'. Then, an interview with Nick Hull of Dream FM and a call from 5 Live about an interview in Frankfurt. As always, having something to do perked me up and by this time, Sandra and Phil had decided on a motel about half a mile on from our stopping point.

I had a cold and hot shower, changed and sat down to write the web-diary. Phil and Sandra set off to Lille, about 30 miles away, to pick up Dan, Jono and Jay who were due at Lille at 6.30pm. I had decided to stay at the motel to finish my diary and rest and was soon dozing comfortably after the previous night's unsettled sleep.

It was good to see Dan, it seemed longer than five days since we had parted at Gillingham and great that the other two guys had joined him, to show their support for him and for the walk. They were ravenous and we were all ready to eat so we headed off to the Chinese Restaurant and the 'as much as you can eat' buffet. The place was reasonably full and as soon as more hot food was brought out, it vanished and it needed luck and speed to keep our plates topped up. With three fit young men with us, this was no problem and we all ate our fill. Then our landlord from the motel came and joined us and bought a round of sake. He was trying to be the life and soul of the party and told us a joke about the fact that *'you don't see as many Germans as you used to around here and they don't stay for as long.'* Memories last a long time, certainly in that part of Belgium.

By this time it was after 11pm. The guys had just finished a busy week in London and travelled 2½ hours by train and with a

John Reeve

full day's walking ahead of us, we were all happy to head back to the motel. I was soon asleep.

Another 7am wake up and a decent continental breakfast. The lads weren't used to getting up at that time at the weekend but were up for it and by 8.15 we were back at our stopping point and ready to go. I was going to walk with the *'Three musketeers'* with Sandra and her brother in the motor home and we set off at a good pace. With three of them chatting away, full of beans, it was easy to get seduced into walking just a little bit faster than I intended and after an hour we had covered 4.2 miles – I would pay for this later! The road continued straight and true and it was easy going on the wide cycle path. During this early part of the day's walk we passed through Geluveld, just a few miles from the village of Passendale.

Situated on the North Flemish ridge, Passendale was in the middle of an area that had been of great strategic military importance for centuries. Achieve this landmark and armed forces had an easy downhill route to the French coast. During the Great War, it was the scene of one of the bloodiest battles of a bloody war, Tyne Cot Cemetery with the graves of over 12,000 British soldiers, is the largest British military cemetery on the European Mainland. Gradually, as we continued eastwards, the signs of the conflagration became fewer and fewer, the fighting had been confined to such a narrow corridor.

As we walked through Menen, we made a detour around the large, outdoor market and then headed north, staying on the N8 towards Kortrijk. We had our first stop of the day after 10½ miles and sat down in a café, enjoyed a coffee and chatted to the locals. We had covered the distance in two hours and 40 minutes – good going.

The weather was grey with the occasional glimpse of sunshine, windy but not as gusty as the day before and so far the rain had held off, despite the gloomy predictions of our landlord from Ypres. However, as we approached Kortrijk, the wind picked up, cracked through the flags of the Mercedes dealership, and the rain came down. It was accompanied by thunder and lightning and we had 30 minutes of 'proper' rain. The lads sheltered in a shop front for a few minutes but I decided that we had a walk to finish and set off in the downpour. We all had waterproofs but continuing onwards, we were soon getting damp, rain mixing with the sweat caused by being zipped up.

We skirted round the south of the city, past the railway station and then headed east and south. Sandra and Phil had been searching for somewhere to stay without success and we met up with them for the second stop at a petrol station after 17.8 miles – still averaging almost 4mph. The four of us stripped off to dry out and change our wettest clothes. My skin-tight top and trousers were fine under my waterproofs but I changed my T-shirt which was sodden. We had a good break with lunch of ham, salad and hot coffee from the petrol station and Phil established that there were some hotels in Zvevegem, our planned stopping point for the day.

So, with spirits and energy restored, it had also stopped raining, four of us set off for round three. Jono, Blisteros of the Musketeers as he was to become known, had opted to be driven to avoid more damage to his feet. Dan was beginning to realise that his comfortable, light-weight trainers were not suited to hours of pounding tarmac and was feeling sore but determined to walk all the way with me. We played 20 questions to pass the time. The lads guessed Alan Sugar just in time but were stumped by Stephen Hawkins. Gradually, the conversation died away as the aches built up and the final few miles became a painful slog, I was glad I had glucosamine patches on both knees. We reached Zvevegem to find that Sandra had booked us into a hotel with baths that sounded good. We pushed on for another four miles, miles in the bank for later.

Yellow Jersey award for walker of the day – Jay for 23.4 miles in brand new trainers.
Distance covered – 23.4 miles.
Total distance covered – 225.4 miles.

Back to the hotel Sachsen with a comfy room and a long bath. After a cold bath and a hot soak, Dan stretched me out and gave me the most painful massage of my life but I felt so much better for it afterwards. I wrote the web diary and uploaded photographs from the day whilst Sandra did the first wash and dry of the walk.

The hotel had a tavern and I went down with Sandra to find the lads onto their fourth halves of Stella. After two more beers we retired to a dining table and enjoyed a steak and Dame Blanche dinner, washed down with a couple more beers. After the meal, I used the hotel PC and sent through the diary and photos and headed upstairs around 11.30. Another long but good day.

On Day 12, the early morning grind of getting up and facing another day's walking was there again. It helped me to feel close to Tim and what he went through but it made it so much harder to start the day positively. As I was becoming more aware, the first hours walk set the tone for the rest of the day – for better or for worse.

Breakfast was good again, the lads had perfectly boiled eggs and it was a very short drive down to our start point. Said goodbye to Phil, he underplayed my thanks as is typically him but he had helped us so much over the last five days especially by taking the pressure of driving the motor home from Sandra, helping her confidence with the vehicle and enabling her to do some walking. He would be back out again with his elder son, Sam, in ten days time and was flying home from Charleroi. Sandra and Jono drove him to the airport and Dan, Jay and I stepped out on the road to Oudenaarde.

We were following the N8 for the entire day. After a slow start I was drawn easily into a faster pace by the two young thoroughbreds and we seemed to fly through Knokke and Avelgem, with its pretty church, walking along the cycle path all the way.

We crossed the river and canal and turned left as the road followed the waterways for another five miles towards Oudenaarde. It was Sunday and there were cyclists everywhere in groups of everything from two to 32 people, all ages shapes and sizes, almost all appearing as if they owned the roads (no cycle paths for them) and making the most of their weekly ritual. It was another cool morning with a fresh breeze and a mixture of sunshine and clouds, good cycling and walking weather.

As we neared Oudenaarde, we had completed nine miles in two hours and 15 minutes – bang on 4mph pace – and I was

A Walk of Faith

getting ready for a stop. I rang Sandra to find out that they were on their way back from the airport but would be another 45 minutes. I knew from our itinerary that the first proper hill since the South Downs was approaching and agreed with Dan and Jay that we would push on and make the climb before we stopped.

The Three Musketeers and me

A tribute to the bike

We skirted round the south side of Oudenaarde and swung south-east. I found out that evening that the famous battle had taken place on ground just to the north of our route. As I read the leaflet in our hotel that evening, my A-level history of 35 years ago came flooding back to me. It had been one of the principal encounters of the War of Spanish Succession and another triumph for John Churchill, the first Duke of Marlborough who, with an army of 90,000, had defeated a larger French force with the loss of only 3,000 men.

Anyway, our focus at the time was on the hill not the battle and after the flatlands it loomed up ahead of us but turned out to be a pleasant change, something to work at and as we turned the last corner and saw the road levelling out ahead, we also saw the motor home waiting for us, right on cue after 12 miles.

All three of us were feeling famished, Sandra had bought fresh bread and pâté and we polished off the lot before she served hot pasta with ham in a tomato sauce. We had a longish break for almost an hour and my left knee and shin were aching badly so, for the first time, I dug out the pair of knee supports we had brought along and put them on.

Getting going again took ages and I realised that the first session had been too long and too far for comfort. The three of us played the classification game to pass time and take my mind of the pain. Jono re-joined the walk after three miles and his natural high spirits helped to spur me on. We stopped for the second break after 17 miles. It had been one of the shortest sections so far but definitely the hardest yet. A much shorter break, I went straight up onto the bed, kept my leg up, drank a hot mug of coffee and then off again, determined to get to our stopping point and keep ahead of schedule.

As we neared Brakel, we saw a roundabout with a massive sculpture made out of bikes, a tribute to Belgium's favourite sport – we must have seen over 500 cyclists out for the day on their bikes. For some reason, my legs felt easier and with a steadier pace, I started to enjoy the walk again. All day we had passed gardens with immaculately prepared lawns, not a blade of grass out of place and there were more as we reached Parike. Just after we had reached the van, Sandra told us it was only an uphill mile

A Walk of Faith

to the hotel. We contemplated doing the extra mile and having 15 minutes more in bed the next day but for me having stopped, it was almost impossible to restart, so we rode up the hill to the Hotel Molenwieck.

Yellow Jersey award to Dan, who wore the soles of his shoes right away.
Distance covered – 21.0 miles.
Total distance covered – 246.4 miles.

We'd seen the signpost for the hotel on our drive through and Sandra had pre-booked rooms. The hotel was quiet, our room comfortable and I had my compulsory cold bath followed by a hot soak. I was getting used to the shock of the cold water knowing that it would wear off after a few seconds and the numbing sensation as the aches and pains faded away became almost pleasurable.

The 'musketeers' fancied going out and finding a pizza place but I was tired and didn't fancy driving around on a Sunday evening looking for restaurants so they agreed we would eat in. The others all had steaks and I went for the house special – fresh trout selected from the tank in the restaurant. Sandra's steak was 'English well done' and was just right for her. We enjoyed the meal and chatted away happily. Then, just as the lads were starting to call our hostess a 'miserable…', she came over and asked if we would like her to call a local newspaper reporter that she knew. I said yes, appreciating that she was keen to get publicity for the hotel but it would also be good to get some profile for our walk in Belgium. I spoke to the reporter and agreed to a photocall at 9am the following morning.

Another late night on the laptop, it was almost midnight before I had finished the diary and uploaded the photographs from the day but still couldn't send e-mails; frustrating!

John Reeve

Hard Times & Good Friends
From Flanders to Liege and Wegimont Chateau

One way to start the day positively was to get up and do some walking before breakfast. I had been annoyed to finish just short of the hotel and at the bottom of the hill, so at 7am on Day 13 of the walk, I was up and Sandra drove me back down to the finish point. It was only half a mile up to the top and the narrow road to the right that led to the hotel. As I reached the turning I decided to carry on for another 30 minutes and work up a proper appetite.

It was a cool morning for the second half of May with dark clouds scurrying past, the wind still blowing me to the east. The N493 was a quiet, country road, winding up and down across open fields from one small village to the next. Traffic was light, the morning 'rush hour' would be short and hadn't started yet. I was pleased to walk on my own and get another mile in the bank. We had finished the previous day about four miles ahead of schedule and it seemed like a good idea to keep building up a buffer in case it was needed. I also sensed that the lads were starting to get bored with walking and another mile less to do for them would make it a better start to the day all round.

Dan was determined to walk with me every step of the way that he could. He hadn't said anything but I think he was feeling guilty about going back to England and not doing more of the walk. He had started a new job with added responsibility in February, was saving for his new flat and due to start a three week holiday to the World Cup in a week's time. So he had done really well to walk for seven of the first 13 days of the journey. He had a busy life in London with lots of friends and a job that he enjoyed but which meant long and unsocial hours and he rarely came back to Essex. Since Tim's death, he had been home more often to see his mum and me, we spoke every day on the phone and he was always willing to listen and to offer his own perspective when

A Walk of Faith

either of us talked to him about his brother; he helped us enormously to keep going and 'get on with it'.

But as I walked through the countryside, I reflected that Dan had said very little about his own feelings and about how he was coping with losing his little brother. They had been close as young boys, had gone their own ways as each developed their own circle of friends and moved away, took each other for granted as brothers do but had always enjoyed spending time together, picking up after months apart with a comfortable familiarity. One of the bitter-sweet ironies of the last six months of Tim's life was the two of them seeing a lot more of each other and realising just how important they were to each other.

How was he coping? Faye was his rock and their relationship seemed to be stronger than ever. She was undoubtedly helping him through his bad times. He had at least three different circles of friends in London, almost all young men in their twenties, not renowned for being the most supportive of each other and yet here were Jono and Jay walking through Belgium to show their support for Dan and at least another six of his friends had walked over the weekend from Wembley. He seemed to be doing OK, keeping busy with things to look forward to and friends around who were there for him.

I rang Sandra at 7.30 and asked her to come and pick me up. By the time she arrived I had covered a good two miles. Back to the Hotel Molenwieck for breakfast at 8am; the lads were pleased to hear that they didn't have to 'go back down to the foot of the hill and march back up again'. After cereal, fresh rolls and ham we quickly packed and loaded our gear back in the van. The journalist and photographer arrived and took photos outside the hotel for the Flemish daily paper.

Thanking our hostess for her support, we were off again and 'the musketeers' were even more pleased when they realised I had chipped off another mile and a half of the day's walk. Consequently, we were all in good mood as the four of us set off, the miles slipped away easily and we soon reached Gerardsbergen, our first town of the day. As we walked down the straight road and crossed the railway line and the wide river, memories returned of driving through the town seven weeks earlier. The main street dropped down into the centre of the town and then climbed up the far side of the valley. It was a busy sight, full of people with a wider selection of shops than many of the towns we had passed through and it was market day. The stalls were spread out along the road, making the place even busier and we were happy to slow our pace, take in our surroundings and watch the locals chatting as they bought their food and other supplies.

At the top of the main street was the town square with a large, imposing church on the left and an even steeper climb ahead. Our route took us off to the right. We followed the winding street past shops and terraced houses until we came a T-junction where we turned left and climbed up out of the valley. It was a good pull up the hill, the weather was improving and it was becoming warm despite the breeze. Through Moerbeke with an increasing number of short, sharp hills, we headed for Galmaarden and stopped for a bacon buttie around 11.30 after 9½ miles. My left shin was sore, looking red and inflamed but after a 30-minute break with my feet up and my head down, it was looking and feeling better and we set off again.

The lads were in boisterous mood, the clouds were moving quickly across the sky but there was plenty of sunshine and a good day for walking. Despite the pain gradually getting worse from my left shin and ankle, the three friends kept me laughing as they attempted to mimic all the animals we passed on our way. Racing with the young horses, creeping up and mooing loudly at the cows, chasing after the hens and ducks and doing whatever they did when they saw the goats and pigs. It was like being with three eight-year-olds with Jono as the gang leader but it also meant that they had to be getting really bored.

We were giving marks out of 10 for the immaculate Belgium lawns and gardens so neat and tidy, not a piece of litter in sight, as we walked past bungalow after bungalow. If the fields didn't have animals grazing, there was wheat and barley or a wide range of different vegetables growing, a rich and productive countryside.

Galmaarden was a nice small town. We turned left in the centre and saw the first sign for Petingen 15 kilometres away, the scheduled stopping point for the day. Our second stop for lunch was near Herfelingen and we had a longer break of 45 minutes before starting again. This was the last session for Dan and his mates until we would see him again in Frankfurt, two weeks later. He had walked 160 miles with me and helped to keep me going. Jono and Jay had been great company.

Reaching Petingen, we decided to carry on to our B&B for the night in Breedhout and put another three miles on the clock. The dominating landmark was the huge TV mast that stood on the top of the hill gazing out over its surroundings and gradually we drew closer to it, passed it and then almost immediately, cheered as we saw the van and Sandra parked in the drive in the distance. Rene and his English wife, Hilda Ann run 'Rosebank', a pretty bungalow in a quiet neighbourhood, and gave us a warm welcome.

Yellow Jersey award to Jono, always in good humour.
Distance covered – 22.0 miles.
Total distance covered – 268.4 miles.

The lads had a quick shower and changed, then we drove them to Alt to pick up a train connection for Lille and the Eurostar for Waterloo. It was a journey of about 30 miles back along the motorway and Sandra having checked train times earlier was chasing the 4.48 train to get the lads into Lille in time for their Eurostar train. Fortunately, the station was on the motorway side of Alt. We dropped them off at 4.45 and they charged off with their bags towards the ticket office. A call to Dan's mobile 10 minutes later told us that they had made it.

A more leisurely drive back to 'Rosebank', my leg stiffened up during the journey and I struggled up the steep stairs which ran from the garage up into their attic space and the two bedrooms and bathroom that Rene and Hilda Ann had added to their bungalow. A short cold shower followed by a longer, hot one and I was feeling a little better but still tired and sore. The various ointments and rubs were applied followed by the glucosamine patches and I was ready to try the stairs again and join our hosts.

It turned out that it was Rene and Hilda Ann's 38th wedding anniversary and they kindly invited us to share their evening meal with them. I was hungry as always, ready for a good meal and we enjoyed a pleasant evening and a good meal with Belgian sausage and a wonderful local cake. Rene explained, in his heavily-accented English, about the Flemish/French division in Belgium. We hadn't realised that we were only 10 miles away from the unofficial border. On the other side, everyone spoke French and adopted a French outlook and way of life. Breedhout was in the Flemish-speaking area, a people who were more modest and cautious than their neighbours. A divide that reached back over centuries of misunderstandings and bloodshed; to us as visitors it seemed petty and irrelevant; to him it was part of his life. He was a powerful man who taught martial arts and appeared to have strong and clear cut beliefs, amongst them not liking the French or French-speakers, but he and his wife were kind and understanding to us.

Relatively early, it was back to our room, e-mails and diary and we were ready for bed. I reflected that there had been no time to say goodbye to Dan with his rush to catch the train, maybe it was better like that. I would miss him over the next few days but would talk to both him and Tim in my mind as I continued my walk – perhaps, as Tim had once said, I did too much of that and not enough talking out loud?

As I rolled out of bed the next morning, I remembered that it was May 23, two days after my sister Isobel's birthday. She was on holiday in Ireland but it was the first time I had forgotten the day in 50 years! It was the day I walked on my own.

We had heard the rain lashing down and the wind howling noisily during the night as we tried to sleep in the double-bed, our tenth different bed in the last 11 nights. It was still raining as we dressed, went down the steep stairs and through the garage to the main room and breakfast. We ate with Hilda Ann and Rene, being polite but none of us relaxed for different reasons. Sandra and I were ready to be on our way.

The rain turned to drizzle as soon as I stepped outside and had stopped within a few minutes. I waved Sandra goodbye and we went our separate routes, me down a narrow lane, her keeping to the main roads. Despite the rural outlook and the dark, quiet morning, we had almost reached the outskirts of Brussels, our first big city since London and a very different, urban world after our walk through small towns, villages and countryside over the previous 10 days. We had checked our route carefully for the day as we hadn't worked out a detailed route around Brussels during our recce, relying instead on a large scale map that Sandra now took with her in the van.

I crossed three minor roads, the commuter traffic gradually building and walked down to the N5 which was in full flow. I turned right and vaguely remembered the busy road, feeling sure I was 'on course'. Right on cue, the turning to the left appeared ahead of me and I crossed over and walked towards the river and canal. Sandra rang asking for directions. She had taken a wrong turning and had headed too far south. I explained where I was on the map and agreed to meet her on the road ahead.

I was enjoying being on my own, space to think; think about my two sons, thinking, thinking, thinking as always. How different they both were and how much they both meant to me. I remembered back to the time before we had children. My life had been good, yet despite everything that had happened and all the heartache and torment of the past three years, I wouldn't have missed the happy times and the bad times we went through together. I was beginning to remember those good times and as I walked, I could feel Tim willing me to be happy and to start enjoying life again. He had been so selfless during his illness, more and more as his condition worsened, always concerned for others, seemingly able to accept his fate and think instead of those he loved. How could he do that? And Dan who seemed to be so engrossed in his own world and his own affairs, much like me in my own way, but I knew that he cared just as deeply. Sandra was the one who added the balance, brought out the best in us all and made us a family. She was our heart and our core.

Far sooner than I expected after our conversation, the motor home appeared as I walked up through Beersel, a small village with a long, straight, uphill, main street. I stopped for a few minutes, Sandra explained how she had gone astray and we agreed to meet at the other side of Alkenburg, another five miles ahead. We were following the map and it seemed to take a long time walking up and down through suburbia with fewer open fields but always plenty of trees. The rain was holding off, the morning warming up and I took my waterproofs off and continued through Alkenburg, to the first stop.

Sandra had fruit, buttered soreen and coffee waiting and it was good to sit down and rest for 30 minutes. We were both unsure about the next section. Sandra needed to find her way across two busy routes into Brussels and to the junction at Aux Trois Colone, where our second stop was planned. I would be walking though the edge of the largest urban forest in Europe that stretched for 15 square miles across the southern outskirts of Brussels, forming a barrier to our route to the east.

After 30 minutes and nine miles I was ready to go again. My shin and ankle were feeling tight and sore but we had a plan and off we went. The suburbs merged into each other with small arcades of shops, big houses and lots of traffic. As expected, I reached the main road where Sandra had parked to check I was on course. We both turned right and waved goodbye. I crossed over and followed the edge of the forest to the south for half a mile until I came to a road that cut into the trees. I checked on the map, it appeared just where it should be. I turned left away from the noise of the traffic and was soon in gloom amongst the trees. After 10 minutes I wondered if I was on the right road and checked the map again but continued on as the rain started to fall again. As expected, I reached a long row of large, secluded houses; people paying for privacy with gates, high fences and glimpses of sizeable mansions through the trees and shrubs. I pressed on with the rain coming down more heavily and starting to soak me despite the trees and my waterproofs. Coming to the end of the housing, the tarmac road turned into a track.

The path ran alongside the edge of the forest now, just like the map said it should and as the rain blew in horizontally on the wind, I gradually picked out the noise of distant traffic that grew louder and nearer and realised that I was approaching another major road as indicated on the map. It was a busy six-lane urban motorway with a raised grass bank in the centre. Standing on the edge, I waited for a gap between the thundering lorries and spray and moved faster than I had done for weeks across the southbound highway and clambered up onto the grass bank. It was even busier on the Brussels-bound side but it seemed easier

A Walk of Faith

repeating the exercise and then I was back in the forest, well marked trail through the trees, sodden with the heavy rain. I walked on for another 30 minutes, the trees gradually thinning, fields appearing and then buildings including what looked like a museum in a park setting. If I was where I thought I was then the map suggested I should turn right just ahead and cut down to the next meeting point. The turning appeared and I veered right past farms and on a narrow lane that widened as I entered a village. Unusually in Belgium, not a sign in sight, I couldn't get my bearings from the map and when I came to a T-junction with no signs in sight, I didn't know which way to turn.

The sun was out and drying me quickly and soon I was feeling warm. I had opted to turn right and eventually came to a main road. Where was I? Sandra rang concerned that I was overdue and shortly afterwards I came slowly up to a road junction with full signage. I had come out onto the right road but was two miles further away than I should have been. Evidently, I had turned off too soon and the road had then turned away from my destination. I rang Sandra and told her the news - hot, hurting and in need of some food and a lie down, but there was nothing else to do except soldier on and get there. I tried to pick my pace up even though I knew I was slowing down. After what seemed like hours but was no more than 45 minutes, the junction came into sight and it was a short walk down the hill to the supermarket car park and the motor home. I don't think I was ever more pleased to see the vehicle during the whole of the walk than that lunchtime.

By now it was 2.30, I had covered 16.8 miles and the good news was that I had only another four miles to go. I took a long break, a good stretch down, up onto the bed with my foot well up, some hot food and fruit, a drink of coffee and a doze.

We had parked just across the road from a café where we had stopped for a break during our expedition in March and I looked in through the window as I walked by. Knowing I had only just over an hour's walking to complete, I didn't feel too bad and easily fell into a steady pace, following the busy road into Rixensart. I had spotted a short-cut, turned left, walked over the railway bridge and then after stopping and puzzling over the map, realised that the narrow cobble-stoned track right at the side of the railway track had to be the path I was looking for.

I followed the path downhill past a large playing field and then uphill with thick bushes and trees hiding the view on each side. I was having real trouble with the Brussels street map and I was already unsure about where I was before the track merged into a road and the edge of a residential area. Roads off to the left didn't fit with the map and where I should have been so I slowed right down, keen not to carry on walking in the wrong direction again. It was about 3.30, there was not a soul in sight and as I struggled up to a T-junction, I was ready to pack it in for the day. I rang Sandra who was already at our meeting point but I couldn't even tell her where I was so that she could pick me up.

For 15 minutes I dillied and dallied setting off first one way and then the other, looking for some indication which way to go, hoping to see someone I could ask but there was no one and nothing. Eventually, I reasoned that I should follow the road to the right, get a grip and complete my walk for the day. After another 10 minutes I came to another T-junction and a larger road and decided it ought to be a left turn. Now there were children, walking home from school, and I asked a group of older students in my schoolboy French for directions to the castle. One boy seemed to understand and beckoned me to follow him. He left his friends as they turned off and we continued for half a mile until we came out onto a roundabout in the middle of a complex of shops and offices. The boy pointed to the road ahead, told me I had about another two kilometres to walk to reach the castle and turned back the way we had come. I thanked him for his help – another kind gesture – and crossed over the roundabout.

I rang Sandra, told her I was back on track and to wait for me as I was going to finish as planned. Having felt lost earlier, this road seemed familiar and I was sure we had driven along this way at the end of March. My leg and ankle were hurting constantly and I felt exhausted. Without company the first few miles of the day were fine but after that having other people around, not necessarily talking all the time but just there, made such a difference. It was almost 5pm before I passed the old Rixensart

Castle and reached the shopping arcade and car park, with the motor home and Sandra waiting for me.

Yellow Jersey award to John for sticking at it.
Distance covered - 20.8 miles plus three miles getting lost.
Total distance covered - 289.2 miles.

    I worked through my stretching routine and then just wanted to lie down and sleep but we had a journey to make, through busy suburbs and main roads filling with homeward-bound commuter traffic. Sandra was unsure where we were going and needed a navigator, so instead of my bed, I took the seat next to her and we went back the way we had come to Aux Trois Colone. We were heading for Waterloo, a southerly suburb of Brussels and the Hotel Ibis that we had spotted during our drive through. Ted Herring and Dave Cobb, friends from Essex were coming out to Brussels by Eurostar and meeting us at the hotel where Dave had booked rooms for the night. I had checked directions to the hotel, found the address and established that it was near a large Carrefour supermarket. The route to Waterloo took us back past the point where I had emerged earlier from my walk in the forest and we continued for another five miles towards Waterloo. Dave rang saying that they had arrived at the hotel and were going to look around, I said we hoped to be there in 15 minutes. The traffic was heavy and as we neared Waterloo, I saw a large retail park with a huge Carrefour Superstore. We drove onto the car park and studied our maps. It didn't seem right, there were no signs of hotels in the vicinity but perhaps it was tucked away somewhere?
    Yet I was sure that we hadn't driven near here before and we drove around for 10 minutes checking different options, queuing in the traffic before we doubled back on ourselves, all the time feeling more tired and getting more frustrated. It was a new low point of the walk.
    Deciding that there had to be another supermarket in Waterloo, we reckoned that the hotel ought to be on the far side of the town and drove into the centre with the traffic streaming in the opposite direction away from the city. I was convinced that we must have cut across the north-south route we were driving

on, as we headed east on our recce, and that the hotel must be close by. Dave had told us where the hotel was in relation to the supermarket and when we spotted the Carrefour sign we knew that our destination should be on the left at the next traffic lights – and it was. Sandra missed the turning for the car park and we turned round and drove round the almost full car park looking for somewhere to park the motor home and finally found a suitable place. As I climbed slowly backwards down the steps, Dave and Ted came to meet us.

They said afterwards, that they had been shocked to see the state I was in, and that they had seriously doubted whether I would be able to continue and complete the walk – was this going to be my Waterloo? But not continuing was one thing that never even entered my head. We checked in, the guys carrying our bags and then found that the room had a shower not a bath as requested and we struggled back to reception and then to a second room. Agreeing to meet up in the restaurant in an hour's time, I climbed into the bath and went through my cold and hot water routine which helped enormously with my sore knees and leg muscles but was far less effective on my shin, which continued to look red and felt very tight, and my ankle which was starting to swell.

Meeting Ted and Dave later, it was clear that they were both raring to go and had arrived in holiday mood. They'd been out to explore and find nearby restaurants where we could eat and leaving the hotel had stopped the first passer-by to ask directions to the nearest bar. Typically, Dave had asked slowly in his passable French whilst Ted followed up immediately with, 'Where's the nearest pub, mate?' using sign language and his right arm to indicate a drink. The Belgian man had instantly understood Ted and pointed off down the road following up with directions that Ted couldn't understand but which Dave could decipher – two very different approaches but an effective combination. We would see this many times over the next two days.

With perception and understanding, the guys had realised that their plans for a night-out had to be shelved and accepted that all I was fit for was a meal in the hotel and bed so the four of us sat

A Walk of Faith

down to eat. The restaurant was reasonably busy; the menu offered something to suit all our tastes and the conversation and lager flowed as we caught up with each other's experiences of travelling. Both Ted and Dave were keen to do some walking and with Dave one of the nominated drivers, Sandra would be able to do some more walking. It was good to have them with us. The other good news was that with today's distance added to the total, we were now over halfway to Frankfurt. The hotel had WiFi and so later that evening I was able to update my diary and send it through as well as checking on incoming mail. As always, I wrote up my personal diary before going to bed and knelt painfully to finish the day thinking about Tim.

Up for breakfast at 7.30. More evidence that the guys were 'up for it' with Ted, renowned for being late, already tucking in as we came into the restaurant area. Over breakfast we heard two versions of who had snored the loudest during the night. Ted seemed to be in the lead as a result of his apparent ability to produce sounds from both ends at the same time; it was clear that they were both enjoying this special time together.

At 8.15 we were loaded up and Sandra drove through the busy commuter traffic of Waterloo. After seeing the very visible signs of the battlefields of Ypres and Passendale and looking down over the site of Oudenaarde, Waterloo was very different. Apparently, there is a museum and a re-enactment each year of Napoleon's swan song, with thousands of people looking down onto the battlefield but the town of Waterloo is very much a modern-day suburb of Brussels, with out-of-town stores, busy roads and street after street of neat, middle-class homes.

It took 30 minutes to drive back to Rixensart and by the time we arrived at the parking area, the sun was warming up with the prospect of a fine day. Sandra took a photo of the three 'old musketeers' and then Ted and I set off at the start of Day 15's walk.

After the previous day's solo walk, talking to myself when I wasn't talking to Sandra on the phone trying to find my way, today I had Ted who could be relied upon to talk enough for at least five people and we settled into an easy pace, talking about all sorts of things. We had looked at the route the evening before and spotted a shortcut on the map but, perhaps because we were chatting away missed the road sign and continued on our way towards Wavre along the main road. My ankle felt a lot better, I was comfortable and pleased to be walking with good friends.

Wavre is a medium-sized town situated to the south-east of Brussels. Once through it, we would be on our way towards Liege and the Ardennes. Studying the map closely, we crossed the river and turned left through the large outdoor market. It was busy, everyone talking at once – 'these French people so much more to say than the quiet, polite Flemish folk' – and a huge variety of food for sale including live chickens and ducks to take home and fatten up. Through the town centre and then towards the railway station, we knew we were too far north, turned towards the east following side streets until we came to a main road and figured that we needed to turn right onto this road until we picked up the N268. We stopped and asked passers-by, then Ted dived into a small garage, map in hand, and without a word of French established that the junction we needed was just ahead.

The Tumble Tot Twins ready for a stroll

Almost as soon as we turned onto the N268, we passed the van with Sandra and Dave heading back towards Wavre looking for us. They quickly turned round and Ted and Dave made the first of many swaps. Walking with Dave was quite different, he was much more prepared to let me set the pace, happy to chat if I wanted to or keep quiet when I was quiet, tuning into what suited me; a change of companion, a change of style and just as effective for me. We walked along a long straight road past motor trade alley with a dozen or more car dealerships and the local football ground and came to a large lake with a wood on the other side of the road. We stopped briefly for another photo outside the Mr Foot shop – couldn't pass that one by - and stopped for our first break after nine miles, just short of Grez Doiceau.

A thirty minute break for coffee disappointed Ted who wanted to stop for lunch. He had found a brasserie in the town and befriended the owner, Edouard and his daughter. It was too early, I wanted to get more miles out of the way but Ted went out to buy some cakes and came back with some fruit flan, not just a few slices but two whole flans. Apparently it had caused consternation and then laughter in the shop when they realised he wanted the whole flan. Whilst I was lying on the bed, Essex FM rang for an interview and during the broadcast, I explained where we were and mentioned that I was walking with Ted and Dave, the Tumble Tot Twins. A new nickname had been created. Ted was happier now with the plug for his business but Dave, a University lecturer, was less pleased. Sandra joined me for the next part of the day's walk, leaving the Twins to fight amongst themselves as well as finding us somewhere to stay for the night.

We walked through Grez Doiceau, with much more of a country-town feel, uphill along a winding road and through a sizeable wood. As we neared the top of the climb, my phone rang and it was the Barnsley Chronicle who had picked up on the walk and wanted to run an article. I talked to Damon Wilkinson, who sounded like a nice guy, and agreed to e-mail through some photographs that evening.

We came out of the wood onto an open, rolling landscape with the sky darkening rapidly and the wind picking up. We crossed over a larger N road and walked past a Belgium Air Force base.

We were on a five mile stretch of straight, undulating and exposed road. The wind was blowing more strongly from our right and the sky was closing in. Sandra asked if I was enjoying the walk. My answer wasn't straightforward; it was proving to be tough and painful at times, parts of each day were a real slog and I didn't enjoy seeing Sandra worrying about the motor home, about me and, of course, her deep sadness; but we were meeting some kind and good people, had visited some interesting places and seen lots of things we would never have noticed from a car. Most of all I believed in what I was trying to do, it made it worthwhile and behind all of that, there was Tim. I tried to explain my thoughts and feelings but I think she was looking for a straightforward answer and much of what I was saying was getting blown away in the approaching storm. I didn't think that, all things considered, she was enjoying it, too many concerns, too much to worry about.

The rain came from the west. We could see it approach and hit us and for 20 minutes it lashed down hard; the wind gusting and trying to blow us off the road. We kept our heads down, gritted our teeth and strode on, Sandra 10 metres ahead with me working hard to keep up with her. As we neared Jodoigne, the storm passed over and the rolling countryside gave way to houses and the occasional shop and bar but still the road stretched straight ahead. Ted and Dave had found a good spot to park and tired and sore, we were glad to sit down and have lunch, another 15 miles completed. Lunch was fresh baguette, tuna and pâté, I walked the 200 metres to the nearest bar only to find it closed – so many places are closed at lunchtime - and carried on for the third session of the day.

The two guys had searched Jodoigne and all the surrounding roads, had asked at the local police station and been directed to what was apparently the only hotel in the district, Les Trois Cles, about 25km away. It was a Best Western hotel and sounded good. My ankle was swelling up and getting tight even in my comfy trainers. Initially, I walked with Ted and as we came into the town, Dave directed us to a pharmacy and talked to the pharmacist who suggested some anti-inflammatory cream. I bought some insect bite spray as well, just in case. Then we crossed the river and into the town centre. It poured again as we walked past the shops dodging from one shop awning to another but still getting soaked, turning right and then left, always heading east. There was a short, sharp hill as we left Jodoigne behind and back into open country, slogging away for another five miles, heading for Hannut. A third downpour of the day, this time walking with Dave, although with the wind warmer now, we quickly dried off and finished 4.1 miles ahead of plan near the village of Jauche. Another steady day's walking with good company.

Yellow Jersey award to Sandra for walking the longest, hardest and wettest stretch.
Distance covered - 21.1 miles.
Total distance covered - 310.3 miles.

It was a 30 minute drive to the hotel. I was lying up on my throne but was convinced that we must be near the Luxembourg border, when we finally drove onto the car park. Les Trois Cles was a typical, fairly modern, low-rise hotel with a brasserie-style restaurant and bar area. Our bedroom was large and the water in the bath nice and hot. Having driven so far to find the hotel, none of us were inclined to go searching for somewhere else to eat, so we settled for the brasserie and a reasonable meal. Sandra ate very little, her ability to choose the wrong dish matching her lack of real appetite. Over dinner, Ted recounted the story of finding the hotel, having been told that it was out on the Namur road but almost turning back convinced that it couldn't be so far away. Eventually finding it, they had asked for two rooms and been met by a knowing look from the receptionist. Having given Sandra and my names for one room, she realised that the Tumble Tot Twins would be sharing the second room – the legend continued to grow.

Another hotel with WiFi and so I was on the internet until after 11pm. I said my prayers in bed that night; kneeling down had become too painful.

The restaurant which had been busy the previous evening was almost deserted at breakfast and we found out as we paid our bills that only seven rooms were occupied, despite being the only hotel for miles. It transpired that the popularity for dinner was due to it being a Feast Day with local people having a day off work and we worked out that it must be Ascension Day – 40 days after Easter. I dozed up on my bed on the ride back to Jauche. My ankle was tight and swollen but I was hoping that it would loosen up once I started walking. Dave was driving the motor home and we realised that most of the petrol stations were closed for the day and with only a quarter of a tank of diesel left, that could become a problem.

Ted was raring to go again and we continued as yesterday had finished, up and down, down and up the undulating but ruler-straight roads. There was a drizzle-grey sky but without the wind and rain it was warm enough for T-shirts; it was getting towards the end of May after all. At Jaudrain, there was an Ascension Day Fair with trestle tables lining the streets and people coming from nearby villages with their umbrellas ready in case of a downpour. Through a second village with the roads strangely quite and we saw a straw man tied to a lamp post. If only we'd had a camera, he could have been Dave.

After an hour, the second twin took over and we soon reached the outskirts of Hannut. I remembered that there was a potential short-cut on the other side of the town but needed the maps to check. I rang Sandra and found that she and Ted were in a bar at the cross-roads in the town, talking to some bikers. We joined them for an early break and Sandra explaining the purpose of our walk, found out that one of the bikers, a Dutch man had suffered from Hodgkin's Lymphoma 15 years earlier. We agreed to meet at Lens St. Servais, the other side of our short-cut and Dave and I continued onwards.

We soon found the side road to the left and followed it towards Poucet but already new roads, not on our map were starting to emerge. At Poucet we were faced with four routes where there should only have been two and inevitably took the wrong road. Playing 20 questions we carried on across open fields, realised we were wrong and asked two cyclists who appeared out of nowhere. They couldn't help but as we walked through another village we asked a man who answered in German and gave us good directions that took us past the picturesque church and onto another path across open fields. We estimated that the next village ahead must be Lens St. Servais and fortunately it was. We had hardly gone out of our way and overall, had certainly shortened the distance by a little bit more.

As we came to the motor home, Sandra jumped out and took over as my companion and we walked through Geer and to the next village. Dave and Ted were waiting for us but we pressed on for another 0.8 miles and stopped right by a café where Sandra and I had grabbed a coffee on our reconnaissance. Another good lunch with my feet up. I was beginning to realise that I needed to raise my foot up above my heart as much as possible to stop the swelling getting worse and I felt OK as I set off again with Ted. All three of them wanted to walk with me, it was what they were there for, and it seemed good to have so much support.

Almost immediately we stopped as the main road swung to the left. I remembered that we had gone wrong here earlier but couldn't remember how we had eventually found the correct route. The van had gone straight ahead but my instinct told me to turn left and almost as soon as we made the turn, we passed a large factory on our right and I knew we were on course. We crossed a main road and picked up the N637, a straight road that would take us all the way to Liege. It was grey and dismal and with more traffic around. Dave joined us for the last part of the walk and even though I was feeling more and more tired, the sight of the two of them walking ahead and waving gaily to the approaching cars and lorries made me laugh. The Tumble Tot Twins were at their best and we had some good craic as we managed another five miles before finishing at Jeneffe.

Ted and Dave were so different in many respects; the former an ex-Fleet Street printer and union man who had moved away from his East End home when Fleet Street moved to Wapping, set up a Tumble Tot franchise with his wife Rosemarie and built a successful business. Although Ted had left the East End 20 years ago, it had never left him. Meeting him for the first time, it is instantly recognizable in his accent and his love of talking and of telling stories; he is a five-foot-six bundle of energy, ideas and kindness with the true East End commitment to his community and his friends. He is the genuine diamond geezer and over the years has done so much to help so many charities and good causes. He has always been there for Sandra and me since Tim was first diagnosed with leukaemia - from the time he drove down with me to Portsmouth to pick up Tim's belongings from his room at University - and has helped us in so many ways. During the walk, Ted helped enormously with his energy and enthusiasm and his communication skills that transcended the limitations of language.

Dave, a Cambridge graduate, who had gone on to teach at University is an educated man who talks as persuasively as Ted but in a very different, less emotional way and with a far 'drier' sense of humour. On the walk, Dave helped me enormously with his company and his consideration but also supported Sandra hugely with the driving and maintenance of motor home and his willingness to do things on our terms. Both are devoted family men; the three of us had been brought together by a love of football and had been good friends for over 18 years.

Yellow Jersey award to the Tumble Tot Twins for their friendliness to passing drivers.
Distance covered - 21.4 miles.
Total distance covered - 331.7 miles.

By now it was after 4pm and all day Sandra and Dave had been looking for a petrol station that was open, but without success. They had conserved fuel as much as possible and avoided doubling back or driving off route but there remained a 25 mile drive to Wegimont and the fuel warning light was glowing brightly. I was shattered, lying on the bed with my leg and foot aching, semi-dozing but could hear the concern as each petrol station we passed was shut. The closer we came to Liege, the more frequent the petrol stations became and at one station, Sandra saw a car filling up and pulled onto the forecourt. The shop was closed but drivers were able to use the pumps by paying by card for fuel. Sandra tried with an assortment of cards and then Dave tried his. Soon they realised that the pumps required specific petrol cards – we were out of luck and with not enough diesel to drive anywhere else.

Up on the bed, I heard another vehicle pull onto the forecourt and my three companions began talking to the driver. Talk turned to laughter and then more concern, the other vehicle was English with passengers hoping to do exactly the same thing as we were – find someone with a petrol card willing to exchange cash for use of the card. Once more, Ted's sign-language came into its own. Seeing a car approaching slowly, he jumped out in front and the vehicle stopped. The driver was a little old lady who looked astonished and concerned as Ted pulled out a wad of cash and a plastic card. He started pointing at the petrol pump, his card and the money and talking loudly and slowly in English. Even more astonishingly, the woman understood and was willing to help and as Anglo-Belgium relations reached a new high, Sandra put in enough diesel to see us through another day.

Waving goodbye to our Good Samaritan, we were on our way with Dave driving and Sandra navigating through the centre of Liege and to the Chateau de Wegimont which lies about 10 miles east of the city. It took us another 40 minutes to reach our destination and I climbed painfully off the bed as we neared the main entrance and drove through the imposing gates. Despite the dark clouds, the chateau was an impressive site, formal gardens in front of the main building, surrounded by a moat (our second of the walk) and with a large central courtyard. Parking at the side of the chateau, we unloaded our bags and I hobbled after the others to find our accommodation.

Already waiting for us were Peter and Elaine, two more friends who had flown out to join us, already collected our room keys and found our rooms. The plan was that the four men shared a room with two twin-bunk beds whilst Sandra and Elaine were in a twin-bunk bedroom. The chateau was a mixture of outward-bound centre for schools and Youth Hostel for walkers and cyclists. The accommodation and facilities were typically modest although clean and well-organised. One look at our room made me realise I would not comfortably survive a night with the other three with my aches and pains, the motor home seemed a much better prospect. However, the baths were large with plenty of hot water and I went through my 10 minute cold and 10 minute hot routine and back along the corridor to get changed.

During my soak, Sandra had met up with some of the teachers from Great Totham Primary School and found out the times for dinner in the refectory and the school concert. We had known, when we first realised that our route would take us close to Wegimont, that Totham school visited with Year Six pupils during May each year but had been amazed at the coincidence when having worked out the exact dates of our stay, we found out that they would be there the same week. Even more good fortune meant that they were going home by coach the following morning and as Sandra had taught on supply at the school, it was possible for her to get a lift home.

Consequently, dinner that evening was shared with 40 school children, all excited because their concert was taking place afterwards. Ted and Dave along with Peter and Elaine, having found out that the bar in the chateau didn't open until after the concert, decided the nearest pub was a better bet whilst Sandra went to watch the concert. I didn't feel like sitting through the concert and was struggling to walk anywhere, never mind another mile to the pub and a mile back and went through into the bar area to find somewhere comfortable to sit. It wasn't easy, I was tired out and my ankle was very red and inflamed; it meant I could only walk by putting my foot down flat and I must have looked a sight, hobbling around in my flip flops. Although the bar wasn't open, there was still ice available and grabbing a tea towel, I wrapped it around some ice cubes and over my ankle and lower shin. The most comfortable position I could find was with me lying down across three chairs with the bottom half of my legs across one of the tables. And that's how Sandra found me, not fully asleep but dozing peacefully, when the concert finished almost an hour later.

The others returned from the pub and the six of us spent some time over a drink catching up on news and deciding plans for the following day. I felt just a little like Frodo must have, when the 'Fellowship of the Ring' split up. Just as I was getting a fuller understanding of the size of the challenge ahead of me, my three trusty companions were all going home; Sandra leaving by coach at 7am, to do some washing and check the post; Dave and Ted by Eurostar from Brussels. It was agreed that Peter and Elaine would drive the Twins into Liege at 8.30am to catch the train that would take them to Brussels. Me – it was my day off, I was going to rest. Peter had already found out the name and telephone number of a doctor for me to contact about my ankle. Sandra had decided to join me in the motor home for the night and another group decision meant that Peter shared with Elaine in the twin-bunk bed room leaving the Twins to enjoy one more night together – the things we do for our friends!

John Reeve

A Chateau, Two Casinos and the Millennium Stadium
Uphill into the Ardennes

Sandra hadn't realised how cold the motor home would be, it was ridiculous really; here we were on May 26 and the weather was still more like March for temperatures and April for rain. Nevertheless, I had worse nights on the walk and hopefully, we would both catch up on some sleep during our very different days. We were up and dressed by 6.30am and I helped to carry her bags to the coach, which was standing in front of the main entrance, filling up with luggage for the journey back to Essex.

We went into breakfast, a room full of tired and sleepy children and as we finished, Audrey who was in charge of the school visit came over. She gave me a kiss and hug, said some words about Tim and gave me a look that made me want to cry. The coach drivers were ready for the journey and we were both close to tears again as Sandra and I said goodbye. She knew she needed to go home and would meet up with us in Germany in less than a week but didn't want to leave. I realised just how much I was relying on her and knew I would miss her badly. It helped that there were children around to keep her occupied. Peter and Elaine, and Dave and Ted, came to say goodbye to her and they were off.

I rang Dr. Meurens and he agreed to meet me at the chateau at 9am. Soon Ted and Dave were ready to depart. More farewells, it was a tribute to their company and support that it felt as if they had been with me for a lot longer than two days. And then I was on my own.

The doctor arrived, business-like and punctual. After examining my leg and ankle, he prescribed antibiotics and told me to keep using the anti-inflammatory cream. He charged 20 euros and gave me a form that he said I could use to reclaim the

A Walk of Faith

money in the UK. If the drugs worked, it would be the best 20 euros I would spend throughout the entire walk. His diagnosis, not 100% certain, was that I had developed cellulitis caused by the constant pounding on hard surfaces and it immediately made me think back to the time when Tim had cellulitis in his arm, shortly after he was first diagnosed with leukaemia. I rang Peter and he agreed to look for a pharmacy on his way back from Liege, call for the prescription and collect the antibiotics for me.

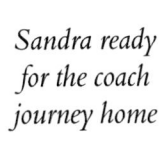

Sandra ready for the coach journey home

Dave was next to return to 'Blighty'

The chateau of Wegimont was first built in the 15th century with the majority of the existing structure dating back to the 18th century in the style of Louis XIV and it must have dominated the valley where it is situated in earlier times. Today it still has extensive grounds as well as the main buildings and these include a camp site, outdoor swimming pool and miniature golf course as well as the garden areas. Earlier on the walk, I had looked forward to a leisurely swim in the sunshine to ease my aches but today I wasn't in a good state for swimming, nor was the weather. After a grey start, the clouds blew in even lower and by 10am it had started to rain. I had plenty to do and spent an hour catching up with my diary, I tried to check my e-mails in the admin office but the chateau's IT security system wasn't having any of it. Peter returned with the antibiotics and I took my first pills straight away.

For the first and only time on the walk, I briefly contemplated not being able to carry on. I realised with some time and space to think, that it had been the three days with Dan, Jono and Jay that had almost certainly started the problem, walking too fast for too long to stay comfortable. If my leg and ankle didn't respond and continued to worsen then there might come a time when walking became impossible. I refused to dwell on the thought but the possibility was somewhere at the back of my mind. I knew my tiredness was partly psychological as a result of my body and mind reacting to the knowledge that there was no walking to be done today and was happy to let the morning drift away, closing my eyes and dozing whenever I wanted. I remembered a moment with Tim shortly after he came home after the Legionnaire's Disease. He was resting on his bed with his mum and dad sitting with him and taking both our hands he looked at us, saying *'I'm draining you both'*. How we wished he could have taken our blood and our energy and changed places with us. Now it was my turn and I knew in my heart that it would be his memory and his courage that I would call upon as my energy source, there was no way I was going to stop.

There was no lunch available at the chateau so Peter and Elaine had offered to take me out for something to eat. We drove along the road towards Liege and stopped at Le Jardin Restaurant, a self-service operation attached to a superstore but one that offered a wide selection of good food as well as serve yourself draught wine and beer. We enjoyed a good lunch and discussed their plans for the afternoon. They had booked into the SAS Raddison in Spa for the next two nights and Peter was going to drive the 20 miles to the hotel where Elaine was booked in for a spa treatment. He would then pick up the motorway system, drive back past Liege and another 50 miles to Brussels airport to meet my brother Chris, his son, Tom and my brother-in-law, Anthony, who were flying in from East Midlands for the next shift. He'd then drive them back to Wegimont. Busy people, Peter and Elaine could only spare three days and would spend their last day in Luxembourg, where they had lived some years before. Today, Peter was generously acting as our driver; without him I would have had to drive the motor home into Liege and to Brussels and back – another 150 miles that would have done my sore ankle no good at all.

They dropped me off at the chateau about 2pm and set off towards Spa. Soon afterwards I was met by a camera crew and reporter from Sky News who had arranged to film an update piece on the walk. They had driven over from their Brussels base and wanted to film an outdoor scene of the reporter and I talking whilst we walked. With the rain still coming down, this meant following their 4x4 vehicle with the camera pointing 'warm and dry' out of the open boot area and a very large umbrella. Fortunately, it meant we needed to walk slowly which suited me perfectly and after a short briefing to discuss the questions I would be asked, we needed only two attempts to complete the filming – all very straightforward.

Peter and the others were due back between 6pm and 7pm so I had a few hours left and after another doze, I decided to drive the motor home back up to Le Jardin restaurant. I had spotted that the restaurant offered WiFi broadband internet and thought it would be an opportunity to send my diary and photographs back to Gemma and check e-mails. It was strange driving the van, I had been kept away from the driving seat by Sandra but it probably did me some good getting out and giving my leg a little bit of exercise.

Back at the chateau the others had already arrived. I thanked Peter for all his help, we agreed to meet in Liege during the walk on the following day and he set off to re-join Elaine. It was good to see Chris and the others. Both he and Anthony would be driving the motor home, so we would still have two drivers who could alternate and Tom, who at 17, was too young to drive the van, would be my constant walking companion for the next seven days. Another 'Three Musketeers', they had arrived in good spirits looking forward to the adventure but were clearly concerned about my condition. They had also arrived bearing gifts including some from Chris' wife, Anne, and her colleagues at work who were following the web diary on a daily basis and had sent a collection of three ointments, guaranteed to sort out every ailment – Emu, Dog and Tiger! Chris presented me proudly with a new Barnsley FC shirt.

Yellow Jersey award to Peter Shields for driving hundreds of miles for the cause, a good friend.
Distance covered - 0.0 miles.
Total distance covered - 331.7 miles.

By this time we had missed the 'take it or leave it' dinner at 6.30pm. There was only one place locally that I knew about, so after sorting out our rooms and the motor home, I introduced them to Le Jardin. They were suitably impressed and we enjoyed a pleasant meal with a glass of beer. Chris was driving to get used to the motor home and we checked the maps and discussed our route for the next day. Back at the chateau, we had moved into a different wing of the chateau with two twin-bedded rooms, I was sharing with Anthony. I slept badly, up almost every hour either to go to the toilet or to ease the aching in my leg, or to throw a half-brick at Anthony snoring peacefully like a babe.

Up at 7.15 and ready for breakfast before the refectory opened at eight. All four of us were wearing Barnsley shirts across the ages, even Anthony, a Derby County supporter was wearing a Tykes shirt for the Division One Play-Off final at the Millennium Stadium and before we climbed into the motor home, I took a photo of my new team members.

A Walk of Faith

It was quicker to drive north up to the motorway and skirt round Liege rather than driving back through the centre but it still seemed to take ages to get to Jeneffe. As I lay up on the double bed, I listened to James Blunt singing tracks from Bedlam with my earphones in and thought of Tim and his very own personal bedlam. I cried for most of the journey and felt profoundly sad as I climbed down out of the van. I was walking with Chris and Tom, Anthony on driving duty and our plan was to walk the eight miles into Liege, through the centre and meet him, together with Peter and Elaine, near Chaudfontaine on the road to the Ardennes.

It was yet another grey day, but without the prospect of rain and warm enough for short-sleeved football shirts. It was comfortable walking with my brother and nephew, easy to talk to and happy to walk at my pace. After 15 minutes my ankle eased a little and we settled into a 3.7mph pace, slow enough not to trouble me too much. We started playing 20 questions, all three of us got into it and the first five miles passed easily. As we came to the outskirts of Liege we veered off our straight road and headed slightly north to walk under the motorway. It was my first experience of the unattractive face of Belgium, after all the cleanliness and order. We walked from one dirty, miserable suburb to another and just as the pavements descended into the worst in the country, uneven with large holes and steep cambers, my ankle started to tighten, worse than before. All in all it was quite depressing and the enthusiasm of the new walkers turned into a gritty realism.

It seemed to take a long time to get into the city centre. Tom was in charge of the map and I was uncomfortable not knowing exactly where I was, so it was better when he got a firm fix and we realised we were bang on target, with the city centre just ahead. We stopped after 2½ hours and 9.05 miles at a café, Aux Parkes de Liege and enjoyed a sit-down and caffeine boost. Feeling more cheerful, more comfortable and less weary we soon crossed La Place De La Republique. Chris stopped at the busy McD's whilst Tom and I carried on towards the River Meuse and Chris only caught up with us as we crossed the river over the JFK bridge. Apart from the occasional chant of 'You Reds', we were being very well behaved and impressed with the sights of a beautiful city with an attractive blend of old and new. We turned right and followed the Meuse for a time and then the Ourthe heading upstream towards the south-east. There was plenty of green, open spaces near the river, lots of trees and we walked along a very slippery patch of leaves for a few minutes and I was glad to get back to solid ground.

During the morning I had two long conversations with Sandra, I was missing her as much as she was missing being with us but she was pleased to hear that the day's walk was going according to plan. I rang Peter when we were about two miles from Chaudfontaine and had just followed the Vesdre from the point where it met the wider Ourthe. My ankle was starting to hurt again the tightness was making me put my foot down flat and I was trying hard to make sure I didn't set off another problem by over-compensating. One mile later, they came into sight and we knew we were closing in on the motor home and the second break. It was parked exactly where I had expected it and I was looking forward to getting my foot up. Waiting whilst Anthony opened the external store to get out some food and drink, I lost my temper when he messed the lock up, despite being told exactly what to do, stormed up into the van and ignored everyone else for 15 minutes whilst I sulked – turning into a right little Prima Donna!

Eventually Anthony sorted out the lock, the good thing being that he now knew for himself how it worked, I apologised and four of us walked over the bridge, past the casino and into the café where Sandra and I had stopped in March. It was quiet with just a few locals chatting and I had two café crèmes and an espresso, I was taking my drugs in different ways. We were ready to set off for the final six miles of the day just as the match was starting at Cardiff. I had spoken to Dan earlier; he was watching it on TV and promised to text through the scores. The first text after 10 minutes confirmed that the match was underway and the score 0-0 but it wasn't long before a second text followed and the Reds were 1-0 ahead.

The game crept up and grabbed me over the next 60 minutes. I had watched Barnsley only twice during the season - at

Southend and Colchester, the former with Tim - and it was the first time for over 40 years that I hadn't made a single match at Oakwell. I was so focused on the walk that despite enjoying the semi-final on TV with David Rawnsley and the four of us wearing the colours through Liege, there was no excitement or anticipation for me before the final started. But as we walked that afternoon along the road that criss-crossed the river and the railway line as the valley twisted and narrowed, the game gradually came to the forefront of my mind.

The play-offs have been a great addition to the football calendar in England, extending interest for clubs and supporters who otherwise would have nothing to play for over the last quarter of the season and providing the soaring highs and plummeting lows of victory and defeat in those winner-take-all finals. They say the Championship final is the biggest match of the year; it certainly is in terms of the financial impact of victory and promotion to the Premiership for the winner. I thought back to Wembley and that afternoon with Dan and Tim when Barnsley had lost 4-2 to Ipswich, just a few years before. We had gone ahead that day and then suffered the agony of seeing our dreams shattered in front of our eyes as Ipswich stormed back. A newspaper advert of two Barnsley fans, father and son, sitting all alone in the stadium after the game, slowly coming to terms with their disappointment summed it all up; there is too much at stake, the fear of defeat too strong, to enjoy a play-off final as every true football fan knows. As the texts came through with news that Swansea had equalised and then taken a 2-1 lead, the game began to matter a lot more. I had been sure that Leeds and Barnsley were both going to win the play off finals for Tim, and badly disappointed when Leeds United lost 3-0 to Watford in the Championship play-off final. Surely it wasn't going to be a losing double?

It was 2-1 at half-time. The walk took us past long rows of old and derelict industrial units based along the river side, not an inspiring route, all the time the road climbing ever so slowly upwards as we headed for the hills. I was feeling sore but the caffeine from the coffees and adrenaline from Wales were helping. Peter and Elaine were keeping up well and the five of us

John Reeve

Three quarters of Andy Ritchie's Belgian Red and White Army

By the Vesdre as Nardiello equalised

were walking in twos and threes chatting away with regular shouts of 'You Reds' to make the locals take notice.

As I took this photograph to mark the end of the day's walk on the bridge at Goeffontaine, Dan's text told us that Nardiello had equalised to make it 2-2 - game on!

As we drove back to Wegimont for our third night, the tension was building and another text confirmed that it was extra time. I lay up on my bed thinking about Tim and Barnsley. Tim had once quoted the Phil Collins lyrics to me *'Watching over you till all your work is done'* and I felt that it was now his turn to watch over me. I felt even more sure that Barnsley would come through. We reached the chateau knowing that there was only a few minutes of extra time left and then as I ran my cold bath, Dan texted to say that it was 2-2 and penalties. I shouted to tell Chris and Tom, then rang Dan and asked him not to send any more texts until it was all over.

I sat down in the cold bath still wearing my red shirt and thinking that it always takes longer than you expect to decide who's taking the penalties, consult with the referee and begin a penalty shoot-out. The cold water was replaced with hot and then the phone rang. I could hear Dan's mates shouting in the background as he described the situation, Barnsley were 4-3 ahead with one penalty left for each side; the fifth Swansea player was about to take his run up and then pandemonium, as I heard the cheers down the phone that could only mean that he had failed to score and the Reds were promoted. I shouted as loud as I could to let everyone in the chateau know the result and Chris came knocking on the door for details of Barnsley's triumph. I peeled off my shirt and sank down into the hot water as several phone calls and texts followed over the next 10 minutes from friends and fellow fans back in the UK.

What a result. Brilliant! But every high in my life is followed almost instantly by the realisation of a loss that far outweighs any triumph. How much sweeter it would have been if I could have shared it with Tim. He wants me to be happy and enjoy myself and I want him to be happy and free.

A good day's walking with the Red and White Army and the Yellow Jersey award of the Day had to go to Andy Ritchie and the Barnsley squad – well done lads.

Distance covered - 21.3 miles.
Total distance covered - 353 miles.

We decided to give dinner at the chateau a miss although we were in time and headed back to Le Jardin, my fourth visit in two days, and enjoyed another good meal. Afterwards, we went back to the chateau bar and celebrated with a couple of beers. There was a group of Dutch people singing songs and we responded with a full version of *'Ilkley Moor Bah't 'At'*, which brought cheers and applause from our drinking companions. Quite a day, all in all, and I finished it writing my diary, back in the motor home on my own before I snuggled down under the duvet.

It felt like a new walk was starting as we began Day 19 of the Walk to the World Cup. The walk from home to Wembley was a warm-up, from Wembley to Dover was getting started and Calais until now had been across the flat lands getting progressively greyer and wetter. Today felt so different again. The sun was shining and after a day's rest and antibiotics inside me, my leg and shin felt less sore and tight. I was ready for some serious walking.

Breakfast at 8am after a lie-in for Sunday, we exchanged greetings with the Dutch people and then the cook refused to take any money from me! Into the motor home by 8.30 and a short, 20 minute ride back to the bridge where we had finished yesterday. Music and thoughts of Tim but much happier, more positive than the previous few days and within 10 minutes of starting the walk, we were right beside the Vesdre with the sun shining, the brown, storm-swollen water flying by and so many shades of green all around us. The road was quiet and it was a morning to enjoy.

Chris was driving the motor home and was driving back to the chateau to empty the toilet and fill up with water before meeting us on the road between Pepinster and Spa for our first stop. We reached Pepinster sooner than I expected and turned right towards Spa, up through the Sunday-morning quiet streets and out into the proper countryside. The road was getting gradually steeper and when we reached Theux, a lovely little market town; it was a good opportunity to take another photograph by the church as the congregation streamed out into the sunshine.

We'd covered seven miles and I rang Chris shortly afterwards to find he was on his way. He passed us about half a mile further on and we agreed to stop after a further mile and a half but I was tiring rapidly with the gradient so when we came to a fritteria with a large parking area, I called him again and asked him to drive back to find us. It was still before 11am but the number of cyclists on the road was growing all the time and as we started the second stage, we were passed by a large group of 20+ riders making the long, easy downhill run.

This next stretch was a real mixed bag. It was open countryside with the sun shining and the river glistening never far away, but there were also narrow, heavily-wooded ravines where the road hugged the riverbank as it twisted and turned always upwards. Then came the long, straight, tree-lined avenue into Spa and the town with its restaurants, shops and casino, full of people and life in the sunshine of a Sunday lunch-time. After that, the steep drag out of town and along the Niveze road and into the Ardennes, with its clean air, bright light and magnificent views appearing unexpectedly as the road turned a corner. Along the road to Niveze, we passed a dozen or so huge houses, all set in their own grounds with fabulous views down into the Spa valley and beyond, all in different styles, from traditional French chateaux, ultra-modern homes and Spanish villas to Middle-Eastern mansions.

Chris had driven ahead to Malmedy to check out the hotel that he had booked us for the next two nights and I rang him to ask if he could meet us as soon as he could make it, as despite the uplifting views, I was feeling knackered from the continuous climbing. He had just set off back towards Spa and having updated him on our progress, he promised to meet us within 20 minutes. We passed a large sanatorium and crossed a river, following the signs as the roads criss-crossed, always heading uphill. We had covered 15.1 miles and were already ahead of the original schedule for the day when Chris found us. A slow stretch-down and a lie-down for 60 minutes, a doze, some food and drink and more of the animal rubs all helped and I started to feel better and ready to tackle the first proper hill of the walk.

During the first day from Wembley as Dan and I had climbed up Shooters Hill, we had come up with our own classification for hills with a 1-5 rating depending on a combination of the length and the gradient of the hill, with a bonus if the gradient steepened towards the top of the climb. On this basis, we had awarded Shooters Hill a 'Two' rating, just above the minimum, and from the South Downs until today, we had come across nothing worthy of more than a 'One' rating – mole hills really. Now, on Day 19 and after 350 miles, we were going to meet our first proper hill. If our notes were accurate, this one climbed upwards for 1.8 miles, with a right turn at a junction after half a mile, under the Luxembourg motorway and then another mile with the road climbing steeper and steeper until we turn left onto the road for Xhoffaix.

I'd been talking about this hill to the others since they arrived on Friday and the good thing was, having built it up, the reality was certainly no worse than my description. My walking sticks came out and were to be regular companions for the next five days. After a pleasant stroll across the valley bottom, we came to the foot of the climb. As always, I attacked it hard, no point doing anything else and using the sticks as a cross-country skier, I worked my upper body hard and settled into a rhythm which had, even Tom, working to keep just ahead of me and Anthony falling behind. There was a very different mood when Chris wasn't walking; he provided our glue, kept the conversation going, chatting easily with his son and his brother. With Anthony and Tom it was far more up to me, to ask questions and help the conversation along and often, I had other things to concentrate on or couldn't be bothered, so we tended to walk more as three individuals, Tom always walking just ahead as my constant guide and Anthony content to walk ahead or behind or with us as the pace and the mood took him. It was like this that we climbed the hill for 40 minutes, Tom staying just ahead, Anthony gradually falling further behind. As the hill steepened towards the top, I was still able to keep my rhythm going and I shouted as loud as I could, 'Call yourself a hill?' The road levelled off just after the left

A Walk of Faith

Sunday morning in the sun as the Vesdre rushes by

On the edge of the forest after a good day

turn and I slowed to allow Anthony to catch up. My final analysis, totally subjective, was that the hill warranted a 'Level Three' rating.

We were on the top now with even more trees and fewer views; the sun was still shining and it was nice to cool down in the breeze with only another mile to the end of the day's walk. Ironically, although we had walked uphill for almost the entire day, a gradual ascent of almost 2,000 feet, and I was very tired, my ankle was less swollen and painful than it had been for the last three days. Perhaps, the antibiotics were starting to work but certainly walking uphill meant less pounding and less pressure on my leg than the flat lands below us to the north and west.

The motor home was waiting for us at a car park on the edge of another forest and it seemed apt to finish with a photograph of the three of us by a sculpture entitled 'Penseé, Homme et Forêt'- we would see more trees over the next five days than we had seen in the rest of our lives.

Yellow Jersey award to Tom for helping to get me up the hills and never faltering for one step. Tim will be proud of him.
Distance covered - 20.4 miles.
Total distance covered - 373.4 miles.

Our route took us north-east of Malmedy and we had a 20 minute drive which took us past the Spa Grand Prix circuit. Chris had already booked us into our rooms at the Hotel Forge, right on the edge of the town centre and he was able to park the van just down from the entrance so we were soon in our rooms. It was a small hotel with a dozen or so rooms, recently refurbished, a small breakfast area and a public bar on the ground floor where food was available.

The others were ready to explore the town and have a few beers but I preferred to take my time, enjoy a long, hot shower and a rest and write up my web diary so I agreed to meet them later for a beer and dinner. It was a fine evening, warm enough for T-shirt and shorts. The town was busy with day visitors as I walked slowly in my flip-flops through the pretty town centre and found the others at Le Pub. I bought a round of drinks to find that they had been ready to leave; Tom had just made a selection of the worst records on the juke box, intending not to hear them. Now we were going to and we had a laugh as his choices played through. They had scouted round the town centre and picked out a couple of likely looking eating places. We settled for a busy Italian where we enjoyed a good meal and a couple more beers, then wandered back to the hotel, feeling tired but good.

John Reeve

Walking in the Hills
From Malmedy through the Hills of the Ardennes and Eifel to the Rhine

I was sharing a room with Anthony and by the time I'd written up my personal diary, said my prayers and talked over the day with Tim, he was snoring away like a good un'. After an hour of lying awake, trying to get comfortable, drown out the noise and sleep, I decided it was hopeless, woke up Chris next door to get the keys for the motor home and retired to the double bed. It was a mild night and I had a peaceful few hours, sleeping in bursts as always. It was colder in the morning and I crept back into the hotel to warm up and get ready for another day.

A typical continental breakfast in the hotel at 8am and then back to the motor home for the drive back towards Hockai. Anthony was driving again today with Chris, Tom and me out on the tarmac. We had stopped in the middle of a forest and started with a weak sun shining through even though raindrops were falling. Chris was upbeat about the weather and I blamed him for it gradually closing in. It took us 40 minutes to get through the forest, right along the hilltops, with the occasional glimpse of spectacular views to either side through the mist. Then downhill into Xhoffaix and the pattern for the day emerged – climb steeply out of one village, along the undulating top for a time and then drop down just as steeply into the next village.

We were heading for Robertville, a beautiful lake-side resort village with some good hotels and restaurants and passed through Ofivat and Laffaye on our way. We were walking on narrow country lanes with little traffic and the map showed a major long-distance path that crossed our route which would provide a more direct alternative. However, when we came to the point on the map, at a steep dip where the road crossed a fast-flowing stream, there was a whole network of inter-connecting paths leading off

A Walk of Faith

into the darkness of the trees so we decided to play safe and stick to the road.

Everywhere, including us, was drenched in the rain and all the many shades of green seemed muted and merged into one. Sandra rang on one of the steep climbs and, out of breath, I was a bit short with her when she went into, 'You didn't say that before' mode. By the time we dropped down into Robertville it was raining hard and we were pleased to see Anthony and the van. The water was boiling for coffee and after a slightly-longer-than-usual break including time to dry out and change layers, we set off again. The extra time seemed to help as we made good time through Ouverte and Champagne and into Weyverts as the weather improved. The latter was a shortcut that I had spotted on the map earlier; without getting lost it saved us two miles.

We dropped down onto the main road and turned left, eastwards as always. By now all the road signs were in German and we saw both Belgian and German police cars outside the Police Station. There was a lot more traffic with a mixture of cycle paths and single-file walking towards the oncoming vehicles. Although the route didn't twist and turn as steeply as on the minor routes, there was still very little flat ground and with the weather still grey with intermittent rain, the walk turned into a slog. Chris was great and sensing my tiredness started a classification game – countries beginning with the letter A, names of Football Grounds where clubs have moved from and to – and in between rounds we sang Barnsley songs to the passing cars and kept moving forward. We walked into another town with a German-sounding name but still in Belgium – Bullingen – where we had our second stop. After a sandwich and biscuit and plenty of liquid, I had a doze for 20 minutes, keeping my leg up higher than my heart.

The antibiotics seemed to be dealing with the swelling around my ankle and as long as I kept my leg off the ground when I wasn't walking, it wasn't getting any worse, if anything it was less tight and certainly less painful than it had been. I was using Emu oil my knees and it also seemed to be helping, the main thing being that I thought it was.

The last session of the day took us to Murringen. On the way I rang Sandra to find that she was at Dan's in Earlsfield loading the car to take his clothes etc home. He was moving out of the house where he had lived for the last three years since graduating. It was a big day for him, moving out, moving on, and going on holiday for a month. Sandra was amazed at how much stuff he had but it didn't matter, we would find somewhere to store it. I spoke to him briefly as I did every day and wished him a great holiday and God's speed until we met again in Frankfurt.

We thought we must have crossed into Germany, all the signs were now in German and the Belgium influences seemed to have disappeared but we hadn't seen any signs or a border crossing so we weren't sure. What was certain was that by a combination of good walking, over-estimating distances on the plan and finding short cuts, we were a whole 14 miles up on schedule. We might still need that for later but we were going really well, thanks to so many people.

Murringen was a pretty, rural village, at the top of a steep climb and we stopped briefly whilst Tom tried out water divining before spotting the motor home and turning left to the car park.

Yellow Jersey award to Chris for helping me through a couple of painful periods with some great classification questions.
Distance covered - 18.3 miles, although with the ups and downs it felt like a lot further.
Total distance covered - 391.7 miles.

It was a long drive back this time and I dozed on the bed despite the bumpy road as we retuned to the Hotel Forge. After sunshine and T-shirts the previous evening, it was cold, wet and grey in Malmedy. The town was quiet after the bustle and colour and I shivered as I walked back along the main street to Le Pub where the others had returned for a beer. We walked round to the Italian restaurant to find it closed on Monday evenings and eventually settled on Le Laure, a more up-market restaurant than we would otherwise have chosen but there was little else open and we were all getting tired of walking around the streets. Le Laure was almost empty but the four of us weren't concerned and enjoyed a good meal with tomato salad, Argentine steak and Dame Blanche the favourite choices.

Back at the hotel, I collected my things, headed straight to the motor home and sat at the table writing my diary. It was much colder than the previous evening and I spent longer than usual talking to Tim, wondering how he was, what he was making of the walk and thinking that he would be as pleased as me, when Sandra was back together with us again.

I was cold, tired and grumpy when I came back into the hotel at the start of Day 21 of the walk. A hot shower warmed me up but didn't lift my spirits; I felt flat over breakfast and allowed myself to slip further into the gloom listening to James Blunt as we drove back to Murringen. It was a bad morning like Tim used to have and although I knew I would climb out of it later, I couldn't be bothered to put on an act for the others.

The slight detour to the motor home at the end of yesterday's walk had totally thrown my sense of direction and being in a 'couldn't care less' mode, I let Tom and Anthony take the map and just followed them, unsure about where we were going but content just to walk. It wasn't long before the others realised that we were off course and at a junction drew me into the conversation. We decided to head back towards the village on another road. Luckily as we came towards the village green I saw a road on the right that seemed familiar and checking the directions felt confident that this was the correct route. It led us downhill on a very quiet road and onto an area of open moor land with views across to the surrounding forests.

The walk had changed dramatically over the last three days with different companions, a different atmosphere and very different countryside to walk through and now as we entered a different country we were going to add yet another difference. With large-scale maps that seemed easier to understand and simpler to interpret, we were taking to the footpaths and mixing up our road walking with cross-country trekking. It was not a time for feeling disassociated. Getting lost earlier had jolted me out of my gloominess and as we crossed a small bridge and walked past a series of ponds which had been mentioned in the instructions, we all knew that we were heading in the right

John Reeve

direction. It was a desolate area and we walked for four of five miles without seeing a sign of life. The road petered out into a track and into a forest and we walked on, everywhere was wet through from the day before but at least it wasn't raining although the sky was grey and it was still more like March than May.

The track came out onto a main road and we saw almost our first traffic of the day. Somehow, we managed to go wrong, turning left instead of right and walked for half a mile along the road, looking for a turn to our right before realising our mistake. It was disheartening having to turn around and walk back. Chris rang whilst we were on our way back, he was waiting for us at Udenbreth and we were late.

As we walked back along the straight road, we noticed concrete slabs sticking out of the ground in the middle of the trees on our left. They stood like tall grave stones side by side and as we walked further we noticed that they continued along the ridge, disappearing behind the trees only to reappear a few seconds later. We speculated about what they might be or have been and our preferred explanation, knowing that we were close to the border, was that they were part of the defences between Germany and its neighbours dating back to the Second World War. They continued for a mile as we retraced our steps, for another half mile until we came to the turning we had been looking for earlier, and we could see them snaking off into the distance climbing up the hill ahead. Later that day, we were to meet a German journalist who confirmed that they were part of the Siegfried Line Defences. The area we were walking through had been the scene of the Battle of the Bulge and the Germans' last major counter-attack in the Ardennes. It was tough country and the fighting in the middle of winter must have been especially bitter.

Back on course for the second time, we were well behind the plan we had set ourselves but it was distance I was keen to cover, the time it took didn't matter so much. Consequently, when we found Chris and the motor home at Udenbreth, I declined the hot coffee on offer and much to Anthony and Tom's disappointment said that we would carry on to our intended stopping point by the radio mast. Out of the village, we saw the first of many wind farms off to our right and then spotted the huge mast about two miles ahead. It was a gradual uphill stretch and we were all pleased to reach the van. Not only had we covered 10 miles of the day's walk, the clouds were also closing in and it poured down whilst we were having coffee and an early lunch.

By the time we were ready to set off again, the clouds were clearing into the distance, we could see the trees to our right and ahead, and distant views across rolling countryside to the right which had appeared as the mist and gloom vanished.

The next stage took us by road through another large forest heading towards Dahlem and it was a hard walk. I was tired and sore and both Tom and Anthony who wanted to help and support as much as they could, found it hard to strike up a conversation with me so when I couldn't be bothered to make the effort, we tended to walk in single file in silence, me concentrating on trying to relax and walk easily, trying to let my mind free-wheel.

I was starting to think about the end of the walk, calculating how much further there was to go. I reckoned I had covered 400 miles from home and around 350 miles from Wembley and so had about 150 miles further to walk. About seven days good walking although the schedule with another rest day built in, allowed for eight days. With three more days hard walking in the hills, once I was through this patch, the rest would be easy. Until then I had resisted the temptation to dwell on the length of the walk, how far I had travelled and how much further was left. 'Just do it,' I had told myself was the best way to get through each day, enjoy the experience, don't think too much about the future or the past. Well, I had failed badly with the latter but I reasoned it was good for me to think about the past and the happy as well as the sad times, so long as I didn't dwell too much there. But I didn't want to start counting down to the finish, with each mile seeming to take longer and longer as I became more obsessed about the time when I could stop. I remembered again, Tim saying, 'You think too much, Dad'.

When we passed the Mercedes-Benz airfield on our left, the directions told us that we were getting close to Dahlem and as we started to drop down towards the village, we saw a short cut that

John Reeve

Tom and Anthony. Another day, another statue

The road winds forever onwards

led us to a busy dual carriageway cutting through the countryside. We crossed as quickly as possible through the traffic

The village was close to the far side of the major road and I remembered the main street. It was a pretty village, immaculately clean and tidy and the motor home was parked at almost the same spot where we had parked the car, three months earlier. We had noticed in Udenbreth a tall pine tree in the centre of the village with all its branches and bark striped off, except for the very top of the tree. There was another one, here in Dahlem and we wondered what local custom it related to.

The last walk of the day was the toughest but the best. The sun was showing more often with increasing blue sky breaks in the cloud and the temperature was moving closer towards the seasonal norm despite the stiff breeze. The route out of Dahlem took us along a twisting road over the railway line and then up a steep lane that merged into a cycle path and then onto the edge of a forest.

We stooped briefly for a photograph and then plunged into the forest on a footpath. It took our eyes a few seconds to adjust to the darkness and the temperature drop was noticeable but soon we were watching the shafts of sunlight as they made patterns all around us and the peacefulness and calm was tangible. We walked for 30 minutes through the trees and came out into the open with the path leading out onto an exposed ridge.

The blue sky was moving away to our left and dark clouds were approaching rapidly, the wind gusting up. The views to each side were spectacular; we could see villages, two lakes, another wind farm, lots of trees, all bound together by the rich green of the countryside. The wind howled loudly as the rain started, we had to lean forward into it until we came to a large hedge and turned left to follow as it dropped down towards the village of Waldorf.

We were starting to become experts at spotting the stripped trees, this one had tassels tied to the top and we walked down through another perfectly clean and tidy village, very quiet, only some boys kicking a football on a patch of grass. I went over to check our way ahead, they understood my poor German and pointed towards a switchback country lane that ran ahead of us.

The rain had stopped and the sun and wind was drying everything out, us included, as we walked towards the junction up ahead with the van parked in a small turning. The air seemed even clearer and the light brighter after the rain. The walk that had started in such gloom was ending on a high note.

Yellow Jersey Award to Anthony for always being ready to help, nothing is too much trouble for him.
Distance covered - 20 miles (plus one in the wrong direction).
Total distance covered - 411.7 miles.

Chris had pre-booked us into a small hotel in Stadtkyll, a small town about 15 miles away and the journey took almost half an hour along twisting country roads. The Art Haus Am See was, as the name suggests, located on the edge of the town, in a picturesque spot overlooking a small lake.

The boys, much quicker than me as usual, were supping their second beer and had already met Mehmet when I came down to the bar area. We found out later than evening that the hotel, a well-known local landmark, had fallen into disrepair and remained closed for more than 10 years until Mehmet Fistik had bought it about two years ago. After bringing the hotel back to an acceptable condition, he had re-opened the place and started to re-build the business using his charisma and personal contacts to encourage both locals and people visiting the area to stay with him.

Mehmet is a larger-than-life character, a former actor and sometime mime-clown who both dressed and behaved flamboyantly. It was impossible to miss him wearing a black hat, red jacket and white scarf, talking to some locals at the bar and he soon came over to welcome me warmly. In a mixture of bad English and German, we talked briefly about the walk. He asked if I would like some publicity and offered to contact a local journalist. As we moved to the restaurant area at the other side of reception, he told me that Fritz-Peter Linden would be coming out later to meet us.

Another good meal, one of the great side effects of the walk was being able to eat as much as I wanted, and a bottle of wine with plenty of laughter and jokes as the four of us relaxed. The

A Walk of Faith

journalist arrived during the main course, agreed to wait in the bar with a beer and as soon as I finished my pudding, I left the others to go through and talk to him. Fritz was chatting to Mehmet as I walked through and seemed very content drinking a small glass of lager. He spoke very good English and it was apparent immediately that he was very sympathetic and wanted to hear all about Tim and the Walk to the World Cup. As we talked he disclosed that he had suffered the loss of a child, it was easy to talk to him and we chatted for over an hour, regularly refilling our glasses and during this time, the others came through but left the two of us to talk.

He worked for the Frierische Volksfreund, a large regional paper and said he was certain he could print a story in his paper and would also send a piece through to the Cologne-based sister newspaper. By now, we had all had a good drink and finished with photographs for the paper, Mehmet, the publicist, enjoying the opportunity to join the walkers. A final beer and Mehmet's wife joined us agreeing with Fritz about the superiority of Cologne beer compared to the local brew – a very warm welcome to Germany.

We left Mehmet and Fritz, went next door to plan the route for the next day and it was 11.30 before we went up to our rooms. I hadn't written up my diary and it was 12.45 before I said goodnight and switched off the light.

The sun was shining am See as I looked out of my window around 7.00 am on May 31. Mehmet came into breakfast to say goodbye to us, still wearing the same clothes from the night before – had he been to bed? We said a fond farewell to him and his wife. I may return to Stadtkyll with Sandra.

Another bumpy ride back to Ripsdorf and the spot at the junction where we had finished the day before. By now the clouds were massing and I gave the map to Tom as we set off into the village. We had picked out a cycle path that led from Ripsdorf, turned right by the church and saw the sign heading off through the outskirts. We didn't see a single person, everywhere as quiet as a mouse, all the rubbish neatly placed for a collection later in the day and, of course, the compulsory pine tree stripped of branches and bark with streamers hanging from the top.

The route took us down into a long, shallow river valley and we spotted several buzzards soaring in the sky, forever watching and waiting. Continuing to follow the cycle path signs, we climbed out of the valley to our right and were passed by a solitary jogger, the first person we had seen on the day's walk and then into another pretty village, Dollendorf. Again very quiet with no one about. Did people really live here?

We turned back left again and dropped down towards Ahrhutte. As we passed a field full of young deer, we saw our first watchtower and then noticed one of the deer caught in the fencing with others gathering around. It must have been trying to escape and got caught in the barbed wire. We walked into Ahrhutte, turned sharp right down to the river and onto a newly laid, yellow stone road that took us along the edge of the river valley with the river now immediately below us and then further away as it meandered across its narrow flood-plain. The path took us three miles downstream to Ahrdorf with the surface firm and true at first but gradually becoming softer and more uneven. Nearing Ahrdorf, we came across the workmen laying the final stretch of the path and had to make a well-signed detour onto an older track, then rang Chris to find out where he was, as we stood high up on the valley side, looking down on the village.

As we walked to meet him, he must have set off to find us and drove past the narrow lane we were descending. Tom set off running to tell his Dad and registered 23km on a mobile speed trap set up at the bottom of the hill, causing laughter and cheers all round, including the people operating the speed trap. We had covered eight miles and took a welcome, first stop and a hot drink at a car park, close to a camp site, right next to the village. The nearby inn seemed to be closed, no one about again, so it was the motor home for a 30 minute rest.

Anthony was flying home that evening to be home in time to take his son, Richard - who was going on holiday to Hong Kong and China - to the airport the following day. Consequently, he was walking again with Tom and me and the three of us set off, planning to meet up with Chris after another six miles. Almost immediately, the cycle path merged with a busy trunk road and although we could see footpaths running alongside the river, we were unsure from the map where they led to and how far they would take us so decided to keep to the main road.

The session turned into a real slog. The route twisted and turned as it followed the edge of the valley, for the most part gently downhill and with a steep rock face immediately to our left. We were walking into the oncoming traffic with nowhere to go if a wagon came too close, it was a dangerous hike with the rain falling and little conversation amongst the three of us. We soldiered on, the second sessions always seemed to be the worst, still with a long way to walk, the expectation and comfort of the first few miles a distant memory. It was all about just doing it.

I remembered back to Christmas and a day Sandra and I had spent with Anthony and Anne in Derbyshire. Anthony and I had gone out for a walk along the roads and paths around the beautiful countryside in which they live. The fields were white with frost and light snow and the ground mercifully hard underfoot, turning the mud into ridges and craters, concrete-hard. We were walking a six-mile circuit that would bring us out at a pub, where the four of us would meet for a late lunch. Heading across another field, I remember talking to him about walking and a strong urge to walk myself into oblivion. Just keep on walking until all memory and all feeling became numb and was obliterated.

This stretch of the walk felt just a little bit like that walk into oblivion. I felt all on my own, just walking, walking, walking; thoughts moving just as steadily into and out of my mind, sore and aching but no worse than many other days, heading onwards because that's what I had to do.

Eventually, we came to the junction where the road turned left across the river towards Wirft and as we headed across the bridge, we knew that Chris and the motor home were just ahead. Lunch was a German croissant with cheese, a ham roll followed by one of my favourite oatmeal biscuits, a hot mug of coffee and a doze. The doze lasted longer than I had intended and it was an hour after we had arrived, before I limped to the steps and made by customary backwards descent of the three steps.

I really didn't fancy the final walk to Adenau; Chris had suggested an alternative route that avoided the steep climb awaiting us but looked much further on the map to me. As always, preferring the shortest route and not minding the climbs unduly, I opted for Route One and, as always, hit it hard. We kept going well up the steep climb, out of another river valley and through a large, forested area but I ran out of steam, somewhere along the top and at times, Anthony was 20-30 yards ahead, with Tom as always keeping just ahead of me.

Through the trees we began to pick out the town of Adenau, far below us and realised that it was almost totally encircled by hills and forests. Tom started the 'Red Army' chants and the two of us enjoyed a long spell of football singing as we headed down the twisting road towards the town, competing over shouts of 'You Reds' to see who could create the longest and loudest echo. I suspect that one or two people in the town below must have heard us coming and probably wondered who the hell was coming towards their busy country town. Unfortunately, I'd left the camera in the motor home and missed the opportunity for some spectacular shots as we walked from one breath-taking scene to another, real *Sound of Music* stuff.

Down in the town, Chris came to meet us and we stopped for the day at a car park right in the middle of the town. Our accommodation for the night was a small, biker's hotel on the southern edge of the town. As we arrived, I realised why it was so popular with the motorbike fraternity, it was situated within 50 yards of one of the tight bends on the Nurburgring Grand Prix circuit and there were grandstand views from many of the hotel bedrooms.

King of the Mountains - Tom who could probably have run up the last hill.

Distance covered – 18.2 miles.
Total distance covered – 429.9 miles.

A quick shower and change and just time to look out from the balcony to see five Mercedes cars taking the tight bend at speed, then back into the motor home for the drive to Cologne. Chris, having driven all day, kindly agreed to drive up to Cologne. I settled onto the bed and dozed as we worked our way through the roads of the Eifel region to pick up the motorway system that would lead us to the Rhine and north to Cologne airport. The motorway system was complex as we passed Bonn and neared Cologne but we found the airport easily and said farewell to Anthony who had been a great supporter, always willing, in good time for his flight.

We were due to meet Sandra who was flying out that afternoon in just over an hour and set off to find a suitable car park. Almost immediately, we found ourselves back on the motorway system and then followed a hilarious but increasingly frustrating 30 minutes as we made a huge circuit, somewhere around Cologne trying harder and harder to get back to the airport. At one stage, I was convinced that we were heading for the Polish border and every sign for the airport was on the opposite carriageway but Chris had it under control. Eventually we followed the same entrance signs and this time, parked right next to the terminal, with just time to get something to eat before Sandra arrived.

It was so good to have her back and it was clear that she was equally pleased to be with us. Ted had driven her down to Gatwick for the flight and the journey had been smooth and easy. She laughed as we told her about our ride around Greater Cologne, even more so when having left the airport, we were back on the entrance slip road five minutes later. Fortunately, after that out journey south to Adenau was straightforward. It was 11.30 pm before we arrived back at the hotel, Am Der Nordschliefe. Everything was dark, the bar obviously closed and we were all ready to go straight to bed.

A second good night's sleep and it was nice to wake up with Sandra beside me. We enjoyed a lie in until 7.30, as we were coming back to the hotel that evening so didn't need to pack and even more importantly were only intending a short, 10 mile walk. In the original schedule, Day 23, June 1, was a rest day but talking to Chris and Tom, we had decided to split the 20 miles scheduled for the next day and walk 10 miles each day. One of the reasons for suggesting this was because we had the toughest climb of the walk to make with the steepest descent to follow about 12 miles later and to walk them both on the same day seemed a good thing to avoid. The other reason was that I had a radio interview scheduled for lunch time with Johnnie Walker for his Sunday show and I wanted to be back at the hotel rather than trying to talk on the road or in the motor home.

There was only the four of us at breakfast which was typical continental and I had cereal and a roll. We were rushing after that to get on the road and start walking as I had a second interview, with Alan Brazil, of TalkSport scheduled for 8.45 am. Sandra drove us back to the finishing point and we set off along the main street around 8.30. Adenau is a largish country town with lots of old buildings but plenty of newer development as well and had a bustle and energy that we hadn't seen since leaving Spa, four days before. There was plenty of traffic, people travelling to work on a cool, grey morning and we were just reaching the edge of the town when my mobile rang and it was the TalkSport studio.

I chatted to the studio technician comfortably as we walked along the road and after a minute, he transferred me through to the studio. Then all went quiet and I stopped, trying hard to hear above the traffic noise but after a few seconds, the engineer cut back in, saying there must be a problem and they would try again. I walked a few yards away from the road and listened carefully when he put me through, this time I could hear the occasional word but not enough to make sense of it. I could hear Alan Brazil saying that they were having trouble with the connection and would make one more try and then it was back to the technician again. At this point, I waved and pointed at Chris and Tom, crossed the road to a large car park and headed to the back of the car park, well away from the noise. Third time lucky and I spent the next five minutes walking and talking around the car park, telling Alan and the listeners about Tim and his love of football, describing the walk and our overnight stay at the Nurburgring and asking for support for 'the 'Forgotten Tribe'. He was very kind and supportive and we received many donations and messages of support from people who had heard the interview that eventually took place.

Eventually, we left Adenau behind and following the instructions turned left and started the approach to Hohe Acht, a 760 metre high hill, we would be walking close to the summit, reaching the highest point of the walk. Heading along the river

A Walk of Faith

valley which stretched ahead for a mile with a very shallow incline, I felt a mixture of apprehension and exhilaration, get to the top and it would be almost literally, all downhill from there. Chris was great and started us playing the classification game, so by the time the river swung to the left and the road made the first of many sharp turns, we had settled into a fast but comfortable rhythm.

In standard formation, Tom just ahead, me in the middle and Chris right behind, the three of us tackled the lower part of the climb. The sharp bends soon became hairpins, each one seemingly steeper than the one before. We were in thick forest with trees all around, wet through although it wasn't raining, and with intermittent traffic on the narrow road. My notes spoke of footpaths that appeared to cut through the hairpins, providing a more direct route and after 20 minutes of solid climbing, I saw one particularly clear path at a hairpin and suggested to the other two that we give it a try.

It turned out to be a bad call. Within 50 metres, the path opened out into a small clearing where logging had taken place and we found out that the only path leading out of the clearing stopped at an almost sheer climb a few yards further on. So, it was back down to the road and get back into a rhythm again, this time without the lead in of the flatter river valley. But working hard together, we found the right pace again and started reeling in the hairpins, one after another after another after another. At times, the forest seemed to close in as the road cut through a narrow ravine, at other times, the view widened out and a couple of times we wrongly thought that we were nearing the top.

The mist closed in, drenching everything around and limiting visibility even more, then we reached a junction with a side road heading straight ahead and our route, the main road, twisting yet again, to the right. At this point, I knew from the notes that we were almost there and within five minutes we saw the car park emerging out of the gloom and the motor home with Sandra waiting patiently for us. It had taken us 60 minutes, my GPS measuring a distance of 3.2 miles from the foot of the climb. Knowing there are plenty of far longer and steeper climbs, I nevertheless reckoned that a 'Level Four' classification was deserved.

We waved to Sandra as we passed the motor home and stopped briefly to put on an extra layer. We were all warm but knew that the majority of the next stretch would be a gradual downhill and the weather was even cooler in the mist. Later that day, we found out that after we had passed Sandra, she had the same trouble with the hand brake she had experienced earlier in the walk and had tried unsuccessfully to release it. There was no one else in the car park and only one other car that had been empty when she arrived. So not wanting to phone and make us turn back, she waited and the longer she waited, the further it meant our return walk would have been, if we had eventually needed to come and 'rescue' her. Fortunately, after 45 minutes, a couple appeared and made for the other vehicle and speaking good English, they were happy to help and chatted to her about their friends in England before she set off to catch us up.

By then we had walked out of the trees into a wide, open, moorland terrain, past the Hohe Acht hotel, when Tracey from Dream FM rang for her regular radio update, crossed the main road and dropped down into the village of Siebenbach. Walking through the village, Tom said that he would be stopping here and that he could walk no further. For a moment, I was concerned that he had a problem and then he announced that in his interviews to local newspapers in West Yorkshire, he had told reporters that he was walking from Liege to Siebenbach. The village had been the end of our scheduled walk for the following day and, therefore, he had finished his walk.

On the other side of Siebenbach, we entered a tiny valley with the road running right at the side of a small but noisy, rushing stream. The sky cleared, the temperature rose and we saw the occasional glimpse of the sun. It was like being at the side of the Vesdre on the previous Sunday morning, only this time everything was in miniature. It was such a contrast to the walk up the other side that we enjoyed the stroll even more and we continued for another three miles with very few cars and only one motor home passing us. As we came into Acht, Sandra took one of the best walking photographs of the journey.

A Walk of Faith

We decided to press on for another 2km to Langenfeld but after the gradual descent from Siebenbach, this stretch was back up the side of the valley with a 1km stretch of very steep climbing. As usual, I attacked it hard, reached the top and continued into Langenfeld but my legs had gone, not sore or aching, just 'gone' – no energy and not much feeling left. But Sandra was there waiting for us and after my compulsory stretch down, it was into the van and back to Adenau, enjoying the drive down the hairpins into the town.

King of the Mountains – Tom, 110 miles and he has strolled all the way.
Distance covered – 10.1 miles.
Total distance covered – 440.0 miles.

On the way back, someone rang from the Johnnie Walker Show to say that he had needed to go to the dentist and rearranged the interview for later in the afternoon so we decided to have a shower and go for lunch. We chose a café, on the main road, just along from the hotel and joined several groups of bikers having lunch. Hungry as always, I had a Bearntsnitzel – escalope, fried egg, bacon bits and salad – and then a wonderful frische waffle mit heissen kirschen und sahne. Enjoying the food with the others, the four of us chatting away quite relaxed, I thought about how much Tim would have liked this aspect of the journey.

He loved being with his family and enjoyed food and eating out. A month of doing both almost every day would have been brilliant. I think he enjoyed the anticipation of going out to eat, whether it was a pub lunch or a smart restaurant for dinner. Perhaps, during his illness it had become something to relieve the boredom but he had enjoyed eating out long before then. He liked all kinds of food, Chinese, Indian, French, Thai, Roast Beef and Yorkshire Pud and a good steak but Italian food was probably his favourite, pizza and pasta and he could concoct a good pasta meal himself.

When he was in Barts, we used to go out to local restaurants, mainly Italian, whenever he was well enough and able to. It was an opportunity to escape from the ward and miss a hospital meal.

When he was too unwell to go out, we'd often bring him some food from the canteen or from Carluccio's across the square. As well as pasta and pizzas, he had a sweet tooth and liked chocolate gateau and proper cheesecake. During the last few months, he became partial to a white chocolate tart that they sold at Carluccio's and I remembered enjoying seeing him eating the cold chocolate. His last restaurant meal was in a tiny, wood-panelled bistro on the Ilê de St. Louis, where we enjoyed a typically French meal on the evening before he came home to die. I wasn't sure whether he would have gone back for a second waffle with hot cherries and cream but he would certainly have loved the first one.

I wasn't feeling too adventurous and it was back to the hotel after lunch and a doze until it was time for Johnnie Walker. The interview seemed to go well and, again, many people kindly donated and sent messages of support as a result of hearing the conversation. In particular, messages from Peter Westhorpe, a schoolteacher who wrote about a pupil who died tragically at his school and about giving his own 24-year-old son an extra hug that night, and from Kim Read, a paediatric nurse from the Isle of Wight who works with children and teenagers with cancer and has a football-loving son of 22, made both Sandra and I gulp as we read them and brought tears to our eyes.

After the interview, I woke up Chris and Tom next door and we decided to take a ride up to the Nurburgring. Little did we know that they were preparing for a massive Heavy Metal Festival starting the next day and as we drove up towards the main grandstand area, the narrow roads were chocked with festival-goers, walking, driving, biking – all heading for the camp site area. After a tricky 17-point turn, Chris managed to extricate us from the scrum and we reckoned that a ride round the track was not going to happen. Back at the hotel, we settled for playing cards in the motor home until it was time to eat again. This time we plumped for an Italian restaurant, Gulia's, had a nice meal and enjoyed catching up with more news from Sandra. It would be the last meal with Chris and Tom; they had both been total stars in different ways. Chris able to tune in better than anyone, except Sandra and Dan, to how I was feeling and Tom, 100% committed

A Walk of Faith

to the cause, to the memory of his cousin and never faltering. I knew I would miss them both when they flew back the next day but Phil and Sam were flying out at second-half substitutes and the team would continue to move forwards.

Day 24 dawned cold and grey, yet again, and the mood was continued at breakfast. It was without doubt the most unfriendly place that we stayed in of the entire walk and none of us were sorry to leave. Just like the previous day, the mist developed into full-blown fog by the time we had reached the tops, fortunately it cleared as we dropped back down and approached Langenfeld but the outside temperature gauge registered 8°C as we stopped and I started the walk with four layers on plus Barnsley FC woolly hat and pair of gloves, both Tim's. It was June 2.

Since we had crossed into Germany, we had noticed wooden 'watchtowers' tucked away in the corner of fields all along our route. Most of them appeared to be substantial structures built to last, some able to hold as many as six people and we had speculated idly as we walked, about their purpose. Perhaps, there were a lot of twitchers in Germany, may be to look out for deer or other larger animals? But our favourite theory was that they were an early warning screen watching for the next invasion. We imagined families driving up to their watchtower for the weekend, enjoying looking out for soldiers creeping through the forests – a kind of 21 century, German version of *'Dad's Army'*. Most days during this part of the walk, we would play 'Spot the Watchtowers' as a game that could run alongside the other diversions we used to pass the time and relieve the monotony. Rather like counting pub signs or AA boxes, for those of us who are old enough to remember them. Tom always won; he had the advantage of being able to see them in the distance long before Chris or I could make them out. Funny thing was that we didn't see a single person anywhere near a watchtower, they must have been so well hidden spying from on high on us, but even that theory was challenged when Tom climbed up into one later that morning.

As soon as we started walking we realised that today they were everywhere. Almost every field had a watchtower and we spotted one, admittedly large, field with three look-out posts. This must be the 'hot spot' where the next 'Normandy landing' was expected. Anyway, the banter helped me to find a rhythm, pick up after a cold and slow start and after two miles we reached Kirchwald, situated on the edge of the high hills. From here it was 10km of steep downhill, out of the hills and into Mayen and the beginning of the Rhine flood plain.

We had picked out a path that avoided a long loop that the road took down into the valley and had recognised that this would mean even tighter contours and steeper descent to contend with, but it looked about half the distance and a good trade-off. We started well along a tarmac path that first climbed up into open countryside with views across to neighbouring hill tops and down into the valley which disappeared into the depths in shades of green.

The map showed our route veering to the left from the main path and after 20 minutes walking we came to a point that seemed to be where we should turn off. The tarmac track finished just a few yards ahead, the path to the left seemed to be well-worn and off we went through two fields with grass knee high and watchtowers everywhere.

Gradually the path became less and less obvious and the ground dropped away steeper and steeper. We were skirting around the edge of a wood and as we reached the bottom of the second field, the path disappeared into the trees and we followed for 10-20 metres before coming to a halt in front of a drop of about 30', almost sheer into a narrow ravine.

We retraced our steps back out into the field and consulted the large-scale map. Our only conclusion was that we had turned off too soon and needed to climb back up to our turn-off point and continue along the track. Tom and then Chris sped off to search the perimeter of the two fields searching for another way down whilst I trudged back up the hill. It was warm work for all of us but lung-bursting stuff for the other two and we were all exhausted by the time we reached the top. The weather was starting to warm up and seemed to increase by 1°C for every 100' of descent. After another consultation we resumed our walk along the track, Tom going ahead again to search for a way through. As soon as the tarmac petered out the path continued between two

A Walk of Faith

hedges but when these came to an end, we were unsure which way to go. Then Tom rang to say he had found a way ahead and was coming back up to show us.

His route took us sweeping around the edge of the trees further to the right, then looped back to the left and into a ravine with a tiny stream and a steep but well-marked path. The trees were tight around us, the ground underneath a mixture of stones and black earth and as we headed downwards the path steepened even more. It was difficult not to break into a run and tumble helter-skelter down the slope. My progress was slow, both legs feeling as if they didn't belong to me, uncertain about every step, the aching in my knees and front of my shins increasing minute by minute. Soon, I resorted to walking down backwards, Tom guiding me past large rocks. By now the tiny stream had grown into a rushing torrent and we continued going down, first backwards then forwards, then backwards again, for another 15-20 minutes until after a particularly steep drop where even the other two were gripping branches and sliding down sideways, the path flattened out and we saw a narrow lane.

It was so good to get onto level ground with a firm footing underneath. We knew we needed to turn left to rejoin the main road to Mayen. We were unsure exactly where we had come out onto the lane and as we walked along the lane, we realised that we must have missed the path somewhere and come out much further round the descent than we had expected. The map showed that we had dropped over 1,500 feet in under two miles, no wonder it had been steep!

As the trees around us thinned, we felt the strength of the sun, which was full out in a light blue sky and were soon down to T shirts in the noon-day heat. We were to find out later, when we reached the motor home, that the temperature had risen from 8°C to 20°C in the space of eight miles and two hours of walking. It was as if we have travelled from February to June in the space of a morning.

We reached the main road with the ruins of St. Johannes Schloss on our right and after half a mile on the main road, picked up another Wanderweg, that followed the river towards Mayen. This was a well-used, well-marked trail that twisted and turned following the contours up and down on the edge of the valley which widened out as it approached the town.

We saw high cliffs on the opposite side of the valley and had a birds-eye view of the town as we made our final descent which brought us out at the Sportsplatz on the edge of town, where Sandra was waiting for us in the motor home.

King of the Mountains – Chris, who'll always be a king to me.
Distance covered – 9.8 miles.
Total distance covered – 449.8 miles. Only 100 miles to go!

It was almost 1pm and we decided to drive to our hotel for the night, then come back into Mayen to look around for an hour before heading for Cologne with Chris and Tom. We were booked into a small hotel in Monreal, a village about eight miles the far side of Mayen and we easily found the village and discovered that it was a picture-postcard, pretty village, full of original Tudor-style buildings with a river and ruined schloss on the hill to complete the scene. Out hotel, the Artarus Weingalerie, was owned by a couple who made and sold their own wine and they kindly agreed to let me use the bath in their living accommodation (the only one in the building) so I was able to have a soak before we drove back to Mayen.

It was a warm, sunny afternoon and for one of the few times on the walk, I felt like a tourist strolling, or hobbling should I say, round the town centre. Mayen is an old town with high city walls surrounding the old town which is largely pedestrianised. Sandra had dropped us off whilst she went to find somewhere to park the van and it wasn't long before Chris, Tom and I found a café in the main platz and sat in the sun enjoying a café crème and watching the world go by as we waited for Sandra. Reading the local tourist information leaflets, we learned that Mayen is a very old town with signs of settlement dating back 3,000 years. The town was recognised by Rudolf von Hapsburg in the 13th century and much of the Alt Stadt dates back to the 17 century. Today, it is tourist attraction, market town for the country people to the west and commuter town for locals travelling into Koblenz or the industry of the Rhine valley.

Whilst we waited, I rang Phil who had flown into Dortmund with Sam and was held up in the heavy Friday-afternoon traffic on the autobahn system to our north. As time was passing, we hatched a plan whereby I would accompany Tom and Chris in the motor home up to Cologne whilst Sandra waited at our hotel for Phil and Sam to arrive. So after a quick look around the town centre, we drove back to Monreal for a second time, dropped Sandra off and within five minutes, were on the motorway system, heading east towards the Rhine to pick up the main north-south route.

It was a smooth journey northwards and we could see the queues heading the other way as we neared Bonn and the conurbations around the old West German capital and nearby Cologne. Straight into the airport in good time for the flight back. Tom had his school Prom the following evening and must have been looking forward to getting home and seeing all of his friends. It had been a brilliant gesture by him and his Dad and we hugged and said our goodbyes before they headed towards check-in.

With time to spare I decided to park up and use the WiFi facilities in the terminal to check e-mails, sent my diary update and spent 30 minutes over a coffee before setting off towards the south. After our unguided tour, two evenings before, I found the route I needed without too much trouble and settled down for my first real drive in the motor home. Fortunately, by now, it was after 7pm and the earlier hold-ups had evaporated as the Friday exodus south came to an end and the drive was fine, me being cautious and still not entirely comfortable in such a large vehicle.

As I neared Monreal, I rang Sandra to find that the others had arrived and had gone to the Italian Trattoria in the village. As I passed the restaurant heading back to our hotel, I hooted the horn to let them know I was back. It was a 10 minute walk down to the hotel and by the time I arrived they had ordered me a main course and were telling me all about the village and how pretty it was.

I found out more for myself as we sauntered back from the restaurant after a good meal and two glasses of red wine. Monreal, it transpired has won several Most Beautiful Village awards and it

183

really did look gorgeous in the fading light of a warm June evening. The houses, some dating back to the 15th century, were packed tightly together, overhanging the river, each with a tiny, immaculately-maintained garden.

Striding out with Tom and Chris through Alt

A Walk of Faith

A warm welcome to Germany

The Nurburgring from our hotel

John Reeve

Monreal – picture postcard pretty

Another one of those trees!

The Rhine and the Main
Mayen and the Rhine to Hattersheim and the Waldstadion

A bright morning and noticeably warmer than recent days. I met our host at breakfast, a friendly giant who was a good three inches taller than me. He told us about their wine merchandising business with the majority of their sales made via the internet. He and his wife had bought their first small vineyard, on the Mosel about 30 miles away and just produced their first home-grown vintage, a Kabinett Riesling. Foregoing the offer to try a glass at breakfast, we looked around their display area and I bought six bottles of their own label as a memento of our stay. He also solved the mystery of the stripped pine trees and the tassels and explained that they were part of an ancient custom associated with May Day and the young, unmarried men of the village.

Sam, who was 13, was raring to start walking and after the short drive to Mayen, he and I picked up the walk from the Sportsplatz leaving Sandra and Phil to begin their game of leap-frog, bringing the motor home and Phil's hire car up along our route. We headed initially towards the town centre and just before the old city walls skirted to the north and west to avoid the town centre and found the road to Koblenz. The streets were busy with Saturday morning shoppers and we soon reached the N258 and began our long approach to the Rhine.

We had noticed signposts for Koblenz way back in the middle of the hill country but it had seemed another world, somewhere to head towards, a stepping stone towards Frankfurt; today, all being well, we would reach Koblenz and cross the Rhine. The end of the walk seemed suddenly to be getting very close. After the picturesque river valley, trees and cliffs of our western approach to Mayen, our exit to the east was through a very different landscape. Out-of-town shopping stretched for one-

and-a-half miles, we could have been in Macclesfield or Minneapolis except that everywhere was so clean and tidy but also very dusty, there hadn't been much rain here recently, not like the forests we had left.

By now, Sam's excitement had turned to boredom as he realised that walking to Frankfurt with his old Uncle who insisted on walking faster than he was used to, was no fun. After chatting away for the first 30 minutes, he had started to drop behind and I had to slow down every five minutes to let him catch up. Fortunately, Phil joined us and we settled into a 3.75 mph pace across the wide plain. It was more like Belgium again, being able to see the road ahead for 1-2 miles twisting and turning as it headed east.

We played 20 questions with Sam and it seemed from his choices that he was fascinated by mass-murderers, Jack the Ripper and Sweeney Todd being two of his favourites. Phil fooled me as we neared Ochtendung, saying that there was a very steep drop and then climb back out of a river valley, so it was a pleasant surprise when I realised that the walk into the small town was much easier than I had expected.

We had our first stop here, my shin seemed to be getting better and better and there was no longer a need to lie down at every opportunity. A cup of coffee and short sit down, then up and off. We agreed to have our second break before Koblenz and Phil joined me again for Part Two. By now Sam was alternating between walking for 30 minutes with us and riding in the motor home with Sandra.

We were quickly out of Ochtendung and back onto the plain, more switchback road twisting up and down towards the river. We passed through Bassenheim, under one of the major autobahn routes and the road began to gradually drop away ahead of us. We could see the much steeper eastern edge of the river valley, perhaps 10 miles away in the distance. Between there and us, there was a mass of houses and other buildings and somewhere, not one but two of Western Europe's great rivers.

The second stop after 15.5 miles was a longer 60-minute break and I dozed up on the bed at the rear of the motor home before preparing for our final approach. Sandra was going to walk with

A Walk of Faith

me through Koblenz whilst Phil and Sam drove ahead to find somewhere for us to stay that night. We would drive back later to collect the motor home and bring it up to our accommodation.

Whilst Tim would have liked many aspects of the walk, one thing I wasn't sure that he would be so comfortable with, was the lack of certainty about some of our days walking. Nowhere to stay and it was now 2pm on Saturday afternoon and no definite route through the city. Sandra and I had agreed to head towards one of the bridges over the Mosel, then to the southern Rhine crossing but we hadn't checked out the detail of this part of the walk and our map wasn't large scale so as to give us any certainty. I was very comfortable with the adventure of finding our way, making decisions as we went along and enjoyed not knowing what to expect. To me we had done an amazing job in planning and organising the walk to the considerable extent that we has been able to and I enjoyed the occasional gaps and working things out as we went along.

Sandra, on the other hand, would have preferred to have more things sorted out in advance and I suspect that Tim would have been the same. He enjoyed trying new things and going to different places and often appeared laid-back, taking things in his stride but behind the 'front', he liked to know what was going on, what to expect and was less keen on surprises and unexpected changes to plans. So the afternoon we crossed the Rhine, momentous in some respects, would not have been one of Tim's favourite parts of the walk. The only aspect that was solid and certain was that we were heading for Lahnstein where the river Lahn joins the Rhine, a suburb about four miles south of Koblenz. As events turned out, he would have been right to be cautious!

The N258 continued north-east towards a major Rhine crossing looping around the north of Koblenz. Our plan was to turn to the right and cut down towards the Mosel and cross over onto a narrow triangle of the city that sat between the two rivers. Within 10 minutes we had lost our way on the map and resorted to following the slope downhill heading in what we hoped was the right direction. Two or three times, we zig-zagged across and then down residential streets and found ourselves in the middle

John Reeve

of a large estate. We asked a man working in his front garden, he directed us through a cutting, along another street and through the gaps between the houses we caught a glimpse of the river and the bridge away to our left.

Although not direct, our route had not taken us too far out of our way and we were happy as we crossed the river, broad and impressive. Was the Rhine really wider and grander than this?

Exactly a week after our walk through Liege, we knew we were back in the city when we faced the maze of slip roads and crossovers on the east bank and gradually worked our way across the roads and headed onwards. This area was designed for four- or two-wheel travel, not for pedestrians and there were few other people about. Stopping for the umpteenth time to check the map, we realised that our proposed route took us straight up and over a very steep and heavily wooded ridge, sticking out like a green strip on top of the buildings all around. After 17 miles, this didn't seem like such a good idea and we opted to turn north, skirt round the ridge and head for the northerly Rhine crossing instead.

This route took us alongside the railway line heading in to the Hauptbahnhof and we searched without success, to find a way to cross over. Eventually, as we both began to get frustrated by the lack of progress, Sandra asked two elderly women as we approached yet another major road intersection with fly-overs and under-passes and they guided us across two roads, down some steps and through the train station. Pointing ahead, they explained that the river was two blocks away and thanking them, we set off with renewed energy.

Arriving at the river, we saw two bridges, one three miles away to the south, the other much closer to our left. We could see traffic on the nearer bridge and pedestrians walking across the river and decided to follow the wide embankment, busy with people strolling along the water's edge to the northerly crossing. We asked someone to take a rare photograph of us together and after a minor detour to get up onto the bridge, we crossed the Rhine and stopped briefly to admire the view. After a bright start, the sky had gradually clouded over and was darkening from the west. On the far side, we turned right down the slip road to head south and I stopped, pointing and laughing to Sandra. We had arrived at the exact spot where two months before, we had parked our car and I had walked across a small children's play area and down some steps to the river itself. Here was the same place we had parked and I was pointing across to the playground and the river just beyond.

Sandra remembered the moment as together we crossed the play area and reached the half a dozen steps. In early April, the path running along the riverside had been covered in flotsam and partially submerged under the river's flood. After all the rain of the last fortnight, what would we find now? To my delight, the path was dry; the river was high and lapping just below the edge but it was going to be OK for us to walk along and we could see others walking away to our left. It was another big moment on the walk and because we were so close to the water itself, brought it home that we had reached a major landmark on our journey.

The river was flowing swiftly, swollen and muddy brown, carrying water down from the Alps and beyond. Almost at eye level, it appeared even more impressive than from the bridge above. Its raw power evident in the tree trunks sweeping past like twigs thrown off a bridge in a children's boat race; the people on the far bank reduced to match stick size, emphasising the scale of the scene. It would be a good walk as we headed upstream. All the same, I was starting to tire and decided to phone Phil and check on his progress. Bad news; they had been driving up and down the east bank for several miles but without success. Apparently, it was another Feast Day on the coming Monday and all the hotels were either fully booked for the long weekend or closed. He had a couple more places to try and we agreed to continue south towards Lahnstein whilst he and Sam continued their search for accommodation.

John Reeve

Sandra crossing the Mosel

By the banks of the Rhine

A Walk of Faith

We followed the path for three miles watching the huge river-barges, often with one or two cars parked on the deck ploughing their way down towards Rotterdam and the North Sea or, fighting the current, heading towards Basle and Switzerland. Flags of all nationality, many Eastern European, Hungary, Serbia and Romania; I imagined the Rhine joining up via tributaries and canals with the Danube, forming a trans-continental water route all the way to the Black Sea. With the majestic castles and folklore stretching back into the mists of time as their backdrop, Masefield might have included a line in his famous poem about the river barges of the Rhine. As we walked, we could hear the engines of the upstream vessels gradually catching up and overtaking us, those heading north appearing to travel at twice the speed as they closed the gap between us and headed onwards.

After 45 minutes I rang Phil again; they had found us a bed for the night, sighs of relief, four of us in the motor home would not have been my idea of fun. It seemed as if the hotel was not too far away from where we were and we agreed to meet after another mile where our route took us away from the river and back into the road system. As we turned away from the river, I remembered the road and we crossed over the railway and over the main road leading away from the southerly river crossing. This was where I was expecting to meet but phoning Phil it appeared that he was somewhere else and unsure about the local routes in a very busy road system.

We pressed on, arriving at a retail park and I rested whilst Sandra looked unsuccessfully for somewhere to sit down and have a drink. My legs were tightening up badly after 23 miles but there was nothing else to do but 'get on with it' and within half a mile, totally by chance, we walked up to the motor home parked right by the blue metal bridge over the river Lahn.

Yellow Jersey Award to Sam for being the youngest walker at 13 years old.
Distance covered - 23.6 miles.
Total distance covered - 473.4 miles.

Instead of the spacious motor home, it was Phil's small hire car that I climbed into after my stretch down and as Phil missed the exit off the motorway, my thigh cramped badly in the back seat and he hastily pulled over to allow me to stretch out again. Despite the road system, the Hotel-Restaurant Weinlaube wasn't far away, tucked into a quiet residential area. As we brought our bags out of the car, I noticed a black, old-fashioned English phone-box on the corner of the car park and we checked in just as a coach full of German tourists pulled onto the car park. By now it was after 7pm. A cold and then hot shower helped and I rubbed my legs, put on a Glucosamine patch and wrote up the web diary whilst the others drove back to Bassenheim to pick up the motor home.

When they returned, I was still fairly zonked, stumbled down the two flights of stairs and managed no further than the hotel restaurant, where they were sitting waiting for me. Most people seemed to be finishing their meals but a glass of wine and a good steak revived me. Sandra and Phil told me that, as they sat near the end of road looking at the map to decide the best route back through the maze of roads and intersections that hugged the river side, another car pulled up and a man asked if he could help. He gave them directions to Bassenheim and then, going right out of his way, led them in his own car, for 10 miles back to the motor home. Another stroke of luck, another piece of unexpected kindness, along our journey.

Later as I talked to Tim before climbing into bed, I reflected that it had been quite a day; a new team, a very different type of walk, the anticipation of crossing the Rhine and the ache of walking further than I had wanted. But we were closing fast on Frankfurt, only three more serious days walking and we would be at Hattersheim.

I paid for the last hour's walk with an unsettled night, legs that continued to ache and refused to calm down until the last dark hour when thoughts of the walk to come, mixed with the desire to turn over and sleep the day away. What was the point of it all; without Tim, my life was a failure and a mess. The other three were already in breakfast by the time I had negotiated the stairs and I had a gunslinger moment as I walked into the main restaurant area. Every table appeared to be occupied by the coach passengers, the room full of noise as yesterday's experiences were revisited and plans made for the day ahead. As I made my way through the tables searching for Sandra, the room suddenly went quiet and everyone turned and looked up at me. With my shorts and Walking to the World Cup T-shirt, I guess that I must have looked quite a sight, stumbling along, clearly with no idea where I was going. Within an instant, conversations resumed and I retraced my steps to find the others sat at a table on the far side of the bar area, near the other non-coach guests. I felt a little better after cereal and fresh bread and jam.

Back to the blue bridge over the Lahn on a cloudy and cool Sunday morning to continue the walk along the Rhine with Sam whilst Sandra and Phil drove the vehicles ahead to drop off the hire car and rejoin us in the motor home. We walked very slowly through Lahnstein, Sam happy to dawdle, chatting much more than he had the day before. I was happy to ease into the day gradually. The motor home soon reappeared, Sandra climbed out to join me and Sam climbed in to ride with his dad. The pattern was set for the remainder of the morning, Sandra and I walking, Sam in and out of the van at regular intervals.

After the town, we re-joined the riverside path and it was a pleasant, easy walk with lots of families out walking, younger and older couples, families with younger children riding bikes, the occasional jogger and plenty of 'Guten Morgen's as we passed by. We slowly picked up our pace and I enjoyed the proximity of the water and marvelled again, at the power of the great river. The unstoppable flow of the water heading back the way we had walked and the branches and assorted jetsam that sped by, created the illusion that we were travelling much faster than we were and we continued the walk for 4-5 miles talking about our arrival in Frankfurt and our plans for our stay in the city. At one point, I imagined Tim watching us walking and talking and hoped that he was enjoying seeing his mum and dad getting on with things. We passed three of the many Rhine castles perched high up on their vantage points and imagined the scene two hundred years ago, the river a reassuring constant.

We had picked out Braubach at the place where we would leave the river on its south to north journey and turn eastwards again. The old town fortified with its old walls was busy with

Sunday strollers, the cafés full of people enjoying a coffee or a late breakfast and we slowed and looked at the old buildings before heading up the slope and through one of the old gates.

The hinterland of the small town was industrialised and we met Phil and the motor home alongside one of the factories that sprawled up the tributary valley. He was happy to continue to drive and let Sandra walk with me. After a short break we set off for the last serious climb of the walk, into the woods and out of the Rhine valley. It was a good walk along a quiet road with light Sunday lunch-time traffic, the gradient gradually increasing as the valley narrowed and the road began to twist and turn. The river gurgled away to us as we crossed and re-crossed its clear, rushing water and we past isolated houses hiding alongside the stream, climbing steadily higher. As I had come to expect, after 4km of uphill we reached the steepest part of the ascent. I resisted the temptation to put my head down and push on as hard as I could and instead stayed close to Sandra, happy to let her set the pace. Then, ever so faintly, I heard country and western music somewhere behind us and over the next five minutes it slowly drew closer and closer. Almost as we reached the top, a low slung motorbike pulling a small trailer, bedecked in chrome and glitter with rider wearing leathers, dark glasses and peaked black cap, came slowly past us, doing no more than 15mph compared to our 3.5mph. Now that's what I call travelling in style and I wondered where he was heading for.

Phil and Sam were waiting for us in a lay-by at the top of the climb and we had our first proper stop of the day after 8.2 miles. Hot coffee and a piece of strawberry flan that Phil had bought in Braubach hit the spot and Sandra took over the driving to let Phil walk with me for the remainder of the day. He had been studying the map and picked out several short-cuts across paths to shorten our route. They turned out to be a mixed blessing, some working better than others and the rest of the day was bitty, with lots of stops to check our progress and route but we avoided having to re-trace our steps.

The countryside was different again, mixed farming with more arable than to the west, plenty of trees still but woods rather than forests, far more open with a rolling, limestone landscape. The roads were wider and in better condition than many of the country lanes we had followed in the Eifel region. We set off towards Schweighausen but turned off across the fields towards our right to cut off the last mile into the village. Another road and a second path took us further east and we stopped for lunch after 13 miles.

Walk three of the day was definitely 'off piste'. We were following footpaths with Sandra driving ahead to Singhofen where we expected to pass through an hour later. Instead, we spent two hours finding our way down one side of a ravine, stopping every five minutes to check the route as we crossed another path and then into a secret valley. This one was so secret it could have survived the 30 Years War and WW2 without waking up. There was a very narrow entrance commanded by a country house with garden running down to a stream. It was the end of the road but no, a path skirted up the valley side and then dropped down and crossed the stream as it gurgled and splashed by, gathering pace, as it headed north towards the Lahn, meandering left and right.

The wooden signs looked as if they had survived from another century and the stone path smooth with the footsteps of people over the generations, glittered in the shafts of sunlight that broke through the mantle of green. Right in the depths of the valley stood a tiny Augustine Schule, reachable only via a three mile track over a very steep pass. As we peered down onto the school to our left, we saw the elaborate network of canals and dykes that the monks had created over the ages, serving to both irrigate the rich strips of vegetable garden in the valley bottom and channel off excess water in times of flood. As we neared the head of the valley, the stream snaked first left then right through a gorge and into another tree-covered ravine. It was a long and tiring walk to get us not very far but I wouldn't have missed it for anything. Not only secret, but also totally enchanting; another memorable episode on my walk of memories.

John Reeve

Sam on the blue bridge over the Lahn

A proud father and uncle

Sandra was almost as pleased to see us when we reached Singhofen as we were to see her and any thoughts of continuing had long since evaporated. It was a warm and bright afternoon and we drove back to Braubach following the river Lahn though Bad Elms with its grand buildings and tourists so that Phil and Sam could pick up their hire car. They were heading back to Dortmund and from there to their home in Spain – a real flying visit but their support and company had been really appreciated.

Yellow Jersey award to Sandra for climbing like a mountain goat.
Distance covered - 19.3 miles.
Total distance covered - 492.7 miles.

Our bed for the next two nights was at the Berghof at Berghausen, a pretty, three-storey, village hotel. We had picked up a leaflet and used the toilets on our earlier expedition and easily found the village and parked the motor home on the busy car park. The hotel had 30 or so rooms, surprisingly large for a small village and was Tyrolean-style with steep wooden gable ends and wooden flower boxes, bedecked with red and green beneath each window. As the night before, the hotel was full with people enjoying the Bank Holiday weekend and the restaurant was busy with a comfortable, friendly atmosphere and good food. Unfortunately, Sandra's very nicely-presented salad was drowned in dressing, we were learning fast about German customs.

Dan rang on his journey west from Riga with the guys in their motor home. It sounded a lot smaller and less modern than ours but they were using Dave's connection with the Marriott hotel chain, to stay Five Star as they travelled through Poland, Hungary and Austria, and would only be sleeping in the van when they had no other alternative when they arrived in Germany for the World Cup. It was good to talk to him but the pleasure was followed, like clockwork, by sadness. As I wrote my diary for the day, I thought of Tim, of how kind and considerate he was beneath the brash and stubborn exterior he presented and what a waste it was. He had only wanted a chance to live.

I wrote in my diary at the end of Day 27, 'nearly there' but at the start of the day I was in a determined mood, wanting to get in a good day's walking after the meanders of yesterday's footpaths and the forgotten valley. We had re-cast the route last night and decided to stop messing about up secret valleys and get on with it – thanks Tim. The only disappointment was that it meant I wouldn't walk through Katzenelnbogen – yes, the cat's elbow really does exist! The B260, the Deutsche Limestrasse, cuts through this part of Rheinland/Phalz and Hesse like a knife from Nassau to Wiesbaden and I was going to walk a seven mile stretch this morning. After the wonderful support from so many family members and friends, it was down to Sandra and me (and Tim, of course) for the final stage of the walk into Frankfurt. Sandra helped me put Vaseline on my feet in the motor home and I felt more energised than I had done for the last few days, knowing it was up to me to set the pace, there was no one else I could tag onto and let them lead me onwards.

It was the Whitsun Holiday and the road was very quiet as I came out of Singhofen. The Limestrasse, wide and straight, dipped ahead of me and then rose up to the first of many crowns before it slipped away again like a snake stretching across the countryside. It was another cool and fresh morning with light cloud and a good day for walking. I was soon into my stride, 4mph, up and down, up and down, feeling fine. Tim was there and I talked to him out loud; about the text messages he used to send me. Now he was my guide and my advisor, helping me work out the right thing to do, always clear about his priorities was Tim.

I was startled out of my conversation by a stubborn motorist who despite being able to see me at least quarter of a mile away, refused to move out at all from their careful passage along the road side and with me being equally stubborn, I managed to clip the wing mirror with one of my walking sticks as it almost forced me off the road. From peace to anger in seconds, it summed up how fragile my moods were.

Hohenstein was the first town on today's route, Sandra was waiting in a car park and I stopped for a moment to talk to her. She probably missed the absence of someone to talk to more than I did but she seemed equally pleased that we were on our own for a change. She had managed to find one shop that was open and bought some sandwiches for lunch. Out of Hohenstein and up to a roundabout with a landmark windmill, I took the left fork and headed into a sizeable forested area, heading for a pathway shortcut. It was another long straight stretch of road, gradually rising rather than the switchback earlier. Chris rang about season tickets for Oakwell; he had called in at the stadium and rang again a few minutes later to say that the tickets were bought.

The trees were tightly packed in regiments stretching into the darkness of the forest; I noticed silver bands tied onto trees all along the route. After a minor junction, my footpath was unmistakeable, even for me, and I turned left, climbed up passing two cyclists checking their bikes and began a long gradual descent on a soft and springy track, good for the knees. The trees never far away began to thin out and were replaced by bushes, now more heath than forest. The cyclists came slowly by and I kept them in sight for five minutes looking ahead to catch a glimpse as I turned each corner. I passed a number of walkers, all couples out enjoying the week-day holiday and after one 'Morgen' as I passed another pair of ramblers, I heard 'Are you really walking to the World Cup?' spoken in a Home Counties accent and came abruptly to a halt. We chatted for a few minutes; originally from Wiltshire, they lived in Wiesbaden and had driven up for a day in the country. Wishing me well, they continued on their way and I was, almost immediately, out of the trees and bushes and into open farmland, the next village straight ahead.

The path merged into a metalled lane that widened as I approached the village of Laufenselden. Along with the Three Crutches pub back in Strood, it was undoubtedly the most appropriately named stopping point of the walk. Sandra was waiting in a car park right by a junction in the middle of the deceptively large village. I'd covered the first seven miles in an hour and three-quarters and nine miles in two hours 18 minutes – a good start to the day – and enjoyed a coffee and a sandwich feeling tired but fine.

The next session took me along a country lane, up into a wood and then down a long, twisting descent, walking round bend after bend after bend for over 30 minutes down into the bottom of a river valley where the main road and the railway line competed for space with the river heading north to the Lahn. The slope wasn't so steep that it hurt my knees and shins but the constant downhill began to make my feet sore as they pushed forwards in my trainers. As I crossed the railway line, I saw three cyclists preparing for the ascent and said 'Good luck guys', as I passed.

After the peace and calm of the wood, the main road was windy with sweeping bends and a high cliff face on my immediate left as I headed towards Burg Hohenstein. Fortunately, there were no lorries on the road due to the Public Holiday but it looked a great route for bikers and there were hundreds of them, heading in both directions, from lone riders to groups of ten, their engines shattering the quiet and echoing off the cliff face. At least I could hear them coming and they tended to give me as wide berth as they swung left and right around the bends.

I reached Burg Hohenstein with the Ober Burg with its old castle high on my right and at the edge of the Unter Burg, I spotted the motor home tucked away at the back of a large car park and stopped for lunch.

I had made the rendezvous sooner than Sandra had expected and lunch of pasta, ham and bean salad was still at an early stage of preparation but I was happy to wait and rest and enjoyed the hot lunch followed by a doze on the bed. The sun was out by now and shone through the tiny roof window making me feel even more comfortable and disinclined to walk any further. But always, that voice, quietly firm and insistent, 'Get on with it, Dad'.

The third session turned out to be mainly uphill through the tiny villages of Breithardt and Steckenroth. After the strong start to the day, I was happy to ease down slightly as the afternoon warmed up and enjoyed what would be almost my last few miles of countryside walking. Over the last 10 days, I had seen countless buzzards circling above along my route and that afternoon, in between the two villages, I spent five minutes gazing up at a solitary buzzard, dark and powerful looking with broad wings being challenged by a much smaller, faster and fiercer bird of prey. At first, it seemed that the larger bird would carry on its patrol, circling its territory but gradually the smaller bird forced the buzzard higher and higher and eventually its sniping attacks forced it to retreat and it headed off into the distance being pursued by its adversary.

At Steckenroth, after 18 miles, I was ready to stop for the day but Sandra advised there was another steep hill ahead and knowing that I didn't like to finish and start at the bottom of a hill, suggested that I continue for another one-and-a-half miles and finish where my country road meets a larger highway. It was a warm climb in the late afternoon sunshine and I was glad to see the motor home again in a small parking area near to the road junction and pleased that I had another hill behind me.

Yellow Jersey Award to Tim for always giving me good advice.
Distance covered – 19.4 miles.
Total distance covered – 512.1 miles.

We were going back to the Berghof and with the road through Katzelnbogen closed, it meant a detour on the slow country roads. Our room at the hotel was a good size, well furnished with a balcony and views across to the hills on the other side of the valley, a flock of wind turbines turning slowly on the tops. After a bath and rub down, it was diary time and afterwards, I spoke to our hostess who kindly allowed me to use the hotel internet connection and my data stick to send through the web diary update. We had lots of messages of support and there were a few tears as I read them and made a few notes to remember to tell Sandra. I checked the 'Just Giving' web page to see that the online donations had surged by over £2,500 following the radio interviews back in Adenau and many more kind messages of encouragement and support. There were also e-mails from a US producer making a documentary about football fans from around the world, a Hong Kong Cable TV Station, Radio 5 Live and a German Cable TV company all wanting to meet up in Frankfurt. As we drew nearer and nearer and the hype surrounding the tournament built and built, it seemed that out short visit to the tournament would be a busy one. Before dinner, I also rang Ursula, our contact at the Goethe Gymnasium and arranged to meet her at 6.30pm on Wednesday in a car park on the outskirts of Hattersheim, just two days and 30 miles away.

It should have been a nice meal but Sandra, perhaps after my time and update about the e-mail messages, was feeling excluded and on the edge of it all. Maybe it was also the nearness of Frankfurt and the uncertainty of what awaited us. The meal was fine, the service friendly and the restaurant less busy than the previous evening but our mood made it difficult to really relax.

A bad night followed, possibly the worst of the walk. My legs ached constantly until about 5am when after some hot rub, I finally slipped into a fitful sleep and woke at seven. It wasn't just my knees and calves but my thighs and quads that were sore. That fast start the day before, which had felt good at the time, had paid me back. But sunshine and a brilliantly blue sky, the brightest since Calais, made all the difference and I felt fine getting up. We filled the water tank and then enjoyed a good breakfast, paid the bill and said thank you and good bye to our hostess. It had been a good place to stay and another example of the kindness and hospitality we met throughout our journey.

The drive was slow along our re-directed route with morning traffic and short queues at many of the junctions and it was almost 9am before I set off. The path across from the junction climbed uphill in a straight line for half a mile until the main track turned sharply left and a narrow track signed, No Vehicles, continued ahead. The map told me to continue forwards but thinking that the main path might zig-zag back towards my route just ahead, I followed it. The sun glimpsing through the trees, it was cool in the morning shade but I was warm from the uphill trek. As I had hoped the path soon turned back to the right but after another 400 yards turned left again and I could see the straight path cutting through the dark trees for another 100 yards, I must have gone wrong already!

Where the path turned left, there was a much fainter track leading to the right. It might take me back to join my route and reluctant to re-trace my steps I decided to give it a go. I would either end up where I wanted to be or completely lost, which would it be? At least I was paying attention and not marching along lost in my thoughts. The path faded even more and I had to climb over fallen branches and wade through deep puddles – I had my waterproof shoes on for the last path of the journey – but

A Walk of Faith

there were always some signs that other people, some with horses, had passed this way. After five minutes, I saw a clearing ahead and came out onto a wide and well-marked trail; my gamble had paid off.

By now I was on the far edge of the trees and came out in the bright sunlight to open fields, the land dropping away ahead of me; the village of Orlen to my right. The air had that early summer freshness but was warming and hinted of a hot day ahead. There was a choice of paths leading across the fields and I asked an elderly man, who looked as if he might be out on his daily constitutional from a nearby nursing home, and he pointed ahead. I passed two female joggers, the first runners I had seen for over a week, and reached the road. Orlen was down the hill to my right and Sandra was waiting on the road-side. She had checked out the next section as far as Neudorf and gave me directions and a short-cut to take.

Continuing up the hill out of the village, I rang Joan Conway, my client on the Isle of Man, she seemed surprised and pleased to hear from me. She had been following my progress and it was good to talk about the people I knew and recent developments, a touch of normality in the midst of everything. It was TT week and the island was buzzing. I was due to go over in 2½ weeks time to attempt the 84 miles in 24 hours Parish Walk and told her that at the moment I was far from certain that I would be in a fit state. No sooner had I finished talking to Joan than Tracey from Dream FM called for a live update interview and before I knew it, I was walking on the hard shoulder of a busy road heading towards a motorway that cut across the road in the distance with Neudorf in the valley to my right. My phone rang again, this time with a message from Sandra telling me to take a cycle path to avoid the busy road, too late. But her short-cut worked fine and I skirted round Neudorf and up a short, steep climb. Thinking happy thoughts about Tim, the sunshine always helps, I fairly sailed up the slope and onto a long downhill stretch into Engenhahn. The village looked pretty in the sunshine, wearing its best clothes and with a bright smile on its face, and I followed the road down the hill and off to the right approaching the junction where I had expected to meet Sandra. There was no sign of her and I rang and had a confusing conversation leaving us both uncertain about where each other was. I pressed on for another 20 minutes, annoyed at first but then smiling to myself, as Tim would have quoted, 'It's just a game, focker'.

I found the motor home in the railway station car park at Niederhausen, full with cars and busy with passengers leaving the station. I'd walked further than planned but another 9½ miles were completed and it meant I could coast along for the rest of the day. Freshly-made sandwiches and cakes made a good snack; it was nice just the two of us. A call from the documentary-maker; they have tracked down 10 people from 10 competing nations, all heading for Germany, all with their own stories and different motivations but all drawn together by football. Sounded interesting.

The second stage took me to Eppstein, initially along a quiet country road, the last of the walk, and then onto a nightmarishly busy road with no pavement or path walking along the narrow hard shoulder towards the traffic, the road twisting around a series of blind bends – not nice. On cue, my left knee began to ache badly turning it into an even harder walk, such a contrast with earlier in the day. Sandra was tucked away right at the back of a car park on the edge of Eppstein and I almost missed her. A longer break and a doze, I only planned to walk for another three miles as far as Lorsbach, no point in getting too far ahead of myself.

By the time I was ready to go again, the sky had clouded over but it was still warm and I set off feeling much better. I decided to leave the main road which ran around the tightly packed, old town of Eppstein and take a short cut through its narrow streets built long before cars had been imagined. It seemed such a contrast to the speed and noise that surrounded it. I settled comfortably into its slower pace and headed up a side street towards castle ruins on the hill and the high street.

Leaving Eppstein behind, I was relieved to see that the minor road I was taking to Lorsbach had a wide cycle path and my third walk of the day was as pleasant as the first. I was heading almost due south along a valley that was gradually widening as it came closer to Frankfurt and the river Main with steep slopes to the valley sides, the trees and heights of the Taunus stretching away into the distance. I was content walking along my safe, flat cycle path rather than being up in those high hills again and I thought about Tim.

We had texted each other daily over the last eight months of his life. Whenever I went out to work, wherever I was going, I would text him when I knew he was awake and always when I left him in hospital to make the sad journey home, I would text him when we were back. In the mornings, he began a routine texting, 'Make sure you win, Dad, I'm going to,' and it had become one of our sayings to each other. As I walked I thought about what he had meant by that saying and what it said about him and his take on life. He was very competitive and wanted to win and do well at everything he did. I used to talk to him about having a goal for each day, something no matter how small that you wanted to get done and to achieve, that was winning. Often when we saw each other at the end of the day, we would ask, 'How was your day? Did you win?' Had life itself become a competition, to be won or lost?

To me, he will always be a winner. He wanted to win, that was important; to do the very best he could, to try his hardest and know that he had, that's what mattered. Not to go into things half-heartedly, not to accept second best; always to expect and to hope to win but to accept also that nobody wins all the time. Tim had experienced his triumphs, far fewer than he should have enjoyed and had, through bitter circumstances, learned to deal with his disasters. In the end, I believe that he had come to treat them both the same. A winner.

Lorsbach is a small town with a long, main street and it started raining just as I spotted the motor home tucked in on the roadside, towards the end of the street, by a garage with an old-fashioned Michelin man that marked the end of Day 28. I had covered 17.5 miles and an overall distance of 529.6 miles. I wrote on the web diary that the Yellow Jersey was getting a bit smelly and needed a good wash.

We had decided to treat ourselves on our last night before Frankfurt and booked into a Ramada Jarvis hotel close by the Frankfurt-Cologne motorway, Four Star luxury after our motels, small hotels, B&Bs and the motor home. Reception was efficient, the hotel seemed fairly busy with business guests and our room large, air-conditioned and with a bath. We had noticed a Spa and decided to take a look, taking our cossies with us. It was large and appeared well-equipped with a large central pool, various saunas and steam rooms and it seemed quiet as we went our separate ways to the changing areas. When we came out into the spa area we noticed several people sitting reading books or papers, dressed in white robes. We decided to take a swim first, got down in the pool and I enjoyed the sensation of swimming and walking through the cool water and its soothing effect on my sore legs. I had been to a German sauna once before and so was not surprised when a man and woman got up from their chairs, took off their robes and jumped naked into the pool. But Sandra was astonished, taken totally by surprise and over the next few minutes we saw first one, then two, then more people in their birthday suits making us feel seriously over-dressed.

A little later, Sandra climbed out of the pool saying she was going for a sauna. I noticed her checking the various log cabins presumably to find one that wasn't too hot and was empty. After she disappeared into one, I swam for five minutes to loosen up my legs and then went to join her. Imagine my surprise when opening the door, I saw Sandra in 'when in Frankfurt, do as the Frankfurters do' mood, with her swimming costume lying at her side and as I laughed with her, my shorts joined them on the wooden bench. I'm sure that we had already been spotted as Britishers, or possibly Americans, and we continued to give ourselves away as we tried to look at ease as we came out of the sauna, had a shower and tried out the nearby steam room. After 28 days of walking shoes, yellow jerseys and striding out on the highways and byways of Western Europe, tip-toeing in the nude around a spa pool felt as surreal as the belly-dancers running towards me back in Chelmsford. What was going on? But it turned out to be a relaxing as well as stimulating experience, I certainly felt better for it and went back up to our room to write my diary before dinner.

Over a pleasant meal we talked about the next day to come. I had 10km to walk to Hattersheim and we decided to press on from there and get close to the Waldstadion before catching a train back to Hattersheim to meet our hosts at 6.30pm. Our city street map told us there was a station called Frankfurt Niederrad about a mile from the stadium and we decided that should be our target for the new day.

The last proper day of the walk turned out to be a 16-miler with the best weather so far, Frankfurt welcomed us in style. Breakfast was down a long spiral ramp and was busy with business people when we walked in. I must have looked conspicuous in Walking to the World Cup T-shirt and shorts but I was in my familiar working clothes and everyone else was too preoccupied with the extensive, help-yourself buffet, the daily news or chatting to colleagues, to pay us more than a cursory glance. I enjoyed a good breakfast without the need to resist cereal, bacon and egg, tea and croissant and we checked out and loaded our bags into the motor home for the 22nd time.

It was a short drive back to Lorsbach, the proximity of the motorway and the big city obvious by the volume and speed of traffic, both far greater than anything we had experienced so far since leaving London. Within two minutes of setting off from the van, Sandra rang to tell me to take a left turn by a large haycart and follow the lane to a footpath that ran along the valley side. Her timing was spot on and I crossed over the river Schwarzbach, still narrow and flowing quickly towards its huge cousin the Main, and picked up the path. Out of the warmth and brightness of an early summer's morning and into the cool, calm shade of the trees.

I followed the path for 30 minutes all the way into Hofheim am Taunus, the path switching up and down the gradient, the surface soft and easy for walking, the river, the railway line and the road close by and always trees. The sunlight found its way through the thick canopy, dappling the ground around me, instantly warming my bare arms and legs as I walked through the shafts of warmth, creating patterns all around.

A last opportunity with space and time to contemplate before the hustle and bustle and Frankfurt swept us up in its irresistible pace. I said 'Morgen' to a couple of runners and six walkers, the largest group I had seen along my journey, crossed slowly heading upstream. As I came close to Hofheim, the path veered sharply and steeply to the left and a second trail dropped down to merge with a quiet, suburban street.

Out into the sunlight, noticeable warmer than when I had left it, an affluent, well-cared for residential neighbourhood; each home a castle protected by hedge or wall or elaborate gate. I passed a postman and as I neared the town centre, the homes became smaller and less secretive but still as neat and tidy and then shops and offices began to appear and I crossed into the Zentrum. Around the platz, an out-door market was in full swing and I slowed and took a few minutes to look around the stalls and called in to some of the shops that surrounded it. I was looking for something that might make an appropriate gift for our hosts to add to the gifts we had brought from home but without anything in mind, there was little likelihood of me buying anything but I did buy some wrapping paper which turned out to be a good purchase; it was very pleasant to be a normal shopper for a brief time, enjoy the morning and then move on.

My route took me back to the busy road but after a short walk, I saw the Schwarzbach over to my left and crossing the bridge, noticed the obligatory footpath running alongside the water and followed it all the way into Hattersheim. Earlier during my walk in the traffic, I had taken a call from a German Cable TV station who wanted to meet and film Sandra and I, for a news piece on their 'Guten Abend', 6pm programme. I had told them that we would be in Hattersheim by 11.30 and agreed to meet them at the Rathaus at 12. It would be a 'nice surprise' for Sandra. She was waiting for me at the car park by the Sportshalle on the edge of the town and I reckoned that my walk along the river-side should take me straight to the car park.

This time my confidence was well-placed and after a slight detour around a long, high hedge, I arrived at the large car park, the motor home parked in the shade, the water boiling for a cup of coffee. As I stretched down, I told Sandra about our appointment and was not surprised by her 'I'm not going in front of the cameras' response; a quick slurp of coffee, collect our things for the rest of the day and then off to the Town Hall. We would be meeting Frau Shoeltzke here at the car park, in seven

A Walk of Faith

hours time. Enough to film the interview, grab some lunch and follow the Main as far as Niederrad.

But the first task was to find the town centre and that wasn't as straightforward as it should have been, especially with our street map in hand. After a short conference, we turned to head in the opposite direction and a car stopped, a reporter jumped out and it transpired that we had almost literally bumped into the people we were heading off to meet. Thank you.

Another short conference lead to the decision to film in the car park and forego the pleasures of the Rathaus, it suited us just fine. Then followed 15 minutes of walking backwards and forwards being filmed 'on the move' and then a short and very comfortable interview. finally, and it all happened very easily, Sandra agreed to a request from the friendly reporter and conducted her first ever TV interview. I left her to it. She was brilliant, just so natural. Afterwards, she couldn't remember a word that she had said, but she did it and for a largely German audience. New experiences, new challenges and small steps all along our journey.

It was 12.30 before we left the motor home for the second time, on this occasion we knew which way to go and headed for the river, through Hattersheim, past the café where we had finished our sortie back in March, along a busy roadside to Sindlingen and down to the mighty river Main. Our challenge was to get around the huge Höchst chemical plant that span both sides of the river and dominated the surroundings for three miles. I had optimistically hoped that there might be a pathway along the river's edge but no chance. It meant we would have to take a long two mile route around the edge of the plant before we could re-join the river. Disappointed, we re-traced our route into Sindlingen and decided to stop at a small Italian restaurant for lunch. There were only three other diners in the restaurant but we enjoyed the break, the food and the chance to get out of the warm, lunch-time sun and felt fortified and ready for the slog as we picked up the edge of the site and followed the road, north and east.

It was a hot, dusty and grimy walk, so different from the pathway from Lorsbach just a few hours earlier, but it had to be done and we soldiered on; miles of concrete reflecting the sun, lorries grinding by, chimneys depositing their carbon legacy into the blue sky. Conversation died down and we marched in our own thoughts with the occasional look at the map to bring us out of our reveries. As soon as the fences and security came to an end, we took the next major road to our right and this brought us into the old town centre of Höechst, the river flowed just ahead of us. It wasn't as wide or as powerful as the mighty Rhine but the Main, to us little Englanders, still appeared an impressive sight. The buildings and vehicles passing on the far bank seemed a long way away, the current moved more slowly and languidly than the Rhine but looked deceptive, tempting people to 'try me'.

Our route now was easy, turn left, follow the river all the way to the railway bridge, hope we could cross it and walk down to Niederrad station. It turned out to be as straightforward as it seemed, longer in distance but interesting and easy walking, the river always there as a companion and diversion. In the old town, there was a pretty park area with a large and impressive old tower, almost lighthouse style and as we left the town, the river swung round to the right and we crossed a small bridge as another tributary joined the main flow. There were all sorts of people out walking along the wide pathway, mothers with prams and pushchairs, couples and families, business people out for a stroll after lunch. For a mile of so, we walked past gardens and allotments, full of vegetables and flowers, another example of the German need to get close to nature so close to an example of their industrial strength.

All along this stretch of the placid river, there were boats moored along the bank, others passing by in the stream. Passing under a huge motorway bridge, we came to a massive weir, the river flowing far faster on the upstream side. We walked through the riverside area of Griesheim and under a second, even larger, motorway bridge and then the railway bridge loomed ahead of us. If we couldn't cross over this bridge, it would mean turning back to the motorway bridge, with no certainty that we could cross there, or continuing for another two miles, so we peered ahead to see if we could see any pedestrians making their way alongside the occasional trains. It was only when we were within five minutes of the bridge that we finally spotted some people walking across and realised that our route would work. Just as we approached the steps leading up to the bridge, a German lady stopped us and in good English asked if we were the two English people she had seen on the TV and read about in her newspaper, the Frankfurter Rundschau. Surprised, we chatted to her for a few minutes and she offered her best wishes for a good stay in her city.

Crossing the bridge, I was suddenly overcome with emotion; I was so close to the end of my walk, to finishing my journey to honour my son's dream, when would I see Dan? For a moment, it all seemed too much and I stopped and cried. Then just as suddenly I was fine again and Sandra took my photo to mark this final stepping stone on our way.

Crossing the Main towards Niederrad

It was 10 more minutes along the hot streets of Frankfurt before we reached Niederrad station. As we turned to climb up to the platform, we saw signs for the Waldstadion, German, English and Spanish and other posters for the World Cup.

Distance covered – 16.3 miles.
Total distance covered – 545.9 miles.

It took us an extra trip down and back up the steps to realise that we could buy tickets on the platform and caught the next train into the Hauptbahnhof. Here we saw out first football supporters, hundreds of mainly English fans, like us arriving in town for the match on Saturday, clutching maps and looking lost and bewildered. Again, we took time to find our bearings across the three levels of tracks and trains and eventually jumped onto a train heading we hoped to Wiesbaden and calling at Hattersheim on the way. Back in Hattersheim, by now it was 5.30pm and we enjoyed a cappuccino and cake at an outdoor café, sitting in the warm, late-afternoon sunshine, weary but excited about our stay in the city and what the next few hours would bring.

We found our way easily back to the car park and the motor home and I typed up my web diary and uploaded the photographs before a car pulled up and three people jumped out. I had spoken to Ursula Shoelzke three or four times on the phone and exchanged e-mails with her. I had also exchanged e-mails with Rosella Lauciello, an 18-year old student at the Goethe Gymnasium. The third person was Oleg Gieberstein, head boy of the Gymnasium. We exchanged hugs without the slight embarrassment that I often associate with meeting new people, we all seemed so genuinely pleased to see each other, it made meeting up easy.

We were going into to the Gymnasium to meet the Director and other pupils who had helped with their fund-raising efforts, the following day and after chatting for a few minutes, we agreed to follow Ursula who would guide us to our hosts' home back in Höechst, where we had walked earlier. The journey took about 15 minutes with a short motorway stretch, we were in the suburbs and were totally lost by the maze of one-way streets by the time we arrived outside the flat.

Ursula rang up to the flat and Karim, Markus and Vanessa, our hosts for the next four days came down to meet us. More hugs, farewells until tomorrow to Ursula and the others and then the Adenaar family helped us to carry our bags up to their flat. It was large and spacious with dark wood furnishings making it look slightly gloomy in the evening light. Karim had generously moved out of her room into her mother's flat next door, giving us

A Walk of Faith

a large room with sofa and desk as well as bed and separate access to the bathroom next door. Whilst Sandra unpacked some of our things, I had my very necessary shower and then we joined the family for an evening meal.

Markus was 15, a pupil at the Gymnasium; Vanessa, 12, went to a local school, both children clearly very bright, speaking excellent English. Karim, their mother, was a slim, dark-haired, thoughtful woman who made us very welcome in a calm and friendly manner. She spoke English even better than her children, understanding the idiom as well as the literal meaning and we settled down to a pleasant meal; as always I was starving.

Suddenly, I realised that my second right hand, my mobile phone was missing. I went back to our room, not there. I told Sandra and Karim and went down to the motor home, not there. As I walked back up to the flat, I thought about all the people I was due to be meeting in Frankfurt over the next few days, Dan at the front of the queue; all of them relying on being able to contact me via my mobile, no meeting arrangements already set apart from the school visit, all my numbers logged into the phone. Karim noticed my agitation immediately. We worked out that I must have left the phone at the café in Hattersheim and she offered to drive us back to check.

I needed my phone and off we went through the maze of roads and parked close to the town centre. Entering the platz, we could see that the café was still open and as soon as I walked in the door, the owner noticed me, went back to the till and picked up my phone. What a lucky break, what a long, deep sigh of relief. Thanking everyone profusely, I noticed that there was already a message on the phone. It was from Tristan, he was flying into Frankfurt that evening, had hired a car and would be coming over to meet us.

We had arranged for him and another of Tim's friend, Will, to stay with Frau Shoelzke during their visit to the World Cup. Will was flying in from Frankfurt tomorrow and because Tris would be arriving late, we'd decided that he would sleep in the motor home and move over to the Shoelzke's tomorrow.

It was 9.30 and Sandra and I were tired out and happy to go back to the flat. We waited for another call from Tris and it was midnight before he rang to say he was on his way after trouble sorting out the hire car. His cheap flight had landed at a 'Frankfurt airport', somewhere near the French border, and it would be another half an hour before he reached us. I gave him the address to punch into his Sat. Nav. and continued writing my personal diary as Sandra tried to sleep. When Tris rang again I went down with the key to the motor home and showed him his bed for the night. It was good to see him, despite the late hour; he was very committed to our cause and the memory of his friend and clearly excited and looking forward to his time in Frankfurt.

A City En Fête
Frankfurt and the start of the World Cup

We were all up by 7am on Thursday June 8, the Ademmer family slipping into their daily routine; Vanessa organised and ready for the day, Markus playing the 'stay in bed' who didn't know what was happening, Karin making breakfast and getting ready for her work at the hospital. Together they were friendly, interested and easy-going, we were given our own key and told to come and go as we liked, the children were inquisitive and enjoyed speaking English with their American pronunciation.

I rang Tristan in the motor home and went down to see him. It was another cloudless sky with the sun already taking the edge off the freshness of the morning, a scorcher in prospect. Tristan was bedraggled after a less-than-average night's sleep and ready for a shower and we went back up to the flat together. Another English person for them to talk to and we enjoyed breakfast of cereal and toast and discussed our plans for the day. We had arranged to meet Frau Shoelzke at the school at 10am and after a meeting with students and the Direktor, we were going with them to a reception at the German FA at 12.30. Markus was angling to skip his first lessons and drive in with us but his mother would have none of this and the family left, all heading in different directions, leaving us to take our time before the drive into down-town Frankfurt.

Tris had worked out the Sat. Nav. on his drive from the airport and it made sense to take his car rather than drive the cumbersome van into the city. We found our way out of Höechst onto the Wiesbadener and headed towards the imposing skyline. The Gymnasium was close to the centre of the city, just off the Mainzer Landstrasse and we drove a circuit around the Festival Hälle before we spotted the school tucked in between larger buildings and found somewhere to park on a nearby side-street. We were a little early and had time for a swift coffee before walking back along the busy street to the school

We were greeted by Rosella and Oleg and taken to meet Ursula. The school was busy, it must have been break-time or class changeover, with students everywhere and Ursula suggested a short tour before our meeting. The school itself looked run-down and in need of a good coat of paint and some TLC but the students were well-behaved and lively and many said hello to us, all appearing to speak very good English. I had prepared a short slide-show with photos from the walk and brought my laptop with me, we were shown into our meeting room and I set up the laptop through a projector.

Herr Wirt, the Direktor, joined us along with about a dozen students who had all taken part in the fund-raising efforts that the school had undertaken on our behalf and we were formally welcomed to the school. I had prepared a few words of thanks in German and enjoyed the look of surprise on the faces of the students when I managed to speak ein bitschen of their own language before reverting quickly to English, so that they could continue to practice their English, I said. As well as the slide show, we had framed one of Sandra's original watercolour paintings of a local Essex scene and presented this to the school along with some Maldon sea salt and Tiptree Jams to Frau Shoelzke.

In turn, we were presented with the money that had been raised by the students, over 300 Euros and we thanked them for their kindness and hospitality. It was a very friendly and relaxed meeting, the students were interested and asked questions; there were a few tears as I talked about Tim and the emotion of the walk. And then it was time to leave and make our way to the reception with the German FA.

Frau Shoelzke and a group of students joined us for the visit which involved catching a train from the Hauptbahnhof and we found out that the FA Headquarters were right next to the Waldstadion; we would be very close to our final destination. With local knowledge, the station seemed much more straightforward than the day before and the group grabbed some lunch from the many food shops and kiosks before jumping on a train to Ffm – Sportfeld. It was a 15 minute journey and as we came out of the station, I began to realise that this was no

A Walk of Faith

ordinary stadium along the English lines, or Italian or Spanish for that matter. We were basically in a forest with trees all around and buildings, many large and modern carved out of the arboreal surroundings. All rather weird, it made it difficult to be quite sure what was what and where to go as buildings appeared and disappeared behind trees as we walked along.

We arrived at the FA Headquarters and were met by one of the officials who showed us around the Museum and Display area with photos of all of the World Cups, cabinets full of the trophies won by the German national team and a wonderful collection of football memorabilia.

We were presented with programmes for the tournament and German pendants but despite my requests, initially joking but then more serious, there was no possibility of any tickets for the England-Paraguay game. We had set off without any tickets and I had always hoped that I would pick one up from someone, somewhere. Various people had said they would try to get one, our hosts from the Gymnasium were initially confident that they could but then admitted that they couldn't help, apparently they were less easy to come across that the proverbial rocking-horse s**t! In reality, I wasn't overly concerned, it would have been a wonderful bonus to see the match live in the stadium but my main priority was to watch it with Sandra and, hopefully, Dan and unless I could get three tickets then one wasn't much good to me. Ironically, other people seemed much more concerned that I should have a ticket than I was, in some ways it was nice but rather unnecessary.

We left the FA building around 1.30pm, the sun blazing down, summer had arrived at last, and the group of us sat down outside before heading back into the city.

John Reeve

Rosella presents Sandra with the donation from the students

Outside the German FA with students from the Goethe-Gymnasium

A Walk of Faith

Our plan was to complete the final 1km from Niederrad on the following afternoon, Rosella, Oleg and some of the others were going to meet us at the station and join us for the last walk to journey's end. For now, the others were going back to school or not, if they had finished classes for the day, Tris was going to the nearby airport to meet Will, and Sandra and I decided to take a look at the city centre. The advice was to go back to the Hauptbahnhof and then head for Hauptwache and the Altstadt.

We managed this without too much trouble, the German underground was cleaner and cooler than its London counterpart and on our journey there was a very noticeable increase in the number of English fans. At the Haptbahnhof they were everywhere, like yesterday, more and more arriving looking tired and lost but 'Up for the Cup'. As we came out of the underground station, we were met by football fans everywhere, every bar, every café was full; there was a huge information centre close by, a football game in action in a tiny, plastic-walled area and a German band playing. The whole place was alive and as well as the multitudes of English fans, we saw Mexican, Trinidadian, Brazilian, Argentine, Swedish, Australian and Italian shirts, everyone enjoying the sun and looking forward to their World Cup Experience.

The overall effect was both exhilarating but also breathtaking and at the same time alien to us, so different it seemed to magnify the chasm between 'them and us'. We found a nearby café, ordered a beer, a glass of wine and a snack and started to soak it all up, to try and adapt, to chill out and give ourselves permission to enjoy. It was exciting but a strange 30 minutes and almost as soon as we left the café, we found ourselves in St. Katharine's church, standing tall amidst the festivities and took a few minutes to regain our equilibrium in the cool and the shade.

Back into the throng and we strolled along the walkways of the old town heading generally towards the river until we came to Romer Platz, a large square surrounded by a church, cafés, restaurants and bars. It had become the self-appointed headquarters of the English fans and it was almost full with at least 2,000 people, many wearing red and white, some with no tops in the sun; families, older couples, lots of twenty

John Reeve

somethings; accents from all over the UK. Many just standing, talking, watching, like us soaking up the atmosphere, others drinking outside the bars. It was a spectacular and quite unexpected sight, 48 hours before the game and the place was heaving, the support for England superb.

We joined the horde and wandered around the square spotting a quieter restaurant in the corner as a possible eating-place for later in the day. Soon it was after 4pm, the heat started to subside just a little and we decided to head back to Höechst and out of the city before the workers hit the trains. At the suburban station, it took us a few minutes to find our bearings but we made it back to the flat without getting lost. We had agreed to meet up later with Tris and Will and I called him to find out that he had picked up Will, with help from Markus, and arrived at the Shoelzke residence; we arranged to meet up at Romer Platz around 8pm.

This gave me the chance to have a bath before the family arrived home and I enjoyed a good soak hearing the others return as I lay in the hot water. My legs were still very sore, I was slow getting moving but had walked 3-4 miles around the city, much better than stopping suddenly after my walk and doing nothing at all. It was nice to hang out with the family as they got on with their early evening routine. Vanessa, as bright as a button, chatting animatedly, wanting to know and willing to share; Markus, smart, trying to be cool, his ambition to become a drugs dealer in Harlem, a wicked sense of humour, a nice boy wanting to be a rebel; Karin, a psychiatrist from the hospital, kind and considerate, aware of how we must be feeling, well-organised and self-disciplined as bread-winner, professional, mother, cleaner and cook.

As we strolled back to the station, it was still warm, a gorgeous early summer evening and the train was almost empty as we made our way back to the Hauptwache. There the party was still in full swing, not as many people around as earlier but making up for the numbers by working even harder at it. Down at Romer Platz, we found Will and Tris, they had found the square earlier, made some instant friends and were already into the beer. The mood of the square had changed as the sun slipped in the sky. There were far fewer families, children and older people, large groups of mainly lads drinking, the square littered with plastic glasses and rubbish, German police standing in one corner of the square watching the fans watching them, an uneasy atmosphere. A football was being kicked high up into the air, caught, kicked again and again and again. Who could kick it the highest? It disappeared onto roof tops but then miraculously dropped back down a few minutes later. The police were watching and trying to capture the ball, the fans mission to stop them stopping the game.

We had a beer and glass of wine and chatted to Will and Tris and their new friends, from Liverpool, Stoke, Kent, it seemed like half the young people of the nation had moved over to be here. Will, tall and blonde was very different from Tristan; quieter and more considered, a good counterpoint to the passion and spontaneity of his friend. He worked for UBS, had a good job and would be moving to Zurich later in the year. After 30 minutes we suggested food and the restaurant over in the far corner of the square, it was relatively remote from the games of the football fans and was busy with a mix of tourists and local people. City prices but the food looked good and we sat down at an outside table. The waiters were waist-coated, the service good and the food excellent. We enjoyed one of the best meals of the walk, chilled out over a few more beers, talked about the city and the lads plans for later in the evening and agreed to meet up back in the square at 11am the following day.

By 10.30, Sandra and I were both exhausted. We left the guys to the nightlife and made our way back to the suburbs and our bed for the night. It had been quite a day, a great welcome to the World Cup, getting to know our hosts; the hospitality and kindness of the school, glimpses of the stadium and the atmosphere of the World Cup and fans from around the world.

After the cool and windy weather, perfect for walking, we woke on Friday, June 9, to another perfect summer morning; deep blue sky, a freshness in the air and the sun shining down on us all. I had my first lie in until after 8am for over four weeks and had just surfaced when the Ademmer's left for schools. We took a leisurely breakfast with Karin preparing for work, then I strolled down to the Stadtmitte and found an internet café where I sent the web diary and checked my e-mails. There were over 20, many from friends saying, 'Well done', and messages from Radio 5, Tim Spanton from the Sun, a reporter from the Daily Mail and two documentary makers all wanting to arrange interviews and meetings, it was going to be a busy day.

Back to the flat and Sandra and I loaded up with flags, wrist bands and collecting buckets, walked down to the station and made the short journey into Frankfurt. As we reached the station, a train pulled in and we dashed up the steps and onto the train without buying a ticket. Over the previous two days, we had made five train journeys without a ticket barrier or inspector in sight. Two stops later, not one but two inspectors entered our carriage. To make matters funnier, we had enough change for one ticket but nothing else less than a 50 Euro note. Soon every person in the carriage was looking for change for us but no one had enough, certainly not the two ticket inspectors. By this time the train had reached the Hauptbahnhof, where we needed to change trains, and we waited whilst forms were competed in triplicate. Just when I expected to be marched off to the ticket office at least, they gave me a copy of one of the forms and sent us on our way; the money didn't matter as long as the paperwork was complete.

Now we had to get tickets for the remainder of our journey and wasted 15 minutes finding the Office, seeing the long queue and buying two bottles of water so that we had some small change to buy tickets from a machine. At the end of all that at least we managed to buy the correct tickets. At the Hauptwache, we were met by even more football fans than the day before, the atmosphere friendly and full of anticipation unlike the night before. Will and Tris were already at Romer Platz and we spread out an England flag and laid the other flags, wrist bands and hats and set up our Walk to the World Cup banner.

After a few minutes a Lancastrian in a group behind us remarked in a loud voice, 'Bloody typical, they've even brought stuff over from England to rip off the true England fans'. It couldn't go unchallenged and I went over to him and as calmly as I could told him our story and that all the money we were raising was going to charity. To his credit, he immediately apologised, said, 'Well done' and 'Good luck' and a few moments later, came over and put a 20 Euro note in one of the buckets. Soon we were doing a roaring trade, selling flags, tied round the waist they became an essential fashion accessory and the red and white wrist bands went down well. Lots of people wanted a photograph of us with the banner and by now we were so used to smiling in front of the camera, that it was easy to stand in the square, in the sunshine, watching the world go by, talking to people from England and all over the world about the walk.

In the corner of the square along from the restaurant where we had eaten the night before, there was a café that Radio 5 Live was using as its Frankfurt base. I had agreed to meet them at 11.30 for an interview on the Victoria Derbyshire show and Rosella was joining me. We went over and introduced ourselves, sat down at another table and watched the professionals in action. Victoria had a German sports journalist with her and was talking to him about the latest pronouncements about the German team in advance of the opening game due later that day. She was talking knowledgeably to him, had an earpiece and was probably getting messages sent through to her from the control room upstairs in the café or the studio in the UK as well a laptop in front of her and we could see messages coming through, one after another. With the noise and bustle from the crowd providing the perfect backdrop for a 'Live' show, it was quite a performance and we sat and marvelled at how relaxed and in control, she appeared.

The show was running late but around 11.45 we were both given head-sets and able to listen to the show and the other contributors in Berlin and Munich. We were cued in for our interview and it seemed to fly by in a flash. Rosella was asked a couple of questions and answered them very confidently in her excellent English. One moment stands out when Victoria looked at me and said that, as a mother, she couldn't imagine how I was feeling after all that had happened and being here in Frankfurt. For a moment, I gulped and hesitated, almost blubbering as Tim would have said, but then pulled myself together and tried to describe the rollercoaster of emotions that had become our lives. After the interview, we spoke to the crew for a minute whilst Victoria went into the final phase of the show and walked back over to Sandra and the guys. A few minutes later, one of the team came over to us and said that Victoria would like a word. It meant something to me when she said 'Thank you', gave me a hug and wished us every success in our mission. A kind lady as well as a true pro.

Talking about pros, one of my next encounters was with Tim Spanton, the reporter from the Sun, who had also walked to the World Cup. I had contacted him earlier, we had agreed to meet up in Frankfurt and I had spotted someone who I had assumed was him, with the Sun red double-decker bus over on the far side of the square, whilst we were waiting for the radio interview. I was cynical about his walk, not because it was publicity-seeking, that was his job and it was also what we were about but because he had taken twice as long to walk as I had done – wasn't I the tough one? Ha, ha! Going over to the bus, I managed to extract him from the embraces of the Page 3 girls, chatted to him for a minute, had a quick photo but was glad to leave him to the audience of lads all far more interested in whether the girls would show off their Page 3 credentials than in him.

By 1pm, our stock of flags etc was running low and we needed to make our way to Niederrad and the last stage of the walk. We had taken around 500 Euros in two hours from the kind football supporters and were ready to get out of the baking heat of the square. We'd been waiting for a message from Dan, hoping he would be able to join us for the final mile of the walk, as he'd walked from the start at St. Bartholomew's Church with us, so far and yet just four weeks away, but when he rang, he said that he wouldn't reach Frankfurt before 6pm and so it was time for us to go. We grabbed a sandwich at the station and Rosella rang her friends to tell them that we were running late but would see them shortly. By the time we arrived at Niederrad, some of the students had decided to go but Oleg and three of the others were waiting for us and a group of nine of us set off for the Waldstadion.

The route which was well signposted was more akin to a country footpath than a walk to a major football stadium, trees all around, unmade pathway underfoot. It only took us 20 minutes in the hot sun and when we arrived at some steps and climbed up towards some large, imposing metal gates, the sight was unlike any other football stadium I had seen anywhere in the world. The gates formed part of a security ring that ran around a huge area, looking inside through the trees, the various open areas and assorted smaller buildings; I could just make out the stadium itself in the distance. We had arrived but the stadium itself was still half a mile away.

Security guards were on show everywhere and I went up to the gate, explained that I had walked 500 miles to get here and asked if I could go inside. The guards spoke only a little English, realised quickly that I was not going to take their standard 'no' response, called through to their control centre on their two-way radio and asked for instructions. Oleg came into his own at this point and argued my case sensitively and persuasively like some 21st century Henry Kissinger. I told him later that he should become a diplomat, he is certainly a young man with many talents. We were told to go to the main accreditation area and it might be possible for one or two of us to be given passes.

The walk around the long perimeter was further than our stroll from the station, despite the shade we were all hot and tired by the time we had walked right round to the other side, passing the main entrance where there were long queues of people collecting tickets and a large lido, busy with people enjoying the arrival of summer. We stopped at the secondary entrance, near to the accreditation centre and Oleg went into action again, talking to the guards. It transpired that the stadium management had been expecting us to visit the previous afternoon after our reception at the FA and had made provision for us to have a tour of the stadium. Instead, I had chosen the worst possible time to complete my walk, the England team were due to arrive at 4pm and security was at the highest level. No one, repeat no one was allowed to go in!

I felt deflated, annoyed with myself and disappointed for the loyal team of supporters who so wanted me to be able to go into the stadium. But Oleg wasn't taking no for an answer. If we could contact Peter Crouch and he asked permission for me to be allowed into the stadium, then the authorities would agree.

John Reeve

Romer Platz
– HQ for
English fans
in Frankfurt

The closest
we came to
seeing the
England team

Outside the
Waldstadion
– let us in!

A Walk of Faith

I wandered away from the others, mobile phone to my ear to ring Dan who was on the outskirts of Frankfurt on his drive from Prague and asked him to contact Rob Aitken, who was our contact with Peter. I knew it was a hopeless mission but had to try, not least for Oleg who was using every angle he could think of to get me inside. We waited and found out within 10 minutes that Dan had spoken to Rob who had rung and left a message on Peter's mobile. We stood and waited and Oleg continued his charm offensive with anyone who even remotely looked like an official. Before long, word spread that the England coach was close by and then flanked by a police escort, it swept past us into the grounds, the group of us waving our banner and shouting 'Let us in'. I picked out Ray Clemence who waved, Rio and Steve Gerrard and then they were gone. It would be the nearest I would get to seeing the England team during my visit to the World Cup.

Still hopeful, we were told to go into the accreditation centre; a senior official was considering our request. Ready for a sit down and a cold drink, we were glad to escape the sun and sat for another 30 minutes waiting for an answer. Will and Tris and the German students all wanted me to be allowed into the stadium, Sandra was supportive but also thought that it was my own fault for not finding out more about events at the stadium and making firmer arrangements. I knew she was right and felt both deflated and angry with myself but I tried to keep a smile on my face and remain positive, more for the others than myself.

Eventually, Oleg was told the news that I could wait until 7pm, after the England and Paraguay teams had finished their practice on the pitch, and be allowed into the stadium but on no account, was I to be allowed into the grounds whilst the two teams were at the stadium. It was more than I'd expected but we had other things to do and having already hung around for two hours, the prospect of another two hour wait, just so I could walk into a stadium, look around and walk out, seemed all of a sudden, to be insignificant.

I thanked all the others, especially Oleg, for their support and company. We arranged to meet Rosella at the Romer Platz on Saturday lunchtime to watch the England game and the group split up. Tris and Will were going back on the tram to Frau Shoelzke's before a night out 'on the town', the students back to their homes; Sandra and I were heading into Frankfurt to meet Dan, we were both so looking forward to seeing him after our respective journeys across Europe. On the way back into the city, my mood of desolation returned and I thought (too much again) about endings.

As a 'starter wanderer', I believe in the power and importance of having dreams; love new ideas and getting new projects underway; imagining what the outcomes might be, putting together plans, getting other people involved, motivating them, putting everything into it myself to drive things forward. Sometimes, I became totally engrossed and very focused and this could be both good and bad but it meant that I could usually make things happen. But I was crap at endings!

Perhaps, it's because I don't like 'goodbyes' and all they signify. Certainly, I can get seduced by the next new idea and lose interest to a lesser or greater extent. Sometimes, I also have the strange idea, arrogant in its implication, that the end should take care of itself, if I've put everything into the rest of it. I had tried unsuccessfully to penetrate FIFA, one of the few organisations I'd approached where I hadn't even been able to find someone who would talk or correspond with me. Then, somehow, I had just assumed that it would all be all right. That the Goethe-Gymnasium would fix it or the German FA would make it happen or that I'd just be able to walk up to the stadium and they'd be waiting for me with the red carpet rolled out. 'Twat!' as Tim would say.

And then, there was the saddest ending of all, the ending that would never leave me, the ending that I knew was inevitable but I still wasn't prepared for. The ending that couldn't have been worse, that allowed for no farewells, that carried the three of us downwards on its spiral to oblivion. I never did say goodbye. I might have told him that I'd loved him ten thousand times but I didn't tell him then. There was no opportunity to share a tender moment, a look, a smile, only the fight for each gasp of air, the gradual loss of awareness, the business of getting on with it, of dying.

Maybe I expect too much. Some things don't need to be said, some things we just know. Sometimes, just knowing that you're not on your own, that those you love and care for, are with you, is quite enough. And so, my moment of Triumph, the end of my 550 mile walk of faith had ended, if not in Disaster, then badly. But I had got there, I had walked all that way, had all that support and kindness and friendship and love from so many people. Had raised goodness-knows how much money, it wasn't all bad. But it hadn't finished as I'd hoped. There's no point hoping, if you don't do something to turn your hopes into reality. I must have been awful company as we sat on the train back to the Hauptbahnhof and then the subway to Hauptwache. Wrestling with myself, up and down, good and bad, holding on to the rollercoaster in my mind.

Frankfurt and its World Cup, grabbed me as we came up out of the subway. Impossibly, the place was even busier, the fans louder and seemingly to be getting into the full swing, as if they had needed an induction into partying German-style and had now got the hang of it. Flags and football shirts from around the world were everywhere, trumpets and horns were blasting out, enough beer had been drunk to relax most people but it was still too early for the stand-off with the police from the previous evening. The place was just going crazy; happy, full of expectation, soaking up the sun and the beer. It was intoxicating just being there, impossible not to get caught up in the excitement as we walked through the crowds in Romer Platz and then down to the Mainkai and the river.

Here, our German hosts had surpassed themselves, there was a mile of food stalls, beer tents, various rides and other entertainment. Looking across the river, we could see as many people on the southern bank. As we continued upstream we came to the Main Arena and the grandstands that had been erected along the river bank, three huge ones on the north bank and two others on the south. Between them were the massive screens, moored to pontoons in the middle of the stream. It was an impressive sight, made even better by all the people out for a good time.

I rang Dan to find that he and the other guys were heading over a bridge just ahead of us and then, unexpectedly, we saw him. The three of us hugged and all of the pent-up emotion of the day flooded out as tears flowed down my cheeks. Feeling better, we found a bar on the south side of the Main and sat and caught up on each others news. They had driven almost 2,000 miles in the last five days, from Mannheim to Riga, then back through Poland, Hungary and the Czech Republic and looked pretty tired and in need of a good shower. They planned to find a B&B as close to the city as possible. I suggested they try the south side of the river and head out towards the airport. We arranged to meet up at the Main Arena to watch the match and, as they went to explore the south bank before returning to their motor home, Sandra and I retraced our steps to the Hauptwache and went back to Höechst.

We had invited the Ademmers to join us for a meal and earlier had agreed that rather than them come into Frankfurt, we would meet them at the station, walk into the old town and eat at one of the restaurants by the river. It was another contrast at the end of a day of contrasts; a good, typically German meal sat outside on a long trestle table in an old square close to the water. The light fading towards 10pm, Vanessa asking questions about our day, Markus interested in Tris and Will and their plans, Karin, considerate and interested, easy to talk to. A comfortable way to come back down after our journey of highs and lows.

An even longer lie-in, until 8.30, on Saturday morning and all was quiet as we went through for breakfast. Another perfect blue sky and it was already getting warm when we left the apartment around 10am, hard to believe that just eight day earlier I'd been wearing gloves and woolly hat in temperatures of 6°C. First stop was the internet café in Hoechst. A Marketing Manager from Avaya had e-mailed to ask if I would like two tickets to a game in either the round of 16 or the semi-finals – difficult decision.

Sandra had bought the tickets for the train and it was full of football fans and Germans wondering what was going on, as we made the 10 minute journey. The Romer Platz was heaving when we arrived at 11.00 and after 45 minutes we had sold the rest of the England flags and wrist bands. The atmosphere was brilliant

A Walk of Faith

and highly infectious; everyone looking forward to the game and it was easy to get picked up and swept along by the mood. We talked to England fans from all over the country, the lucky ones with tickets about to set off for the stadium but most like us, looking forward to watching the game on the river bank.

The tournament had started well the evening before with a victory for the home side and it was noticeable that, for the first time, there were German flags and shirts to be seen. It was as if the nation had realised that their team was not going to be humiliated and what's more, it was OK to support their national team. Dan was down by the Main queuing to get into the Main Arena and he rang around 12 to say that they had been let in and the seats were filling fast. We waited until 1pm but Rosella had not arrived and after various photos and more interviews with random journalists, we walked down to the river and were in the seating area by 1.30. We squeezed in just in time as they closed the larger grandstand area a few minutes later

A superb setting, right by the wide river, with the two huge screens moored in the centre of the flow, one facing north (the larger where we were) and another facing south. 15,000, almost all England, fans were in the larger arena with a third smaller arena further to the east. We met up with Dan and his mates and soaked up the atmosphere; huge queues for the beer and food stalls, music stages, photographers and camera crews everywhere. Dan and I did a couple of laps with two of the collecting buckets, just generally asking people for donations, and raised another 500 Euros.

By the time of the game, it was baking hot and many people were starting to wilt a little not just from the alcohol. We had taken eight bottles of Oasis drink and with hats and shirts to cover our heads were not too bad. After a brilliant start and the early goal created by Becks, the game fizzled out a bit and the atmosphere in the second half became anxious with huge relief at the end. A disappointing performance but it was the result that mattered.

Dan and the others stayed on to watch the Sweden - Trinidad and Argentina – Ivory Coast games and found seats in the shade as the sun continued to burn down and the grandstand half-emptied. We said goodbye to Dan, he was heading south the following day towards England's next destination and we would see him back in England in two weeks time. We made our way back up towards the square, passing Swedish and Trinidadian fans heading for the grandstand. Romer Platz was full with chanting England fans, celebrating the victory. As smaller groups of Swedish, Argentine, German and Brazilian fans walked by, they were challenged to sing a song and then drowned out as England's other barmy army replied. It was going to be a long and happy night in down-town Frankfurt.

After a phone call, we met up with Rosella and three of her friends from the Gymnasium, found a table and had an ice-cream and coffee with them. A little later, Tris arrived back from the Arena and I talked with him about the match. He was waiting for Will, who had gone to the stadium and apparently walked into a champagne reception with German models giving out the drinks – it helps to work for a big company like UBS.

Ursula Schoelzke rang to invite us for a drink and meal, so we decided to leave the city centre and met them at a very relaxed and comfortable Greek restaurant where we were joined by our hosts from Höechst. We sat outside, the evening was warm and we had a good meal with pleasant company.

Ursula and Karin were wary of the city centre and all the football fans and concerned that their children should stay away. I tried to persuade them that this was a 'once in a lifetime' opportunity to be part of such an event and that the atmosphere was not only safe but also something that the teenagers would really enjoy. Not sure how much progress I made but I suspect that when the English fans left town and Germany continued to do well, their attitude might have changed.

The meal over and goodbyes exchanged, Sandra and I were shattered, having been outside all day and glad to be back at the flat by midnight.

Sunday morning, another lie in and another glorious day; all at once we were going home and the sunshine and the spectacle made it even harder to pack up. But there was no reason to stay, Dan was heading towards Munchengladbach, Tris and Will were flying out and our German friends deserved some time to enjoy the sunshine. A leisurely breakfast and we rounded up our things which seemed to have expanded into the space available in the flat. We were still not sure what we were going to do. Tris came over and emotional sod that he is, we had a hug before he set off to the airport. He had been a great supporter, full of enthusiasm, a natural salesman, prepared to have a go at anything, all in the memory of his friend.

Photos and goodbyes with the Ademmers and then it was time to move; after five days and quiet Sunday traffic, I still managed to get lost leaving the town and still unsure, we decided to make for the Lido, next to the Waldstadion, and enjoy some time relaxing in the sun.

The traffic on the major routes was busy and it took two circuits before we found a car park in the trees and walked across the bridge and along part of our route to the stadium. It was 2pm by the time we arrived and we were happy to change into our swimwear and find a quiet spot. It was a large site with four interlinking pools, various food and drink stalls and a wide and deep grassed area with trees providing shade around the edges; it was busy but big enough to take the crowds without feeling hemmed in. We had a sandwich and drink for lunch and spent the next three hours sun-bathing for as long as we could manage before dipping in the pool, repeating the leap into the sudden coolness several times. It was over 30°C and after four weeks of outdoor living, I'd finally developed a decent tan. At one point the tannoy system played *'Amarillo'* in German and Sandra and we smiled ruefully at each other; you can't keep a good man down.

We wanted to leave Frankfurt and, at least make a start on the journey home. But as the afternoon drifted away like Sunday's should do, we agreed that the Ramada Jarvis hotel, right next to the Cologne motorway would be far enough for today. We could be up and off in the morning and soon be in Belgium and on our way. The 20 mile journey to the hotel was accomplished without getting lost and we booked in for our last night away from home. Having been by the pool all day, we gave the Spa a miss and went down for an evening meal. The businessmen of mid-week had been replaced by coach loads of football supporters, Spanish and Japanese; there were two large screens set up in the lobby area

John Reeve

The big screen on the river at the Main Arena

My favourite photo

With the Ademmer family before heading home

A Walk of Faith

showing highlights of matches and the hotel had certainly moved into World Cup mode since our visit only five days earlier.

The journey home was quick and largely uneventful. I enjoyed one moment at a petrol station near the Belgium border when having been ripped off by motorway premium prices that suddenly moved into the realms of UK petrol prices, I paid for our tank of diesel with bags of 50 cent pieces. The attendant refused to take them at first but as I shrugged ignorance and turned to leave, he started to open the bags and proceeded to count them all; sorry to all the other customers who had to wait. We managed to catch a ferry an hour earlier than scheduled and hit the early evening traffic on the A2 which had calmed down by the time we reached the M25 and drove through the tunnel and back into Essex. It was after 8pm when we arrived home. A strange feeling coming home; we took the few things we needed inside and left everything else for the following day.

John Reeve

A Journey without End
Back home; getting on with it; Mixathon and charity dinner.

Lots of people talked about returning home after the walk, some asking how we thought we would feel, others telling us to expect an anti-climax; of course we knew that would be the case and had planned accordingly. But we still had to work through that feeling and no one could have quite prepared us for how low it would take us down and how long it would persist. Still being busy and getting on with it was my antidote to most things.

Tuesday was emptying and cleaning out the motor home day; Wednesday and Thursday I was off working near Oxford, preparing for a new project that I'd taken on specifically to keep me busy. Whilst I was away, Sandra took the motor home down to Chipping Hill School, talked to the children about the walk and let each class climb in and explore the motor home.

On Friday, we drove down to Newbury and returned the vehicle. It had been an essential part of the team, a late but very welcome addition to our plans and we left a present for Emma, who was busy and couldn't be there to see us.

During this time, I was in contact with Avaya and their kind offer of tickets for a World Cup game. Their offer was two tickets plus hotel and hospitality package for the Germany-Argentina match in Berlin. A Friday night game promising a weekend in a fantastic city and a great match in store; ironically, we couldn't get flights to Berlin on the day of the game and I couldn't afford to take more time off to fly earlier, or to walk as some jokers suggested, so we never did get to see a 'live' World Cup game

The following Wednesday I was in Swansea starting work on the new project. I would spend seven weeks there over the next three months. It was a good piece of work and gave me the opportunity to work with some talented people. For the first month, we were based at the Liberty stadium, a new facility shared by the Ospreys and Swansea City. I resisted wearing my Barnsley shirt on the first morning, didn't want to start rubbing it in too early. My Monday morning routine became getting up at 3.45am and on the road by 4.00, that way I could be passing Cardiff before 8am and at the stadium for an 8.30 start. Fortunately, it was summertime and I enjoyed some glorious sun rises. The hotel where we were staying was quirky but OK and had a decent gym and good swimming pool. One unexpected bonus was that they allowed Sandra to stay for £10 per night and she came down twice, for four nights and two nights, and enjoyed exploring Mumbles and the Gower in their summer finery. We had two good meals at the Mermaid at Mumbles, the Dylan Thomas quote written large on the wall.

Sandra started supply teaching, there wasn't much during the last half-term of the school year but it was important for her to start getting back into a routine and it led to a maternity leave contract for the New Year in September. But all through those weeks that turned into months, there was emptiness, a feeling of futility that would sweep in unexpectedly and stop us in our tracks. The nights were, and always will be, the worst, the time to reflect, the times he struggled the hardest, the time he died. The darkness, the despair, the sheer bloody wastefulness of it all still brought my anger too easily to the surface, too often directed at the wrong person, but more often now, it brought on a deep well of sadness and at times, it felt far easier to succumb. Do we stop, do we push on? Take a break, just be! But there were always things to be done, opportunities to push the pain to one side, to ignore, to pretend, to just get on with it.

I had needed something to concentrate on, to provide a positive goal. I had never been so focused in my life as during the last six months. Why hadn't I focused like that to try and save my son's life? So many answers, so many excuses; hindsight toys with us, providing glimpses of insight then mixing them with 'how it should have been' and 'if only'. As I write, seven months after the end of the walk, the memory of Tim's illness and decline, the walk to Frankfurt, are illuminated sharply in my mind and I'm convinced they will always remain clear. But the time after we returned has already begun to fade, so little has changed but so much has happened.

Bright spotlights illuminate the gloom, such as the 24 hour 'mixathon' that Dave Valentine held at Dukes, with the full backing of the team. He had a great night and day and another night. Then there was Tris stopping busses to collect donations, and the sun shining down on the bongo player.

In July, we held an Open House for some of the many people who had made the walk possible; at one point we had 45 people sitting out in the garden on another beautiful day. Ted raised funds through their Tumble Tots groups, Rosemarie organised a Tumble Tots Olympics and invited Sandra to hand out certificates at the Witham group. Also in July, Sandra and I went to see James Blunt, one of Tim's favourites, enjoyed a wonderful Sunday afternoon and evening and as the evening cooled enjoyed the haunting melodies as the sun disappeared behind the backdrop of the moat and ancient castle.

All the time money continued to come in. £4,500 from Dukes, the same again from Tumble Tots, money from Chipping Hill school and the Anglo-European, donations from Wollastons, money from Scouts and Brownies and Rainbow groups, many people had raised their own sponsorship. Letters arrived from people from all over the country, many with touching words and small donations, every penny counts. Our total continued to increase from 50 to 60 and then to 70 and 75 thousand pounds. We had smashed our initial target of £50,000 and were now heading towards six figures. Sometimes, the money seemed irrelevant and a distraction but at other times, we took comfort from the wonderful support we had received, far exceeding our expectations and our determination that the money would be put to good use and help to make a difference, however small, for other young people.

At the start of August, Sandra and I, along with her dad, visited the Teenage Cancer Unit at St. James's – Jimmies- hospital in Leeds. We had bought two Leeds United season tickets with our own money, one in Tim's name and presented them to Sue Morgan, the Clinical Nurse Specialist at the Unit. Our idea was that patients would be able to go to a game, perhaps with a parent

A Walk of Faith

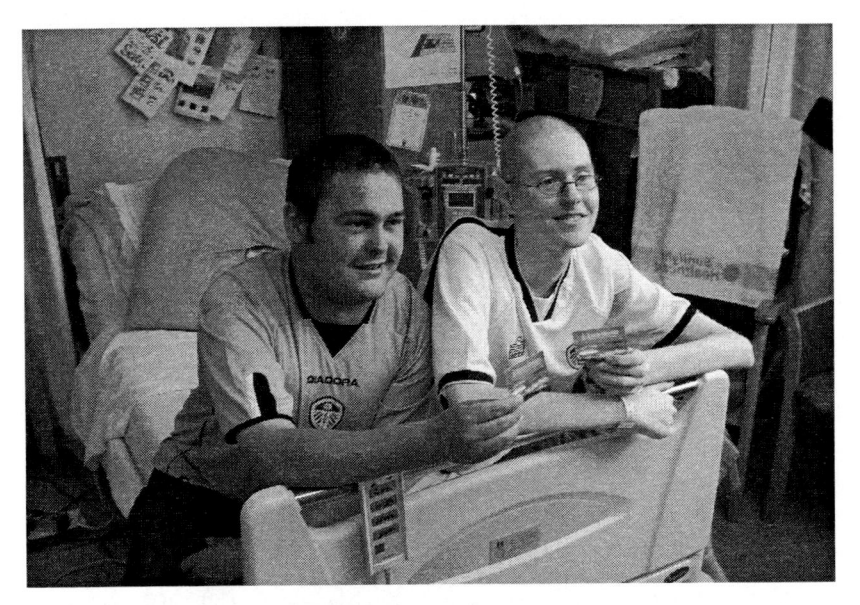

Matt and Aaron – he kept us waiting until his Leeds shirt arrived

Sandra talking to the children at school about the walk

or friend, and have something else to look forward to during the long and anxious days in hospital. It was an emotional visit; we were delighted to see the wonderful facilities available for the teenagers but thought back to Tim, wishing he had been able to enjoy these sorts of facilities and be with people of his own age. We met Matt and Aaron who both had ALL like Tim, one who had just been given a two-year all clear and off to the first game of the season that day, the other recently diagnosed and just setting out on his own journey of salvation.

During August we also managed a five-day break in Norfolk, courtesy of Peter and Elaine's flat at Cromer. Unfortunately, I'd tweaked my back the week before and had to seek out a physiotherapist. We visited Sheringham and Holt and enjoyed the chance to escape from paperwork although I visited the local tourist office every day to check e-mails.

In September, Dan moved into his new flat and Sandra enjoyed helping him to buy furniture and sorting out his new home. We had several trips with car loads of his things. It was good to see him and Faye settling in and the decision to buy the flat seemed justified.

Back at home, it was more trips to Swansea but another fundraising project was starting to draw closer, an auction and dinner at the Emirates stadium. The idea, sparked by that first England shirt we had been promised back in February by the FA, had lay dormant for six months but now we moved back into planning mode. Arsenal generously agreed to give us a 50% discount on room hire and we argued that the new stadium would make a good venue, accessible for people working in London and somewhere that many people wouldn't have visited or seen 'on the inside'. Initial interest was strong and we set a date for November 9. However, turning the interest into hard cash proved much more difficult and three weeks before the event, we had only 150 people signed up. With late bookings, the final number was close to 200, enough to have a good night.

With late changes to the room, uncertainty about the AV system, problems with the coach bringing people from Essex and our wish that everyone enjoyed themselves, the lead up to the dinner and auction was fraught. Both Sandra and I were stressed

A Walk of Faith

as we arrived at the stadium. But yet again, other people rallied round and helped to make the evening a great success. Lorna Denny and the team from Arsenal responded positively to our requests for last-minute changes to the table layout; the team from Leukaemia Research organised the main auction, the silent auction and the raffle; Big Guns and Long John did a great job with the AV system and in providing entertainment for the evening; Geoff Thomas, our guest of honour for the evening brought Ian Wright along for the drinks reception. Wrighty was great, spent 40 minutes chatting and acted as a magnet for many of the guests to have their photograph taken with one of the legends from Arsenal's old home just across the way.

A smashing photo of Sandra and Wrighty

As the evening unfolded, so Sandra and I began to relax. The entertainer, Mickey P. Kerr sang, played the guitar and ukulele, recited his own poetry and rapped – a 21 century troubadour. Half the audience didn't like him but the other half, me included, thought he was great. Geoff made a short speech and I followed with some words and showed some pictures from the walk. We had loads of items for both auctions, seven Premiership team signed football shirts, footballs, books, pictures. Perhaps the most unusual items were tea for two at the House of Commons and a bottle of House of Commons whisky. The latter, kindly donated by John Whittingdale, had been autographed by David Cameron and Tony Blair making it a unique bottle of single malt. Our auctioneer did a great job and over £9,000 was raised from the two auctions and the raffle, and together with the contribution from the ticket price brought the total amount raised on the evening to over £12,000.

But the real showstopper came right at the end of the evening, when Smithy and Tris and four more of Tim's friends asked if they could say a few words. Tris started and soon handed over to Smithy who said how Tim would have enjoyed the evening and the venue although he would have liked a fuller plate for his main course. He talked about how Tim liked things neat and tidy and how he used to leave CDs lying around in his room just to annoy Tim. Then he said that he wanted to mess Tim's room up one more time and proceeded to give Sandra and me, the framed England shirt, that the six guys had bid £1,500 for, to hang, 'where it belongs', in his room. It was a total surprise, a wonderful gesture, a moment for quick gulps and tears in the eyes. I think he was right; the shirt does look 'at home'.

It was 1am before we had packed up the car and set off back to Essex, tired but delighted with how it had all worked out. Over the following days, we had many calls, texts and e-mails, all saying how much people had enjoyed the evening. All the hard work and angst had been worthwhile.

It was a busy time that autumn; as well as the dinner and auction we held a charity collection at Oakwell with great support from Barnsley FC and raised almost a thousand pounds at the match against Leeds United. Chris and family, Ann and Anthony, Val Ackroyd and a team of collectors from the LRF branch at Huddersfield all helped to make the collection a great success. Afterwards, it was nice to meet up with Stephen Dobson, an old school friend who we hadn't seen for many years.

In October, I walked for an afternoon with Ian Botham during his fundraising walk around the UK – 17 cities in nine days – on behalf of the LRF and the TCT. I felt honoured to be invited to walk with the great man who has done so much as President of LRF and enjoyed the 10 mile march around Cambridge with Alastair Campbell and Nasser Hussein as other walking companions.

On December 4, we walked from Oakwell to Elland Road for the return Leeds v Barnsley match. At the request of West Yorkshire Police, kick-off time was changed to 12 noon only two weeks beforehand and what should have been an 8.30 start turned into a middle of the night, 5.30am start from Barnsley. Chris had done a great job to sort out the route and find a suitable stopping point as well as taking charge of organising the collection at Elland Road. Tom, as always, walked with me from the start and we were joined by David Rawnsley and his niece, Megan, whose sister, Joni, has aplastic anaemia and was recovering from a bone marrow transplant. Joni had hoped to be well enough to walk some of the way with us but she was suffering from the effects of graft-versus-host disease and was poorly at the time.

Spookily, it was 12°C, when we set of in the dark and we were joined by another eight intrepid walkers at our stop near Wakefield. The walk should have been uneventful except that Megan developed blisters after six miles, David and Chris managed to get lost in the middle of Wakefield, Tom disappeared

John Reeve

Always my football home

With the great man

A Walk of Faith

down a man-hole, badly grazing his leg, and Dorothy had someone run into her car at the White Rose Centre. Nevertheless, the 12 of us arrived in Leeds, right on schedule at 11.15am. By then, the collectors including Ted, Billy and Tom who had driven up from Essex and a team from the Teenage Cancer Trust were moving into action and the walkers were able to sit down and enjoy a mug of hot tea.

The following week was Sandra's birthday and the first anniversary of Tim's death. Dan came home for the day and we arranged to inter Tim's ashes in the new churchyard at St. Bartholomew's. We planted a tree and Father Stuart conducted a short service. Then the three of us continued on Tim's walk, past the bare apple orchards and back to the only home he had really known. It felt like the right thing to do.

Christmas was a strange time with more highs and lows. We were invited to the LRF Carols with the Stars at the Albert Hall and enjoyed a wonderful evening, with Geoff and Sue Marshall-Clarke and Daphne and Bernard as our guests.

We went to Dan's for Christmas, he worked until 1pm at the gym and we had Christmas dinner at the Blue Harbour on the Kings Road with Faye and her family. On Boxing Day we travelled to Yorkshire, picking up Sandra's dad at her sister's and spent time with him, with Isobel and with Chris, Anne, Tom and Kathryn. We saw Joni, much better now, she seems to be winning her battle and looking forward to the future. Down south for the New Year and 11 friends who came round for dinner on New Year's Eve. All very busy, keeping occupied. Letting the sadness in but trying to control the doses, searching for a way forward, hoping for a soft landing, 'getting on with it'.

And still the donations continue to arrive. As I sit in bed, typing this on my laptop at the start of February 2007, our total funds raised has passed £100,000. Dave Valentine has given us more money from his sponsorship back in June; Lloyd Scott has donated the money from a raffle held at a talk he made at Brighton University; Charlie Arme and the sixth-formers from Anglo held a Rock Concert and raised over £500 for Tim's Trust; Ursula Schoelzke on a visit with some students from Frankfurt gave me 50 Euros that had been collected at school and many more kind people keep on making donations.

We met with Cathy Gilman at LRF in January to discuss how the money that we have donated to the fund should be used and have agreed to support the Cytogenetics Group, led by Professor Christine Harrison at Southampton General Hospital. They have been carrying out leading-edge research for many years, have the world's largest cytogenetic database and are turning their attention to ALL in teenagers and young adults to discover why the disease is different in this age group from younger children and older adults and how to treat it more effectively. Other conversations are continuing with Professor Stephen McKinnon at the Royal Free/UCL and with Barts as well as our ongoing relationship with the Teenage Cancer Trust to decide where the remainder of the money should be used. We want to get it right, to make sure that every penny counts.

Work continues for us both; Sandra is teaching a reception class in Witham, enjoying the children and the teaching but, like so many teachers, not the paperwork and endless meetings. I'm as busy as I want to be, working hard, enjoying the people I am lucky enough to work with and the variety of what I do but making time now for other things in a way I've never done before. Sandra and I are making the effort to go out on our own, for a meal or to watch a film at least once a week. We're planning weekends away and short breaks, things that we can look forward to. A trip in a few weeks time to see Phil and Jane and the boys in Spain and the seat that Phil has built in his new plunge pool, made painstakingly as a mosaic, Gaudi-style and dedicated to Tim with an inscription, 'Live Strong' TPR. In March we go to Skye to meet Nicola Bradbury in her recently completed home overlooking the Cuillins. In May, we hope to go back to Poperinge and see Sylvia again, during her month of duty at Talbot House.

Without me doing a thing, we already have four awareness and fundraising events being planned for 2007. Roehampton Uni, through Big Guns and Gemma Kelly has nominated Tim's Trust as one of their Rag Week charities; Kate Bome from Great Totham School is organising a charity Black Tie Ball at Braxted

Hall. She's sold 270 tickets, we will hold an auction and raffle, there'll be a band, dancing and a good evening's entertainment, having some fun and raising money. Gary White and Clive Hopwood, who both came to the Dinner at the Emirates, have offered to complete the Three Peaks Challenge and it looks as if a group of about 12 of us will spend 24 hours climbing the highest peaks of Scotland, England and Wales during the long days of June.

My role has changed from walker and centre stage performer to supporter and back-room organiser and this is even more evident in our great venture for 2007, an amazing triathlon to the Rugby World Cup. Back in Germany, I had sensed Dan's concern about not being as involved as he would have liked and that he would come up with his own fundraising tribute to his brother. He certainly has, because with friend and colleague, Rob Aitken, he intends to swim the channel from Dover to Calais, cycle 1,120 miles from Dover to Cardiff, Edinburgh and back to London and to run 262 miles from Twickenham to Paris and the Stade de France.

A hard training run in the hills

It's called a Deca-Ironman although people have already called it many other things! The two personal trainers have been in serious training since September 2006 and have a series of monthly challenges to build up the necessary stamina and endurance.

Only yesterday, they cycled 150 miles, another step on the way. So for me it's back to letters, phone calls, e-mails and meetings; planning routes, arranging transport and logistics, finding sponsors, planning publicity, designing leaflets and web pages.

Sandra is terribly worried again, this time about her elder son and the toll that this incredible challenge will take on his body. She doesn't want him to do it or at least to share the load as a relay between the two of them. I believe that they know what they are doing and I understand why it is so important for them to do it, can relate to the element of risk and uncertainty that is part of the motivation. But I want them to be as well-prepared and with the best support possible, to make sure they have every chance to complete their journey and so there will be lots to do over the next seven months until they arrive in Paris in early September.

The driver for me which used to be about providing for my family and securing our futures has changed. Now it's much more about helping other people, both the people who I meet on a day-to-day basis and those close to me, Sandra, Dan and Chris; staying true to my family and the friends who have stayed true to me. And then there's the 'forgotten tribe' and what has become my mission to make a tiny difference, the dream that in 15 or 10 or 5 years time, it has to be as soon as possible, 90% of teenagers and young adults with ALL will survive just as the survival of children with the disease has improved; making my dream a reality so that the dreams of so many young people have a chance to come true.

That's my journey, a journey that will never end; a dream to help other people but also a journey of redemption for me. Most of the time now I can handle my memories of Tim; sure there are still many occasions when an unexpected association, a word or a familiar place stop me in my tracks. Like hitting a plate glass window, I crumble into pieces but as soon as I think of Tim, what he went through and how brave he was, then all of my problems evaporate and I move on. Mostly I can recollect the happy times, the wealth of golden moments. I feel blessed to have been married for 31 years and to have two sons whom I have always been proud of. But I don't want to forget the 'darkest moments', to loose their sharp edge, to avoid the pain and the torment, I want it to endure for as I long as I endure, to become part of me, my inspiration, my source of energy and passion to overcome the intolerable and shine a spotlight on the unrelenting spirit of my sweet son.

Each evening when I'm at home, usually after a bath, I sit quietly on Tim's bed for a few moments. When he was very ill, towards the end, there were a couple of times when we'd sit side by side and rest our heads together. It was about making it through another day, knowing we had 'done good' and 'won today'; time to give thanks, to draw strength from each other, to share our resolve to persevere, a tender moment of love between father and son. No words were spoken, none were needed. We knew.